Practicing Peace

Practicing Peace

Theology, Contemplation, and Action

MICHAEL JOHN WOOD
Foreword by Peter Catt

WIPF & STOCK · Eugene, Oregon

PRACTICING PEACE
Theology, Contemplation, and Action

Copyright © 2022 Michael John Wood. All rights reserved. Except for brief quotations in critical publications or reviews, no part of this book may be reproduced in any manner without prior written permission from the publisher. Write: Permissions, Wipf and Stock Publishers, 199 W. 8th Ave., Suite 3, Eugene, OR 97401.

Wipf & Stock
An Imprint of Wipf and Stock Publishers
199 W. 8th Ave., Suite 3
Eugene, OR 97401

www.wipfandstock.com

PAPERBACK ISBN: 978-1-6667-3530-7
HARDCOVER ISBN: 978-1-6667-9224-9
EBOOK ISBN: 978-1-6667-9225-6

MARCH 29, 2022 2:50 PM

Scripture quotations, unless otherwise indicated, are from the New Revised Standard Version Bible, copyright © 1989 National Council of the Churches of Christ in the United States of America. Used by permission. All rights reserved worldwide.

Unless otherwise noted, all italics for emphasis have been supplied by the author, including occurrences found in quotations.

For Rani, Sarah, and Hannah

"Wherever space is opened peace breaks out."
—Harrison Owen

Contents

Foreword by Peter Catt		ix
Preface		xiii
Acknowledgments		xvii
1	Introduction	1

Part 1: THEOLOGY

2	Touchstone 1: God Is Christlike	17
3	Touchstone 2: Christ Reveals the Nature of Violence	33
4	Touchstone 3: Christ Gives a Peace That the World Cannot Give	51
5	Touchstone 4: Christ Enables Us to Practice Peace	76
6	Nonviolence and Scripture	97
7	Nonviolence, Judgment, and Wrath	109
8	Nonviolence and Hell	122

Part 2: CONTEMPLATION

9	Integrating Perception: Affect, Emotions, and Story	131
10	Loving God: Contemplative Prayer	136
11	Loving Neighbor: Conversation and the Inner Village	142
12	The Inner Work of Forgiveness	155

Part 3: ACTION

13	Natural Living Systems	161
14	Collaboration	167
15	Collaborative Emergent Design	171
16	Conversational Frameworks and Tools	201
17	Conclusion: Joining the Dots	221

Appendix A: The Inner Work of Planning for a Conversation	225
Appendix B: The Inner Work of Forgiveness	227
Appendix C: The Dialogic Dance between Power and Love	229
Appendix D: How Circle Processes Help to Structure-Out Rivalry and Structure In Collaboration	230
Appendix E: Talking Circles Principles (Generic)	235
Appendix F: Coaching Approach to a Conversation	237
Appendix G: Sample Questions for Reflective Practice	240
Appendix H: Joining the Dots: Integrating Theology, Contemplation, and Action in the Practice of Peace	241
Bibliography	245

Foreword

THE GREEK ORTHODOX LITURGY BEGINS with prayers and antiphons that signify the gathering of the people. This is followed by a ritual element called the small entrance. During the small entrance, the deacon, who is carrying the book of Gospels, along with the other clergy, enters through the doors of the iconostasis and approaches the altar. The deacon then emerges and says words that can be translated "Wisdom! Attend!" or "This is Wisdom. Let us attend!"

To attend is to be present. It is also to notice what else is present. The Orthodox expect the risen Christ to be present as they celebrate the Divine Liturgy. They expect to encounter Wisdom, Sophia—the feminine, creative principle of the Divine. And they intentionally declare that they will attend to Wisdom and to the Christ.

> Let us attend.
> Let us practice being present to the moment.
> Let us attend to the context in which we find ourselves.
> Let us attend to what is emerging.
> Let us attend to what the Spirit is up to and join in.

The practice of attending and then responding to that which is emerging reflects the framing we encounter in Michael Wood's book. It is a framing that has much to offer us in these complex and challenging days—days characterized by a pandemic, increasing social tribalism, institutional decline, and the intertwined ecological and climate crises.

For many of us who have been formed in the Western tradition, learning how to attend in the way described above requires us to undergo a journey of transformation, a journey from head to heart. Michael takes us on that journey in this book.

I was formed in the Western head-dominated framework when I trained as a scientist. The scientific method is framed by a set of ideas that includes discovery, investigation, and the use of evidence. The fruits of this approach have been many and good: diseases have been eradicated; life expectancy has increased; literacy, particularly among women and girls, has improved; food production has reached previously unimaginable levels; and superstition and bigotry-shaped pseudoscience have been challenged, if not fully overcome.

One side effect of looking at the world through the prism of scientific inquiry has been to see it in reductionist and mechanistic ways. So, the shadow side of the Western paradigm has caused us to objectify the earth, its creatures, and even our own bodies. As a result, we see ourselves as existing over and against what we label *nature*. For many, the earth is no more than a static backdrop over which we lay our plans, imposing our wills on an empty wilderness.

Under the influence of this paradigm, much of the church has come to see mission as taking God to previously godforsaken people and places, and Christian formation is practiced as if the seeker is an empty vessel. Further, churches have copied many other Western institutions, organizations, and businesses by getting caught up in strategic planning. More often than not, this process is a top-down affair that rarely bears the promised fruit. This is because the world is more complex and dynamic than we imagine. And, as we shall see, the future is emergent, not something we create.

The history of the rise and fall of civilizations suggests that increasing complexity is one of the factors that leads to societal collapse. This is because as the complexity of the system increases, so do the inputs of energy and organizational capacity required to manage it. At some critical point in the society's growth, the energy and organizational inputs needed to maintain order exceed the capacity of the system to deliver them, and so the system begins to collapse.

One way to avoid societal collapse is to change the operational paradigm, so that the inputs required are reduced. This is one of the advantages that approaches that focus on emergence offer us.

For me, the disruption of the Western command-and-control model began while I was studying biology. In the early 1980s, biology was moving rapidly beyond the collection, describing, and dissection of specimens to the study of the complex systems found in nature that cannot be described or understood through processes of dismantlement or reduction. The beehive was discovered to be a self-organizing system, with no central command structure and no middle managers. In like manner, the cells of an embryo self-organize into a complex being, without the need for a central authority that implements a blueprint. The self-organizing systems found in nature use webs for information sharing rather than the centralized and hierarchical structures we tend to use in Western institutions. They are nature's way of organizing and operating systems that are too complex for a command-and-control system to execute.

The disruption to the Western worldview continued for me after my ordination. I was fortunate enough to encounter some ideas and practices that were seeking to deal with the church and the world as complex, emergent systems rather than as simple, linear, and predictable ones.

One of these disruptors was the catechumenal process for Christian formation, which I discovered through the work of Ann McElligott, Michael Merriman, and Walter Guettsche. The catechumenal process gifted me with two principles.

The first catechumenal principle is that God had been at work in the life of the seekers since before the seekers were formed in the womb. This means that they bring with them a wealth of lived experience, talents, and insights that can be offered to the community of faith as gifts. Each newcomer therefore shapes the life of the community as much as the community shapes them. A new community therefore emerges as each newcomer finds their place. The shape and character of the new community cannot be predicted. It can be recognized and described only as it emerges.

The second catechumenal principle is the idea that we learn our theology best through a cyclical process of action-reflection-action. This means that one's ministry and theology are shaped by lived experience. Theology, in turn, becomes something that seeks to explain that which is lived, rather than being an abstract idea that is applied to life.

Another piece of the puzzle fell into place when I discovered the work of Peter Senge, C. Otto Scharmer, Joseph Jaworski, and Betty Sue Flowers. These suggest that by attending to the present, one can begin to perceive the emerging future as a field—a field one can enter and explore. By attending to the present, we can sense the future that is emerging and embrace it.

Attending to the emerging future requires organizations to work on developing spiritual maturity. Spiritual maturity develops as individuals become more self-aware and the group focusses on operating in a collaborative manner. Spiritual maturity also requires teams to embrace the use of a completely new set of approaches and tools as they seek to discern what the emerging future means for them and their organization.

It was while seeking to engage more fully with the processes that enable groups to be present to the emerging future and to explore more deeply the spirituality and group dynamics that lead to collaborative maturity that I met Michael Wood.

In 2011, the Synod of the Diocese of Brisbane resolved to explore ways of dealing with the complex issues we face, using dialogue rather than debate. Michael, along with West Australian colleagues Brendan McKeague and Neil Preston, visited Brisbane to assist us.

The processes have been a great blessing to the life of the church in Southeast Queensland. We have used them to explore complex and emotive issues such as the future shape of marriage; the effect of fossil fuel extraction industries on communities, agriculture, and the environment; and the emerging shape and ministry of the church, as well as to enable conversations about climate change and the plight of refugees.

In this book, Michael Wood takes us on a journey that parallels the journey I have undertaken over the past two decades. I am sure it will be a blessing for any who seek to engage the future that is making itself known in the midst of the complexities of these current times.

I give the last word to Michael:

> Through the gift of the Spirit, we have a foot in the new creation, through the mind of Christ, and yet we also experience the tugs and pulls of rivalry and competition. One way this reality has been illustrated in popular culture is the picture of an angel sitting on one shoulder and a devil sitting on the other, each whispering in an ear and competing for our attention. But all this does is make us feel like we are in living in a spiritual war zone. Douglas Campbell gives a more helpful metaphor. He invites us to think of sitting in a room with two pieces of music playing at the same time. One sound system is playing a beautiful piece of music, which inspires peace and joy. Another sound system is playing a piece of music, which inspires fear, anxiety, and fantasies of violence. This presents an invitation not to fight against the negative but to consciously refocus on the positive.

Peace,
Peter Catt+

Preface

I ONCE HEARD SOMEONE SAY THAT people write books to sort out their own thinking—to try to draw together strands of life and offer it to other people in some potentially helpful way. I guess that is what I am doing here. For the past twenty-five years, I have served as a priest in the Anglican Diocese of Perth, Western Australia. For half this time, I have also worked as a self-employed facilitator. Prior to that, I had careers in the shipping and banking industries. Along the way, I have had to figure out what it means to lead, in a formal sense, when one has absolutely no idea how to do it. I've come to understand that we learn best through our failures.

As an officer in the merchant navy in my early twenties, I felt comfortable navigating a ship across the world with responsibility for forty people's lives and hundreds of millions of dollars' worth of cargo. That was relatively uncomplicated. By comparison, leading a small church community is a different undertaking altogether. In my mid-thirties, around four years into my ministry as an Anglican priest, my confidence started to unravel, and I came close to slipping into clinical depression. I had been working in a series of financially struggling parishes with small congregations. I knew something about the Bible, theology, and church history, from my formation as a priest. I discovered, however, that this was not enough to navigate the complex relationships and other daily demands of a small local parish.

Being young and enthusiastic, I tried to lead heroically from the front, coming up with lots of ideas, with which I tried to engage other people. I assumed it was the job of the priest to get things happening and to be the one in charge. The latter role was supported by the language used on the bishop's licenses issued to me, such as "rector" (ruler) and "priest in charge." My endlessly-patient congregations bore with me with humility and encouragement while the parish bills grew and the congregational numbers stagnated. I was working too many hours and was frequently tired and irritable at home.

When I look back on this experience, I perceive what can be described only as signs of violence. This included violence to myself and subtle forms of violence towards others, either in the way I thought negatively about some people (internal violence) or tried to control people (external violence). This is particularly ironic, because I had always been keenly interested in Jesus's commission for his followers to be peacemakers (ministers of reconciliation [2 Cor 5:18]).

I don't think I'm alone in this predicament of noticing a big gap between what I believed and the way I have sometimes lived. It has been my observation that the use and abuse of power is one of the unspoken shadow aspects of church life. By shadow, I mean those things that are largely invisible or denied within ourselves.

Because much of my life is now spent working in non-church contexts, I know that the problem of violence (sometimes physical, but also psychological, social, and spiritual) is endemic in families, communities, congregations, organizations, cultures, and societies. This is not surprising, because the sources of violence lie deep within the human condition.

There is an aphorism that asserts "when the student is ready, the teacher will appear." It was when I was at a very low point and asking God for help that I was referred to Brendan McKeague, one of the early adopters in Australia of a process called Open Space Technology. Open Space Technology is a dialogical (conversational/dialogue) process designed by an Episcopal priest in the USA named Harrison Owen. It is a way in which people can meet to listen to each other, explore complex questions, and collaborate on shared dreams. I once heard Harrison say that "wherever space is opened peace breaks out." He knew this from personal experience, having facilitated Open Space meetings in many high-conflict situations, and it has become true in my experience as well.

Learning and implementing the principles and practice of Open Space Technology in the early 2000s was life-changing for me, the church, and the broader community in which I lived and worked. Practicing Open Space led to a passionate interest in the principles and practices of collaborative (nonviolent) leadership. I started to learn, apply, and teach dialogical processes in congregations, tertiary education, community groups, and health care settings, not only as meeting practices but as paradigms for leadership. I found the whole process personally life-giving, and many participants reported how liberating and energizing it was to engage with each other in these ways. Structured dialogic processes like Open Space, Talking Circles, Restorative Processes, and Coaching are deeply respectful, nonviolent technologies for living and working together, particularly in situations of high complexity and conflict.

In the first Open Space meeting I facilitated, which was for a group of clergy, a participant reflected at the end that the process had "felt like prayer." Just as theology was defined by St Anselm as "faith seeking understanding," I discovered that dialogic, collaborative processes were "practices seeking understanding." That is, I knew that these processes worked in practice, but I wanted to understand why they worked in theory.

This has led me through a journey of gradually joining the dots between theology, contemplation, and action in the practice of peace and, hence, to writing this book. I have come to the view that God's love is fundamentally about the practice of peace. God is love, and, therefore, God is our peace. We practice peace not just because it seems like a nice idea, but because peace is inextricably associated with becoming human.

If this book has turned up in your hands, I hope it is useful. As we say in Open Space, "whoever comes are the right people." My vision is that this book will support those of us who are *learning through doing* to feel more confident and equipped to be catalysts and enablers of peace—in our families, communities, churches, workplaces, schools, universities, health care systems, political structures, companies, and philanthropic organizations. We will do this non-anxiously, as we discover that the only person whom we can change is ourselves. And we will do this hopefully, because we know that small groups of committed people, working together by God's grace, can make a difference beyond what we dream or imagine.

Michael Wood
Perth, Western Australia
Whadjuk Noongar Land
Advent 2021
Maranatha

Acknowledgments

THIS WORK HAS BEEN BREWING for many years, and there are a lot of people to acknowledge and thank. We all stand on the shoulders of the ancestors. If there is anything worth reading here, it is inevitably because I've absorbed it from wise persons along the way. Any errors are likely to be mine. First and foremost, I want to acknowledge my friend and professional colleague, Brendan McKeague. As mentioned in the preface, Brendan changed the direction and quality of my life by introducing me to Open Space Technology. Since then, Brendan has been a constant and wise guide, although he still has not persuaded me to drink Guinness.

Thanks to Harrison Owen (the vision and inspiration of Open Space Technology), Dr. James Alison, Dr. Carly Osborn, Rev'd Dr. Scott Cowdell, and Michael Hardin (making René Girard's work accessible); Dr. Douglas Campbell (helping me to see the nonviolence in St. Paul); Dr. Brad Jersak (unpicking the thorny language of hell); Fr. Richard Rohr (poetic wisdom); Michael Rowdon and Rev'd Dr. Sarah Bachelard (gently drawing me, again and again, into contemplative prayer); Rev'd Dr. Anna Killigrew and Rev'd Peter Harrison (desert mother and father); Dr. George Trippe (twenty-five years of dream work); Dr. Neil Preston (joining the psycho-spiritual dots); Dr. David Moore (mentoring in Restorative Conferencing); Philip Goldsworthy, Michael Vial, Jo Hart, Rev'd Dr. Anne van Gend (founding members of the Peace Education Network); Rev'd Dr. Peter Catt and Jen Basham (not just talking about complexity, emergence, dialogue, and collaboration but actually leading it); Dr. Carolyn Oldham and Dr. Chantal Bourgault du Coudray for consistently championing dialogic processes at the University of Western Australia; Rev'd Dr. Ric Barrett-Lennard (encouragement to write); Archbishop Kay Goldsworthy and Lisa Goldacre (study leave); Dale Hess and committee members of Pace e Bene Australia (encouragement and project funding support); Rev'd Jan Crombie (opening space in Melbourne); Archbishop Phillip Aspinall (for having the courage to open a full day of synod with four-hundred-fifty people and no predetermined agenda); Dr. Anthony and Sue Tuckett (friendship and hospitality); Brett Wood (inspiring conversations); Dr. Clare Mouat, Clare Menck, Karen Whittle-Herbert, Dr. Meriel Griffiths, Rev'd Bronwyn Pagram, Gray Castledine (proofreading and helpful suggestions); Johanna Vondeling and Ted Lewis (editorial advice); Matthew Wimer and the team at Wipf and Stock; John and Ruth Wood (a lifetime of support).

And because the last shall be first, my loving family, Rani, Sarah, and Hannah, for your gentle, persistent, and unfailing encouragement to put my fingers to the keyboard.

1

Introduction

WHO IS THIS BOOK FOR?

Firstly, this is a book for lay and ordained church leaders and for those responsible for their formation. It is for those who want to inspire, model, and foster positive relationships in their church communities; "walk the talk" of the gospel of peace; and be catalysts and enablers of peace. This does not require us to be heroic experts who have all the answers. Rather, I believe that those of us in formal leadership roles need to unlearn a few destructive self-expectations and habits of being in control. I am advocating a gentler and more genuinely collaborative approach to leadership, which can leave us feeling energized rather than exhausted.

Secondly, this is a book for any Christian who wants to contribute more intentionally to peace in the world, at home, in the community, at church, or at work. In our relationships, we sometimes experience a disconnect between Sunday and the workweek. We run into conflict with our partner or children or someone at church or work, and, before we know it, we are immersed in a quagmire. We may feel a vocational imperative or desire to be agents of God's transformational peace in the world but feel lacking in the confidence and capability to do this. This book provides theological and practical frameworks and tools for practicing peace, regardless of whether we are in structural positions of authority.

Thirdly, this is a book for young and emerging leaders of any (or no) faith background who want to make a difference in the world but are not sure where to start. As a university chaplain, I am constantly impressed by the deep compassion and intellect that young people bring to the world's challenges. The complexity of many of these challenges is enormous, and many young people I encounter are feeling overwhelmed, depressed, and anxious. These things can manifest as cynical withdrawal or as a generalized anger that has no outlet beyond street protest and yelling in the echo chamber of social media. Such anger is understandable, and protesting is certainly an important mechanism for raising awareness and driving change. However, it can also leave protestors feeling discontented and powerless, because protest still requires someone *else* to change; it does not necessarily increase a sense of personal agency.

This book is about taking responsibility for what we love, as an act of service to the world. Saint Therese of Lisieux (1873–1897) spoke of doing ordinary things with extraordinary love, and this inspired Mother Theresa to begin an order of sisters that has cared for countless thousands of the poorest of the poor. All initiatives that contribute to the peace and wellbeing of the world start with small groups of committed people sitting together to get clear on their shared story and a shared intention to act. When these thousands of little initiatives are added together, the collective effect can lead to transformational tipping points of change.

STRUCTURE

I propose that the practice of peace requires attention to three interrelated ways of knowing (epistemologies) around which I have structured the book. The terminology I have used for these ways of knowing, or lenses, through which we perceive and make sense of the world are:

1. Theology
2. Contemplation
3. Action

These aspects of the spiritual journey are not independent of each other. I am teasing them apart for the sake of investigation, but one of my goals is to consistently draw links between them. It is possible to start reading the book at whichever of the three parts you are most interested in. For example, if you are less interested in the theological foundations and more interested in the how-to of collaborative/dialogic methods, then you can go straight to the action section (pt. 3). Then, to learn more about the theological rationale for using such methods, or the contemplative stance that would help you to implement such methods, you can go back and read the earlier chapters (pts. 1 and 2 respectively).

You will find prompts to reflect dotted throughout the book. These can be used as moments to pause and reflect on your own responses and/or can be used for conversation in a book study.

OVERVIEW OF PART 1: THEOLOGY

The gospel of Christ is the gospel of peace: the foundation of knowing who God is, who we are, and how God transforms culture nonviolently.

Theology is derived from two words, *theos* (God) and *logos* (reasoning). Theology is "reasoning about God." St. Anselm of Canterbury (1033–1109) said that theology is "faith seeking understanding." As soon as the mystery of God starts to tug at our hearts, we may begin to reflect on what is happening to us. That question is the beginning of theology.

When I started to read the Bible seriously, in my early twenties, I was immediately troubled by some of the appalling violence it contained and how this could possibly be reconciled (or not) with the beauty of the Jesus story and the "peace of Christ which surpasses understanding" (Phil 4:7).[1] The questions that I started asking forty years ago have continued to percolate.

One thing that has become clear over the years is that we human beings tend to make God in our own image, to support our own desires and wish fulfillments. Someone who saw this acutely was the twentieth-century theologian Karl Barth. As Barth observed the rise of the German imperial war machine in the early twentieth century, along with the en'thusiastic endorsement of its operations by 90 percent of the church-attending Christians in Germany, Barth discerned that this massive political and ethical failure was underpinned by a profound theological

---

1. *Christ* is from the Greek, meaning "anointed." When the Christian Testament talks about Jesus Christ, it means "Jesus the anointed one" (or, in Hebrew, Messiah). In this book, I generally use the word Christ as a title and as shorthand for the fullness of the eternal Word of God—God's self-revelation (Logos, John 1:1); Jesus of Nazareth; the risen and ascended Christ, who is continuous with Jesus of Nazareth and now with a transformed body; the one in whom we live, through the Spirit; the one declared in the Nicene Creed as "God of God, Light of Light, True God of True God . . . of one being with the Father."

error. This error was to begin theology somewhere other than the decisive revelation of God in Jesus Christ.[2] This led to Barth's role in framing *The Barman Declaration* and his expansive theological project in his multi-volume *Church Dogmatics*. Barth's project was to keep reminding Christians of the absolute centrality of the person of Jesus Christ, out of which healthy ethics and politics will follow.[3]

Saint Benedict of Nursia in the sixth century also realized the importance of beginning everything with the contemplation of God. Benedict begins his Rule for monastic life with the word *listen* (incline the ear of the heart to God). In the seventh chapter of the rule, Benedict outlines twelve degrees of humility, the first of which is "keep the awe of God continually before your eyes." Why is this so important? As Barth realized, we become what we worship.[4] If we worship a God who is love (peace), our lives are more likely to take on the character of peace. It has become clear to me that when our image of God is shaped by Christ, it is impossible to make God into a god of war.

There are lots of ways of making peace if we think of peace as the absence of immediate conflict. For example, we can make conflict go away in the short term by silencing, expelling, or killing those who disagree with us. In this way, we conceive of peace as the absence of conflict, because we have driven the conflict out. However, this apparent peace can only ever be temporary, because that which we violently exclude will inevitably fight back in a new form.

In contrast, the deep and enduring peace that Jesus gives is a peace flowing out of God's nature. The Christlike God reveals, destabilizes, and remakes human mechanisms of peacemaking. I have come to the conclusion that the gospel of Christ *is* a gospel of peace. I have articulated this gospel in the form of four theological touchstones (pt. 1 of the book). A touchstone is a marker that we can use to keep the big picture in mind when immersed in the detail. The touchstones I am articulating are not the only way of framing the gospel. They are simply my attempt, drawing

---

2. We could point to other examples of self-justifying, self-protective militaristic ambitions of most countries. Australia has a small military compared to many countries, and yet it has a highly sophisticated and economically lucrative arms industry that exports to other countries. Australia also has a legacy of violent colonization.

3. I absorbed the essence of this from a conversation with Douglas Campbell. He may have also written it somewhere, but I can't find it.

4. Ps 135:18.

on the wisdom of many others to clearly articulate the gospel of peace.[5] The four touchstones are:

a. *God is Christlike.* For Christians, our primary way of knowing God is through Jesus Christ the living Word of God. Christ is the image of the invisible God. This is incredibly good news, because Christ reveals the irrevocable love of God for the cosmos and the trajectory of life towards the ultimate union of all things with God.

b. *Christ reveals the nature of violence.* The revelation of God in Jesus reveals (unveils) some very unsettling realities about humans, particularly the way in which we try to make peace through violence. We examine how violence originates in disoriented desire and deep psychological needs for survival and belonging within ourselves.

c. *Christ gives a peace that the world cannot give.* The self-emptying and humble love of Christ, through whom the cosmos is made, is the same Love that deals with our violence.[6] Christ heals our wounds and disoriented desires and sets us free to inhabit a life that is not founded on the making of victims. This is a peace that the world cannot give.

d. *Christ enables us to practice peace.* As we are transformed by the mind of Christ and gifts of the Spirit, we explore what it looks and feels like to live the peace of Christ. This occurs within a community in which participants are growing into human beings made in the image of the fully human one (Christ). The gospel of Christ is centrally about healthy, life-giving relationships within the human community,[7] sourced in relationship with a nonviolent God. Peace

---

5. My theological thinking has been significantly influenced by Douglas Campbell's apocalyptic reading of St. Paul, and Girard-influenced scholars such as James Alison, Michael Hardin, Walter Wink, Scott Cowdell, Bradley Jersak, Gil Bailie, and S. Mark Heim. I note the predominance of male writers. Interestingly to me, I have been more influenced by female writers in pts. 2 and 3.

6. I will frequently use the words *kenosis* or *kenotic*, from the Greek word meaning to become empty, empty handed, humble, non-grasping, even apparently foolish. See Phil 2:6–7.

7. Peace is also about a sustainable relationship with the earth with which we stand in relationship. This is a subject of immense importance, and others more qualified than I are increasingly writing about it. I give it less treatment here than it deserves. Suffice to say that the practice of contemplation, which I emphasize, has significant implications for the environment. See also Wood, "Climate Change."

is the core of the Christian message and foundational to the identity and purpose of the church.

Having articulated the gospel of peace, I turn, in chapters 6–8, to some of the most common obstacles, in the Bible and Christian vocabulary, for believing in the nonviolent goodness of God. For the sake of coherence, we need to make sense of violence in the Bible rather than ignore it or do impossible intellectual somersaults to rationalize it.

For example, what are we to do with passages in the Bible that say that God orders genocides? What about the notion that a loving God will condemn large numbers of people to everlasting suffering in hell? Is it possible for God to be a pathological murderer in one moment and the Prince of Peace in the next? Navigating this territory will require us to think about *how* we read, as much as *what* we read, in the Bible.

In laying out the theological foundations for the practice of peace, I am drawing on existing scholarship. I am trying to be a bridge-builder between the theological academy and the local Christian community. I feel like I am standing on the shoulders of giants. The first eye-opener, for me, to the peace implications of the gospel was John V. Taylor's book *The Christlike God*, which is also a phrase that I use with ubiquitous regularity,[8] closely followed by Walter Wink's *Engaging the Powers*. My thinking has been significantly shaped by Christian Girardian scholars and, in recent years, by Douglas Campbell's work on St. Paul. Anyone familiar with Campbell's work will recognize his influence in the way I have structured the four touchstones—in particular, the necessity to begin with the solution/end to understand the nature of the problem.

The scholarly sources are listed in the bibliography and identify where you can go to dig more deeply into what I often present as givens. The field of theology is vast, and some of the ideas that I present as gospel are not held by all Christians. Therefore, while I have intentionally used the pronoun *we* throughout the book, as a friendly way to enroll the reader as a traveling companion on this journey of peace, I accept that some readers may resist their inclusion.

---

8. The term "the Christlike God" has been widely ascribed to a former Archbishop of Canterbury, Michael Ramsey. I have been unable to find any written source. A colleague who knows Ramsey's work much better than I said that he had spent many hours trying to track down the quote and been unable to do so. He suspects that it might originate from one of Ramsey's many television interviews. Happily, the phrase has been given a new lease of life and interest through Brad Jersak's book *A More Christlike God*.

It is a radical thing to be reminded of the root (radix) proclamation of the church that Jesus is the revelation of God, and therefore the revelation of what it means to be human. I am reminding myself of this as I write—reconnecting with the heart of the story of Jesus, with its stunning insights into the human condition and its power to shape us into catalysts and enablers of peace.

OVERVIEW OF PART 2: CONTEMPLATION

The relationship between the inner life, loving God, and loving neighbor

If theology is faith seeking understanding, what do we mean by faith? In Christian thought, faith is not just, or even primarily, intellectual assent to an idea.[9] To have faith in God (or another person) means that we *trust* them. Trust is a relational knowing, which is deeper than cognitive ideas, or observable facts, about another person. For example, I can describe all kinds of objective truths/facts about my wife, but my trust (faith) that she loves me is more than an idea. I *trust* her! This cannot be proved to an external observer. In the language of poetry, the seat of such trusting, relational knowing is the heart.[10]

While theology is endlessly interesting and intellectually stimulating, if that is all we have, then we risk treating God as an intellectual curiosity that we try to master with our cleverness.[11] At worst, the spiritual journey may turn into an ideology where we latch onto a conception of truth and try to defend it furiously, at the expense of relationships. Wars have been fought over good ideas. However, the God of peace leads us beyond ideas and into loving relationships. The quality of our relationships flows from the *heart* as well as the *mind*. Relationships are fed by the contemplation of beauty, the depths of silence and the subtlety of the body. We often pray in words, but, frequently, words are inadequate.

---

9. An assent to an idea is a belief, e.g., "I *believe* it to be true that my wife was born in India."

10. I use the metaphor of the heart in the sense of intuitive, bodily, and emotional knowing.

11. This is what happens in religious studies, where the investigating ego stands over Christ and subjects him to scrutiny using criterion other than Christ. This is not to deny that religious studies, like any field of inquiry, cannot offer useful questions for Christians to consider.

Then prayer drops to the deeper level of silence.[12] This is the territory of contemplative knowing.

Chapters 9–12 explore how the practice of peace is inextricably associated with the practice of contemplation. Using Jesus's two great commandments as a frame,[13] I focus on contemplative prayer as an embodied way of loving God with all our heart, soul, mind, and strength, and contemplatively informed conversation as a primary way in which we love our neighbor as ourselves.

These two things—contemplative prayer and contemplatively informed conversation—are intricately connected. Contemplative prayer deepens our relationship with God and, in doing so, deepens our relationships with our neighbor by leading to a greater awareness of how our complex desires and needs influence our conversations. Similarly, the challenges of interpersonal relationships constantly drive us back into dependence on God.

OVERVIEW OF PART 3: ACTION

The art and skills of dialogue, both individual and group, through which we navigate relational complexity, grow healthy communities, and collaborate to practice peace
Theology and prayer inescapably shape the way we live. This can also work in the other direction. We might find that the way we are living feels inconsistent with what we profess to be true (theology) or sense to be true (prayer). Perhaps we find that we are in conflict in the workplace, church, or home, and we say, "I know Christ is about peace, but I really hate someone at work. What can I do about this?"

In chapters 13–16, I dive into the how-to (skills) of dialogue, conversation, and collaboration as practices of peace. The examples I provide come mainly from churches, but the principles are transferable into any complex human system, including community groups and workplaces. Every vision statement I have ever seen posted on walls in organizations has been based on an ethos of mutual respect. If the vision statement

---

12. "The Spirit helps us in our weakness; for we do not know how to pray as we ought, but that very Spirit intercedes with sighs too deep for words" (Rom 8:26). The fourth layer of sacred reading (Lectio Divina) in the Benedictine tradition is pure silence (contemplatio).

13. Mark 12:28–31.

is on the wall of a church, it invariably includes an appeal to Christlike love and forgiveness. Unfortunately, these honorable aspirations can lead to people suppressing their disagreements and strong emotions. These collective subterranean conflicts can then fester and pop out in dysfunctional explosions or manipulative indirect forms of communication.

The good news is that collaborative group methodologies, which help to create conditions for deep and respectful listening, leading to shared commitment and coordinated action, already exist. I lay out a Collaborative Emergent Design approach, which I and others have developed, tested, and refined in many contexts. Collaborative Emergent Design is a structural practice of peace, because it involves working *with* people rather than doing things *to* them or *for* them. This basic collaborative process is supported with a toolbox of practical conversational frameworks.

BEING IS THE FOUNDATION OF DOING

It is easy, when addressing a topic like peace and nonviolent leadership, to foster just another form of busy activism. I have tried to avoid doing this. To become human is to allow ourselves to be shaped increasingly into the image of the Christlike God. For activists, this sometimes means doing less rather than more, as we give up our ego attachments. Harrison Owen makes the provocative statement "Never work harder than you have to."[14] Our world is being destroyed by hyper-consumptive activity driven by our acquisitive desires.

The question I am addressing therefore is not so much *what* we do—what causes, projects, or ends we seek—but *how* we do what we do in collaboration with others. Practicing peace can take us into multitudes of worthy causes—spiritual, psychological, social, economic, environmental, domestic, political. We can frame almost any cause as "just" and therefore "good." But how just are we being if we burn ourselves out and burn our relationships in the process? Despite sermons we may have heard to the contrary, Jesus never taught us to *build* the kingdom of God. Jesus always talks about the kingdom as either a gift given or a reality we are invited to enter. Building causes and ignoring relationships is perilous; those who crucified Jesus were convinced that they were doing a good and holy thing for God. I write this to sound a special caution to the

---

14. I have heard Harrison say this in person and have verified it by email.

justice-driven ideologue lurking in many of us. Much violence is done in the name of justice.

As mentioned earlier, the focus of this book is how we practice peace in commonly experienced contexts of daily life. Some of what I have written will be transferable into the specific contexts of the military and police, particularly in day-to-day leadership. However, it is outside the scope of this book, and my expertise, to discuss the ethics of coercive force or of war. As a form of structural violence, the industrial military war machine, and its economic effects, is certainly going to throw up fundamental questions of conscience for Christians.[15] This book *might* help with how people of good conscience engage with such questions. But more important to me is the question of how a more intentional practicing of peace, especially by Christians, in whatever places we find ourselves, might reduce the likelihood of violent conflict in the first place.[16]

TERMINOLOGY

(i) Gender and personhood

This book assumes a basic familiarity with the Bible and the theological vocabulary that readers may have absorbed through church/worship participation, or perhaps by going to a Christian school. If you do not have such a background, then Wikipedia generally has serviceable introductions to key vocabulary. All biblical quotes are from the New Revised Standard Version (NRSV) translation unless otherwise stated. I have occasionally drawn on David Bentley Hart's erudite translation of the New Testament. The latter is refreshing, in that it gives a very tight rendition of the Greek into English, which gives a raw freshness, such as what we might imagine the early churches heard.

---

15. Australia derives significant economic benefits from the development and export of weapons. On the other side of the ledger, there is the opportunity-cost of the military (money that the country could spend on other things), the price paid by nations in the long-term PTSD suffered by soldiers, and the rupturing of societies in which war is waged.

16. Pope Francis has questioned whether any modern armed conflict can be a "just war" and has asked all people to consider how they can promote peace (Wooden, "No More War"). For a comprehensive review of the way Christians have thought about war through history, including the state of the current discussions, see Rynne, *Jesus Christ Peacemaker*.

In the Scriptures and Christian tradition (e.g., Apostles' and Nicene Creeds), we frequently find gendered language and metaphors for God. This language is commonly male but not always. For example, Jesus uses the image of gathering the people of Jerusalem under his wings like a mother hen;[17] John's Gospel draws on imagery, familiar to Jewish listeners, of the feminine divine wisdom in speaking of the Word of God (Logos);[18] and the breath (*ruah*) of God in the Hebrew Scriptures is grammatically feminine. Another way that John's Gospel works with gender is through the image of a marriage feast. John begins with a wedding at Cana (John 2:1–11) and ends, in the book of Revelation (Rev 21:2), with a marriage. The woman who is betrothed to Christ is a symbol of the new Jerusalem, united with God.

These powerful relational images utilize gendered language, even though the church has sometimes used gendered language in destructive ways to diminish women and gender-diverse people. We need, therefore, to remind ourselves in categorical terms that the infinite God is neither male nor female. God is not limited to being a first-century Palestinian Jewish male, even though God became known to us very intimately in the form of Jesus. The point of the incarnation is not that God is male but that God is human.

Similarly, Jesus speaks to God using the term *Abba* (an affectionate term for Father, somewhat like Papa), not because God is male but because the language emphasizes relational trust. I sometimes wonder if Jesus wanted to transform the cultural meaning of human fatherhood by (re)modeling it in terms of Jesus's positive relationship with his Abba.[19]

One useful liturgical experiment has been to express the Trinity in functional terms (e.g., Creator, Redeemer, and Sanctifier). A downside of this linguistic move is that we lose the crucial markers of God being a communion of *persons*. I am keen to retain the emphasis on personhood in this book because of its implications for nonviolent dialogue.

For these reasons, I have decided to retain the language of Father and Son when directly quoting from the Bible. Where possible, I will replace

---

17. Matt 23:37.

18. Wis 7:22–27; John 1:1–4.

19. The potential for modeling fatherhood in a positive way is no less important today. We also note the numerous ways in which Jesus breaks the cultural norms of his day by validating women in radical ways, how the first witnesses to the resurrection (apostles to the apostles) were women (Matt 28:9–10; John 20:11–18), and how St. Paul counts women as fellow leaders of churches (Phil 4:2; 1 Cor 16:19; Acts 18:26).

the pronoun *Him* with *God* and refer to the Holy Spirit as *she*, reflecting the feminine of the Hebrew word for Spirit. I have decided that moving frequently between pronouns—he, she, and the singular they—could be distracting from the main points being made. I hope that readers can do their own mental workarounds when it comes to these constraints in the English language.

(ii) Scripture

The terminology I have adopted for what Bibles usually call Old and New Testaments is the Hebrew Scriptures and Christian Testament, respectively. The reason for this is that when the Gospels and epistles were being written, and the authors spoke of the Scriptures, they were referring to the Hebrew Scriptures (particularly the Greek translation of the Hebrew Scriptures). Far from being *old* (which might imply superseded), the Jewish disciples of Jesus were searching their Scriptures to articulate their experience of Jesus in light of their tradition (as the risen Christ evidently taught them to do on the road to Emmaus).[20] We need to remember that Jesus was a Jew and that his Jewish disciples never gave up their Jewish faith. We need to keep remembering this in view of the tragedy of anti-Semitism throughout history, including from Christians.

(iii) Nonviolence

A key point in this book is that peace is not the absence of conflict but the way in which we navigate conflict nonviolently. Consistent with a linguistic convention in the nonviolence movement, the word *nonviolent* is not hyphenated. We commonly hear people using the word *non-violent* (hyphenated) in terms of avoiding violent acts. However, the word nonviolent is a positive expression, meaning "Christlike love in action." Nonviolence is purposefully active and is *not* a synonym for pacifism. Nonviolence is committed to mindsets and actions that honor the dignity of others—an expression of Shalom.[21] Similarly, I sometimes use the

---

20. Luke 24:13–32.

21. *Shalom* is a rich Jewish word capturing a range of meaning, including well-being, rightly ordered relationships, health, and prosperity. It is a state of communal harmony and not just the absence of dispute or conflict.

expression *Christlike peace* to distinguish Christ's peace from the way cultures try to make peace through perpetrating violence.

Finally, I have avoided giving a decisive definition of violence. This might seem strange in a book that talks so much about it. Part of the reason is that definitions of violence prove to be inadequate, because people's experience of what constitutes violence is so varied and contextual. This becomes evident in an exercise that my colleagues and I usually do with groups when we deliver "Jesus and Nonviolence" workshops. Rather than begin with a definition of violence, we put a flip chart on the wall with two columns, one titled "Violence" and one titled "Nonviolence." We then ask people to call out words that they associate with each heading. After a while, the group notices paradoxes. For example, the word "tolerance" typically shows up in the nonviolence column, but then someone will inevitably say, "But we don't tolerate everything; to tolerate some things would be to do violence to people."

Definitions of violence tend to focus on the phenomenon of violence—its outward forms, including physical, emotional, spiritual, structural, economic, political, and social violence. However, in this book, we will explore how God illuminates the inner spiritual dynamics of violence, what God does with our violence, and how God opens a *way* to a deeper and more profound peace.

So let us now turn to God and the gospel of peace as a foundation for the practice of peace.

Part 1
THEOLOGY

Blessed are the peacemakers.
—Jesus in the Gospel of Matthew

Be at peace with one another.
—Jesus in the Gospel of Mark

Grace and peace be with you.
—St. Paul

Grace and peace be with you.
—St. Peter

The role of the Christian faith is to be peacemakers.
—Archbishop Justin Welby

To be true followers of Jesus today also includes embracing his teaching about nonviolence.
—Pope Francis

2

Touchstone 1
God Is Christlike

JESUS IS THE STARTING POINT (THIS IS GOOD NEWS)

Christianity has done its share of perpetuating violence through history and justifying it in the name of God. I am convinced that we can justify violence theologically only if we start our thinking about God somewhere other than Jesus. For example, we could start our thinking about God by assembling a vast collection of descriptors about God from the Hebrew Scriptures or even from philosophical conceptions of what we suppose God *must* be (e.g., all powerful, all knowing) and then try to squeeze Jesus into that preexisting image of God.[1] This makes God subject to categories that are derived from outside God's self-disclosure in Jesus.

A simple but important example of this would occur when we talk about God being just. Most societies tend to take it for granted that good behavior should be rewarded and bad behavior should be punished, and we appoint judges to ensure that happens.[2] Perhaps you will agree with

---

1. The Westminster Catechism, section 7, is an example of such a list of descriptors of the character of God. This does not mean that the Hebrew Scriptures are not useful for providing useful knowledge of God but that Jesus Christ is the lens for our discernment. I will unpack this more as we go along.

2. As Douglas Campbell points out, such assumptions are tied up with a raft of other (incorrect) assumptions (e.g., that persons are rational individuals bound together

me that this understanding of justice would be considered self-evidently *reasonable* by most people. We might then project this notion of justice onto God, and, in doing so, we have framed God in the image of a human judge, dispensing punishment. In doing this, we have also provided a theological basis for justifying violence in human justice systems. We have created a convenient self-reinforcing loop. This is an incredibly easy mistake to make. The problem with projecting our linguistic assumptions onto God is that it can lead in very twisted directions. It is less than a century since world wars were precipitated by an assumption that certain races were superior to others. Colonial expansion relied, as least in part, on a belief that the invading nation was culturally, if not ontologically, superior to the one that an empire was invading.

We need to work in the other direction. As Christians, we need to start with Jesus as the revelation of God and allow *Jesus* to be our teacher and the hermeneutical (interpretive) key for all our language about God, including the way we read the Scriptures. The Christian Testament was written by people who had already been grasped by God in Christ through hearing the testimony of firsthand witnesses, through worship (including reading the Hebrew Scriptures), through prayer (direct address by the Holy Spirit), and through breaking bread together.[3]

The testimony of the first witness and the early churches they gathered together, was that *Jesus* is the Word—the image of the invisible God.[4] The foundation to which this book will continually return is that the imperative to live and lead nonviolently is not just because we think it might be a good way to live, but because it is ontologically grounded in the revelation of God in Jesus.[5] The Christian Testament concisely summarizes this in several places:

---

principally by contractual relationships of rights and responsibilities; and that if the contract is broken, there needs to be a consequence—generally punitive).

3. Luke 24:13–35, Acts 1.

4. The church has conveyed the apostolic witness to Christ in many ways, including oral tradition/preaching (1 Cor 15:1–8), liturgy, creeds, iconography, prophecy, poetry, Gospels, and epistles. The church through the ages has always needed to *discern* Christ, through the Spirit, in a living community through such mediating vehicles. This has given rise to occasional and ongoing robust debates, including which texts should be included in the Bible.

5. I accept that human language constrains our capacity to describe the infinite. The God who exceeds all our conceptions must enter our human experience in language we can comprehend—primarily in the linguistic form of Jesus, the embodied Word of God. The infinity of God is not *limited* to what can be said of Jesus of Nazareth;

- In the beginning was the Word, and the Word was with God, and the Word was God (John 1:1).
- Before Abraham was born, "I Am" (John 8:58).
- Whoever has seen me has seen the Father (John 14:9).
- Thomas said to him, "My Lord and my God!" (John 20:28).
- I am the Alpha and the Omega, the beginning and the end (Rev 21:6).
- He is the image of the invisible God, the firstborn of all creation (Col 1:15).
- Long ago God spoke to our ancestors in many and various ways by the prophets, but in these last days he has spoken to us by a Son, whom he appointed heir of all things, through whom he also created the worlds. He is the reflection of God's glory and the exact imprint of God's very being, and he sustains all things by his powerful word (Heb 1:1–3).

Monotheists, gentile Christians, and Messianic Jews[6] took a while to figure out some of the baffling implications of these statements. Followers of Jesus cannot separate God from the experience of the crucified and risen Christ. Michael Ramsey, a former Archbishop of Canterbury, summarizes the point as "God is Christlike and in him is no un-Christlikeness at all."[7]

The First Letter of John says "God is love" (1 John 4:16), but John can say this only because he has encountered this love in a very particular form, in the shape of Jesus, crucified and risen. The significance of the *Word becoming flesh* is not that Jesus is a first-century Jewish male but that Jesus is a human being. Jesus's most common way of referring to himself was "the human one" (Son of Man). God is not an abstract construction of philosophy that we can master with our language. God must inescapably use ordinary stuff—carbon atoms—to physically reveal

---

however, the essential nature of God, as love, is not different to the love we see embodied in Jesus. In pt. 2, in the reflections on contemplative prayer, we acknowledge that all that we can say about God (via positiva) is balanced by the recognition that much cannot be said (via negativa) because of our limited perceptual apparatus.

6. The term *Messianic Jews* refers to Jews (such as St. Paul) who came to know Jesus as Messiah (Christ). They did not stop being Jews, but their Jewish faith was adapted because of Jesus being their Rabbi and Lord.

7. As cited in Taylor, *Christlike God*, unnumbered page in preface.

God's self. This is sometimes called the *scandal of particularity*, to which Annie Dillard speaks as follows:

> That Christ's incarnation occurred improbably, ridiculously, at such-and-such a time, into such-and-such a place, is referred to—with great sincerity even among believers—as "the scandal of particularity." Well, the "scandal of particularity" is the only world that I, in particular, know. What use has eternity for light? We're all up to our necks in this particular scandal.[8]

Saying that God is Christlike is a shorthand way of saying "God is love." This love is not an abstract concept or a human feeling but is a *person* (Christ) who remains present to us.[9] This is the first touchstone: *God is Christlike—humble, crucified love*. This is our foundational go-to point when we get bamboozled by biblical details and thorny theological questions. This is the key to reading the Hebrew Scriptures and Christian Testament. Therefore, as disciples of Jesus, we need to read the Bible *backwards*, to discern Christ to whom the text points.[10] For Christians, the creation story begins at the first verse of John's Gospel (John 1:1), not the first verse of Genesis (Gen 1:1). The God who created the cosmos was, is, and always has been the crucified, resurrected, and ascended one.

In this book, I will repeatedly use the phrase "the Christlike God" to make it clear that when I am taking about God, I am talking about the God revealed in and through Christ—his life, death, resurrection, and ongoing presence through the Spirit, discerned in and through the community of the church. Scott Cowdell puts it like this:

> Today's rivalry between theism and atheism is really about defending or attacking God's right to intrude upon our space, with both sides typically unable to perceive or appreciate the kenotic reserve and respect of the Holy God, imagining instead an intrusive insensitivity that is more typical of the false sacred. As Girard emphasizes, however, the Holy God does not reach

---

8. Dillard, *Pilgrim at Tinker Creek*, 79.

9. More precisely, God reveals God's self as a communion of persons (Trinity). Christlike love is an eternal relationship between persons. What is important about the persons of the Trinity is not their gender but their kenotic relationship to each other.

10. I am taking my lead here from Douglas Campbell's work, which in turn draws heavily on Barth.

for the world's levers by any means other than the powerlessness of Christ.[11]

We must allow the revelation of God in Christ to interrogate and interpret everything, including the written words of Scripture.[12] Brad Jersak notes that Greek Jewish scholars such as Philo and many of the great early Christians teachers all began their reading of Scripture with the presupposition that God is the ultimate good and love.[13] What the revelation of Christ does is to put tangible flesh to conceptions of good and love and so fill these terms with a distinctive meaning. All theology is therefore christological and becomes the foundation for doing ethics. The church summarizes this in the Nicene Creed: "We believe in one Lord Jesus Christ, eternally begotten of the Father." There was never a time when God was not like Jesus—which means that self-giving relationship has always been at the heart of God, and God's intention, purpose, and goal for the universe has always been union and life in God.

THIS IS REVEALED . . .

One of the fascinating things about Jesus being the image of God is that it is not screamingly obvious at first glance. The insight that a crucified Palestinian Jewish man reveals the glory of God is not something that came easily to the first disciples—even to those who had been close friends of Jesus. One of the striking things about all the resurrection stories is that they all contain elements of nonrecognition, partial recognition, or gradual recognition. For example:

---

11. Cowdell, *René Girard and Nonviolent God*, 141.

12. While Christians commonly refer to the Scriptures as the word of God, this statement needs to be nuanced. The scriptures are the word of God to the extent that they testify to (bear witness to) *the Word* (Jesus Christ), who becomes present to us as the Scriptures are read and bread is broken, in a community of faith. Through the inspiration of the Spirit, the meaning of the written text, as pointing to Christ, is unveiled. The community then becomes a "letter written not with ink but with the Spirit of the Living God" (2 Cor 3:3).

13. Jersak points out that Philo built on Plato's proposition of God as ultimate good, and the early Christian teachers saw the revelation of Christ as *the* revelation/definition of love (citing Origen, Gregory of Nyssa, Basil the Great, John Cassian, John Chrysostom, and Augustine). Where any text did not point to this goodness and love, teachers would advocate reading the text allegorically, "because to read them literally would be unworthy of God" (Jersak, *More Christlike Word*, 89–95).

- Mary Magdalene initially mistakes Jesus for a gardener (John 20:15).
- The disciples on the Sea of Tiberias don't initially recognize Jesus (John 21:5).
- Jesus walks along the Emmaus road with two disciples for a whole day and is recognized only in the evening "in the breaking of the bread" (Luke 24:16).
- When Jesus appears to the eleven in Jerusalem, they experience a mixture of terror, disbelief, and wonder (Luke 24:36–41).
- On the mountain in Galilee, some of the eleven doubted (Matt 28:17).
- In the shorter (original) ending to Mark's Gospel, the women flee in terror and amazement (Mark 16:8).

Saint Paul makes it clear that he did not figure out, with his unaided human reason, that Jesus was the Christ. Paul did not *get it* by reading his Scriptures, even though he was extremely well read in his own scriptural tradition. Neither did he *get it* by the rational arguments of Greek wisdom. Paul received an apocalypse (which means unveiling—a revelation). The veil between worlds parted. This is the kind of seeing of which mystics speak. It comes unexpectedly, and our egoic wills cannot force it.

When I think of my own gradual journey from youthful atheism through to Christian faith, I can identify this gradual process of deepening awareness. There was a series of events over time, all of which had a sense of grace rather than any work on my part—for example, being involved in a youth group for a period in my late teenage years; standing on the bridge of a ship in the middle of the Indian Ocean, contemplating the awesomeness of the galaxy; being drawn to sit in the deep silence of empty churches in ports far from home; dipping into the Gospel stories and being intrigued by this man, Jesus, whose "peace transcends understanding" (Phil 4:7); being drawn into a local Anglican Church in my early twenties, receiving a warm and hospitable welcome and being moved by the beauty of the liturgy. In such ways and many others, the revelation of Christ is *mediated* to human beings.

... BY GRACE

Does this revelation occur only to people who are particularly spiritually sensitive, or good, or holy, or insightful? The answer is no. In none of the resurrection stories is the appearance of Christ a response to a prayer of repentance. Rather, revelation comes as a surprise to the unrepentant— as a breakthrough. God is constantly initiating the contact with fallible human beings (lost, wounded, judged by humans as unworthy), searching us out even when we don't initially know this movement of the Spirit is happening to us and in us.

- God proves his love for us in that *while we still were sinners* Christ died for us (Rom 5:8).
- Which one of you, having a hundred sheep and losing one of them, does not leave the ninety-nine in the wilderness and *go after the one that is lost* until he finds it? (Luke 15: 4).
- When the Pharisees saw this, they said to his disciples, "Why does your teacher *eat with tax collectors and sinners*?" (Matt 9:11).
- God, who is rich in mercy, out of the great love with which he loved us even *when we were dead through our trespasses*, made us alive together with Christ—by *grace* you have been saved—and raised us up with him and seated us with him in the heavenly places in Christ Jesus, so that in the ages to come he might show the immeasurable riches of his *grace* in kindness toward us in Christ Jesus. For by *grace* you have been saved through faith, and this is not your own doing; it is the *gift* of God—not the result of works, so that no one may boast (Eph 2:4–9).

... THROUGH RELATIONSHIP

To say that God is Christlike is to simultaneously say something fundamentally important about what it means to be human beings—to be *persons*. Persons are, by definition, inherently relational. We cannot conceive of ourselves outside of telling stories about our relationships. This is also true for Jesus, as is apparent in the following text from John's Gospel:

> Jesus said to Thomas, "I am the way, and the truth, and the life. No one comes to the Father except through me. If you know

> me, you will know my Father also. From now on you do know him and have seen him." Philip said to him, "Lord, show us the Father, and we will be satisfied." Jesus said to him, "Have I been with you all this time, Philip, and you still do not know me? Whoever has seen me has seen the Father. How can you say, 'Show us the Father'? Do you not believe that I am in the Father and the Father is in me?" (John 14:6–10)

A key point of these verses is that persons (Father and Son) are mutually self-defining. The only reason that God can be called Father is that God has a Son/child. And the only reason that Jesus can be called Son/child is that Jesus has a Father/parent. To take a personal analogy, the only reason that I can be called a father is because I am father to my daughters (the same for my wife, as mother to our daughters). In an equivalent way, our daughters can be called daughters because they have parents.

Aboriginal peoples help us with this insight. When White Fellas meet each other for the first time, they often ask questions like "What do you do for a living?" In this way, we perceive each other as *individuals* who act in and on the world. Australian Aboriginal persons tend to begin a conversation with questions like "Where do you come from?" which also means "What is your place, land, and family?" In this way, Aboriginal people explore identity in very relational terms.

The church initially expressed these important truths about the centrality of relationship in the heart of God through the wording of eucharistic prayers and hymns (an important early example is Phil 2:6–11). As time progressed, the church also felt it necessary to preserve and protect these central relational concepts in the form of credal statements that are still recited weekly as part of the liturgy.

Because some of the key theologians who worked on the development of the Nicene Creed were Greek speakers, some categories of Greek metaphysics were deployed in the development of the doctrine of the Holy Trinity. These have been helpful in shaping a Christian understanding of what it means to be human. For example, the doctrine of the Trinity required a fundamental reconceptualization of the meaning of person. Prior to the Christian theological work on the nature of God as Trinity, a *person* was synonymous with an *individual*. A person was a citizen of Rome with specific legal rights. In contrast, slaves had no rights and therefore no personhood. Young children had little more personhood than slaves.[14] The Cappadocian fathers,[15] who were instrumental in crafting the language of the Nicene Creed, framed a new understanding of what a person is. Their insight was that a person is a *being in relationship to other persons*.[16] The essence of a person is their capacity to address another person and receive a response—to love and to be loved in return.

Pondering this in relation to peace and nonviolence invites us to consider how we engage with difference (culture, beliefs, age, sexuality) between persons in our churches and communities. We might dislike what another person is saying, but how do we relate to the person as someone with intrinsic dignity, with whom we are inextricably related?

> Let all of us speak the truth to our neighbors, for *we are members of one another* [that is, we form each other as persons within a single body who is Christ]. *(*Eph 4:25)

Secondly, the doctrine of the Trinity wrestles with the paradoxical question of unity and difference. How can the three—encountered as Father, Son, and Spirit—be spoken of as one God, thereby preserving monotheism? Working through this paradox required a new conceptualization of the nature of unity.

In the formulation of the Nicene Creed in the fourth century, scholars were articulating that the oneness of God was not a numerical unity (uniformity) but a *relational* oneness. God is love, and love is always a relationship between persons. The persons of the Trinity are constituted through a constant self-emptying (kenosis) towards each other. There is a union (oneness) of perfect giving and receiving of love.[17] Because the substance of God is love, God can give only God's love. It is not as if God could choose to act contrary to God's own nature.

---

14. This reality lies behind, and gives a powerful significance to, Jesus's statement "Let the little children come to me, and do not hinder them, for the kingdom of heaven belongs to such as these" (Matt 19:14).

15. Basil of Caesarea (330–370), Gregory of Nyssa (335–395) and Gregory of Constantinople (329–389).

16. Carnley elaborates on this in *Yellow Wallpaper*.

17. For visual metaphors for this kind of unity of relationship, I commend the YouTube clips of Torvill and Dean ice-skating; Fred Astaire and Ginger Rogers dancing; and the duelling banjos scene from the movie *Deliverance*. Do we feel drawn into the beauty of the dance/music and, in a sense, *participate* in it? In the case of *Duelling Banjos*, we might also observe the temporary cessation of an undercurrent of violence/hostility, as others are drawn into the music.

As we will see in later chapters, this dance of giving and receiving is the theological foundation of dialogue—a kenotic movement of giving and receiving, leading to creativity. As humans, we never express this giving and receiving perfectly in our relationships, but we have the pattern of it in the divine life. God speaks God's self (God's Word, which is love) into the cosmos and, with a vulnerable humility, invites us into a freely chosen relationship.

Conceiving of love in this way—as a relational dynamic of giving and receiving—means that unity does not rely on everyone being the same. God *makes* us different and invites us all into the communion of the divine life. Pondering this reality raises the question of how we *listen* to difference, even incredibly uncomfortable difference. When someone is challenging something we hold to be true, it can feel threatening to our identity. To stay in the furnace of a conversation, in a spirit of charity, can feel quite discomforting and may cost us a great deal, as it did for Jesus in his death. This gives rise to the question in Christian community about what is central to our common life and what is peripheral.

I am not claiming there are no certainties. We will frequently need to make assessments and take a stand on what we believe to be true/false or right/wrong. There is nothing wrong with dualistic thinking per se, because it forces us to think clearly. The question is what we do with our dualistic distinctions. What do we do with our certainties in the context of nonviolent relationships? Are there situations in which our certainties might be transcended, rather than compromised?[18] The dynamic of both valuing and sometimes transcending differences through dialogue is an important theme in this book which we will revisit again in parts 2 and 3.

. . . CHARACTERIZED BY AN IRREVOCABLE COVENANT

So far, we have seen that we know God because God has chosen to reveal God's self in Jesus. God is Christlike, in whom there is no un-Christlikeness

---

18. Jesus frequently made dualistic distinctions, e.g., "You cannot serve God and money" (Matt 6:24). Even though St. Paul taught that in this life we see only in part (1 Cor 13:12), he also dealt robustly with persons he thought were wrong—such as teachers who were trying to derail his gospel by trying to impose certain Jewish cultural practices on gentile Christians as requirements, over and above the grace of "Christ crucified: (Gal 1:6–9; 1 Cor 2:2). One of Paul's pastoral bottom lines seems to have been "the only thing that counts is faith expressing itself through love" (1 Cor 5:6).

at all. This revelation is a gift and does not rely on any quality or virtue in ourselves. It is utter grace. It typically comes as surprise rather than intellectual or religious deliberation; it is not something we figure out for ourselves.

By definition, unearned grace is grace for all. God's desire is for everyone to freely choose to enter the joy and peace of union with God. As St. Paul says:

> For those whom he foreknew he also predestined to be conformed to the image of his Son, in order that he might be the firstborn within a large family. And those whom he predestined he also called; and those whom he called he also justified; and those whom he justified [redeemed/released] he also glorified. (Rom 8:29–30)

The verse above has been used in some questionable theological ways. One particularly heinous proposition is that God predestines all human decision-making—that is, if a person rejects Jesus, then it was because God declared it to be so.[19] In the interests of a theological premise of God's absolute sovereign freedom and power, we create an image of a God who is apparently content to put up with losing relationship with a good proportion of what God created. But neither do we control our own destiny. If we get overly confident about our own human capacity for free choice, then we can inadvertently create a contractual relationship with God; we might mistakenly think that we control our own salvation and that God will *reward* us for our decisions.[20] Either of these positions can result in an anxious relationship with God. With the first, we end up anxious, because God might destroy our unbelieving friends. With the second, we end up anxious, because contracts are always vulnerable to an anxious performance-based mindset.

The gift of grace is in knowing that we can rest in the love of the God who is irrevocably committed, by covenant, to everything and everyone that God has made. God's gracious sovereignty is found not in God making arbitrary decisions about who lives and dies. God's gracious sovereignty is found in God's plan to draw *all* people freely to God's self—and we trust that this plan will succeed, not because we are good but because

---

19. It gets worse. In this doctrine, the preordained declaration of God also results in eternal condemnation.

20. In touchstone 2, we will reflect on how our "freedom" to choose is somewhat ambiguous.

God is very patient! The verses that follow on from the above quote (Rom 8:31–39) show effusively how *nothing* can separate humanity from God's love. God's election of us flows from being created by God: if God made us all, then God loves us all (everyone, without exception), and that love is irrevocable, just like a parent's relationship with their children cannot be revoked. Once a parent, always a parent. I remember seeing an evening news report in which a mother was being interviewed outside a courthouse after her son had been found guilty of murder. She was asked by the interviewer what she thought of her son's actions. She said, "It's terrible what he did. But I can't stop loving him. He is my son."[21] The following list of examples is extensive, because I am trying to illustrate the strength of this theme:

- The gifts and the calling of God are *irrevocable* (Rom 11:29).
- Where can I go from your spirit? Or where can I flee from your presence? If I ascend to heaven, you are there; if I make my bed in Sheol, you are there (Ps 139:7–8).
- And this is the will of him who sent me, that I should *lose nothing* of all that he has given me, but raise it up on the last day (John 6:39).
- He has made known to us the mystery of his will, according to his good pleasure that he set forth in Christ, as a plan for the fullness of time, to gather up *all things* in him, things in heaven and things on earth (Eph 1:9–10).
- For from him and through him and to him are *all things*. To him be the glory forever (Rom 11:36).
- For to this end we toil and struggle, because we have our hope set on the living God, who is the Savior of *all people*, especially of those who believe (1 Tim 4:10).
- When *all things* are subjected to him, then the Son himself will also be subjected to the one who put all things in subjection under him, so that God may be all in all (1 Cor 15:28).
- Therefore God also highly exalted him and gave him the name that is above every name, so that at the name of Jesus *every knee* should bend, in heaven and on earth and under the earth, and every tongue

---

21. The point is that human parenthood is a kind of analogy of God's parenthood. But it is the latter that is the model and archetype of the former: "We love because God first loved us" (1 John 4:19).

should confess that Jesus Christ is Lord, to the glory of God the Father (Phil 2:9–11).

- For in him all the fullness of God was pleased to dwell, and through him God was pleased to reconcile to himself *all things*, whether on earth or in heaven, by making peace through the blood of his cross (Col 15:19–20).
- The Lord is not slow about his promise, as some think of slowness, but is patient with you, not wanting any to perish, but *all* to come to repentance (2 Pet 3:9).
- He is the atoning sacrifice for our sins, and not for ours only but also for the sins of the *whole world* (1 John 2:2).
- For the grace of God has appeared, bringing salvation to *all* (Titus 2:11).
- And we have seen and do testify that the Father has sent his Son as the Savior of *the world* (1 John 4:14).

As we have seen, God's intention is to bring *all things* into union with God. We can therefore be less anxious about God and rejoice in the promise.[22] But if God's love is irrevocable, then what are we to understand by all the language in Scripture and tradition about God *saving* us? Saved from what or whom? And . . . if God's covenant is irrevocable, then does this mean that we can behave in any way we like—that we can live however we like, without consequence and without judgment? As St. Paul says,

> Should we continue in sin in order that grace may abound? (Rom 6:1)

"By no means," says Paul. Because consequences for our life choices still exist. If we drink too much, then, sure as night follows day, we will get a hangover (we will revisit this theme later in a discussion about the judgment of God). If humanity continues to live unsustainably, we will

---

22. I acknowledge the inevitable challenge from those who will point to exclusionary texts in the Christian Testament, including a number by St. Paul, where Paul clearly says that only believers will live after death (e.g., Paul writing to a persecuted church in a classically apocalyptic genre in 2 Thess 1:6–9). Paul does not develop a systematic theology, and his writing develops over time. Brad Jersak indicates how Paul sometimes deploys divine threat as a rhetorical tool (Jersak, *More Christlike Word*, 230–34). My reading is that the overwhelming thrust of Paul's theology is that God's kindness and grace is extended to all (as per touchstone 1).

destroy the planet. We can choose to live in the grain of God's love or reject it (although, as we shall see later, whether we can actually *freely* choose to reject God entirely is contestable). We could waste our entire lives with our self-constructed identities, lurching from one fascination (distraction) to another; or we could allow God to lead us into an abundant life. Since God wants to relate to us in a way that provides us freedom to respond, it means that God's interaction with us can be only persuasively *invitational* rather than coercive/threatening. The theme of *invitation* is a crucially important theme to which we will keep coming back when relating nonviolently to others.

Let us now draw these threads together. I am contending that living and leading nonviolently is grounded in the fundamental premise that God has revealed Godself as Christlike. By grace, God's intention and promise is to draw all of life into union with God's self. A primary implication of this first touchstone, for peace and nonviolence, is in the way we *look* at ourselves and others. Do we perceive ourselves and others as creatures/children of the Christlike God, loved by God, made in the image of God, and irrevocably called by God into a loving purpose and end? The Jewish philosopher Martin Buber asks us to pay attention to the way in which we perceive the other. Do we perceive the other as an object through whom we get our own needs met or as a "sacred thou"—one who has inherent dignity?

If we value people only to the extent that they are useful to us, it can be easy to violate them by diminishing their fundamental dignity as creations of God. But if we see others as fellow creatures, made in the divine image, and destined for the same end as us, we will celebrate their life, their unique beauty, and their distinctive gifts. Could our first response to a person be "Yes, thank you, Lord, that I have met this person"? Could we constitute all our relationships in the first instance by thanksgiving?[23]

All this may sound lovely and idealistic. Naturally, most of us take ourselves to be peace-loving and nonviolent people. We typically see violence as being other people's problem. Herein lies the problem! The fact that God is Christlike from the foundation of the world sheds light on (reveals) a dark side of our human condition—a predicament from which we will need deliverance. Paradoxically, however, we can recognize this predicament only in the very process of being set free, by God, from

---

23. Rabbi Jonathan Sacks explores this them beautifully in *The Dignity of Difference*.

it. Even our predicament becomes a grace. But more about that in the next chapter.

SUMMARY OF TOUCHSTONE 1

1. God is like Jesus: God is and always has been Christlike. All theology is therefore Christology, and Jesus is the lens for reading the Scriptures and doing ethics.
2. The primary Word of God is a person: Jesus, the Christ. The words of the Bible testify to the Word.
3. This insight comes as a revelation, an unveiling, an apocalypse—by grace; we don't figure it out ourselves by natural reason, logic, or only by reading the Scriptures unaided by the Spirit.
4. The revelation of Christ is mediated to us, through the Spirit, typically in the first instance by some combination of loving human relationship, church, Scripture, and sacrament.
5. God loves everyone, and our destiny is loving communion with God. This election of humanity is rooted in being created by God. God is the model for the unconditional love that loving parents give their children—a love that is universal and irrevocable. Therefore, we can relax into knowing that our standing with God does not depend on either right belief or right action. Our relationship with God is covenantal, not contractual.
6. God's love flows out of the loving relationships between the persons of the Trinity. God loves, because love is God's nature. God does not arbitrarily *choose* to love, as if God might have the option not to do so.
7. We learn from the Trinity that our personhood is constituted, shaped, and formed by relationships with other people. This is unavoidable. To even talk about who we are requires telling stories about formative places, persons, and events in our lives.
8. The dance of giving and receiving love within the Holy Trinity is the theological foundation of dialogue—a kenotic movement that overflows as creativity.

9. God speaks the Word (Jesus) and *invites* all to a freely chosen response. This is the theological basis for freely chosen participation in dialogue.

REFLECT

1. Who have been the significant people in my life in whom I have sensed God as unconditionally loving of me and others?
2. To what extent do I perceive every person as having inherent dignity, regardless of how different they are to me and even if they want to do me harm? Does the other remain a sacred thou rather than being an object whom I utilize for my own ends?
3. What does it feel like to know that I am loved by God, regardless of my personal virtues?
4. Are my relationships characterized by control and demand or by invitation?
5. If the trajectory and end of the cosmos is the peaceful reconciliation of all things in God, and if the church is a sign, herald, and foretaste of this cosmic divine vision, what might be the implications for our shared life together—as humans and as the church?

3

Touchstone 2
Christ Reveals the Nature of Violence

SIN AND VIOLENCE

In the first touchstone, we talked about the goodness of the Christlike God. We do not reason our way to God. The revelation of this Word (Jesus) comes as an apocalypse—a revelation—an unveiling—a parting of the veil. In Christ, we see that's God's relationship with us is one of unconditional covenant, and this covenant is irrevocable from God's side.

This is very good news. But a part of this good news, which is more challenging to hear, is that God's revelation in Christ illumines some dark and violent aspects of our human condition. The love of God confronts us with ourselves. We can be a people of peace only when we are open to God's diagnoses of all aspects of our humanity. When it comes to peace, if we are not part of the problem, we cannot be part of the solution. And we can perceive our problem only in the process of being set free from it (more elaboration on this point is coming in touchstones 3 and 4).

A way into this could be to do a little imaginative exercise. Imagine that we had lived our entire life in a world constructed by rules of engagement that limited our freedom, but we were completely unaware that such rules existed; we just took them for granted. A movie which explores this brilliantly is *The Matrix*.[1] The matrix is the world of everyday perception that the inhabitants take to be real. But it turns out that the matrix is a computer-simulated reality. It is nearly impossible to break out of the matrix, because people do not know they are in it. For people to be freed, there needs to be an intervention into the matrix by an outsider who puts a virus (sometimes called a Trojan horse, because it is in the form of something that looks innocuous) into the programming of the matrix. It is through such an intervention that the main character, Neo, learns that there is a world outside the matrix.

The illusions, lies, deceptions, and life-limiting forces of the matrix are a metaphor for what, in theological language, is called sin. I'm not talking here about sins as individual immoral actions but the background programming of the system itself. St. Paul talks about sin as a kind of milieu characterized by powerful forces that are frequently invisible to us but that orient us towards violence and death. Using the evocative language of the ancient world, Paul says:

> We wrestle not against flesh and blood, but against principalities, against powers, against the rulers of the darkness of this world, against spiritual wickedness in high places. (Eph 6:12)

In modern language, we might talk about the collective violent dynamics of human systems interacting and combining with the complex forces of the individual unconscious. This milieu is invisible to us because it is so familiar. We just take it for granted that this is the way the world works. In the course of everyday life, we become *disoriented*, so much so that a decisive intervention by God from outside the programming of the matrix is required.

SOURCES OF VIOLENCE

Why does human desire, which is positive (created by God), become so disoriented that we are blind to our enmeshment in violence and even call it good and justifiable? I will approach this from two angles, the collective (social) dimension of violence and the personal (intrapsychic) dimension. We need to have our desire reoriented to the deeper reality of God's love that we named in touchstone 1.

---

1. Wachowski and Wachowski, *Matrix*.

(i) Social dimension: mimetic rivalry

The most extreme kind of violence is murder, and it shows up early in the Hebrew Scriptures in the story of Cain murdering his brother Abel (Gen 4). Here we find the first use of the word *sin* in the Bible. In the story, the Lord warns Cain, "Sin is lurking at the door; its *desire* is for you, but you must master it." Where does this sin, lurking at the door, come from? To push the question back to an even earlier story, where does the serpent in the garden of Eden come from? Clearly, the serpent is part of the ecology of the garden, but this is paradoxical, since the serpent seems to work against God's purposes.[2] Who put the serpent in the garden and to what end? The Scripture leaves these questions hanging. What is clear is that the Genesis story points to how desire, which God creates as a fundamentally good part of human nature, can become a seedbed of violence. The serpent is a literary device for how we experience, out of nowhere, a strong acquisitive desire for something that has been placed off limits. Parents will understand this immediately. What happens when we say to a child "No, you can't have that"?

The nature of desire is a central question of interest to all spirituality. God invites us to freely choose relationship with God—inviting us to participate in the divine desire of love. But if God gifts us with freedom, then that must include the capacity to exercise that freedom to desire other things in ways that take us away from God's love. In my own reflections on these questions, I've been helped by the work of the French-American academic René Girard. Girard was originally an atheist and was converted to Christ through his contemplation of the Jewish and Christian Scriptures and the story of Jesus in particular.[3]

René Girard points out that humans are, by nature, imitative —which means we copy each other. For example, at the simplest level, we note that babies and infants imitate their parents. Imitation is the way we learn language. I recall the mild embarrassment, mixed with admiration, that I felt when one of my children, barely two years of age, innocently said a particularly colorful swear word in our local supermarket. Obviously, she

---

2. To be clear, I am treating these stories as theological narratives, not history. As St. Paul puts it, Adam is the archetypal person of flesh; Adam is all of us (1 Cor 15:22, 45).

3. Girard's work primarily focuses on Western literature and culture. In his later years, he started to explore and notice connections between his theories of human desire and the literature of other cultures such as India. Asian scholars of Girard are now deepening that work.

had been listening carefully to one of her parents, and I was extremely impressed with her capacity to pick up language so quickly!

We are also enculturated into our belief systems through imitating beliefs about what is right and wrong—law, morality, ethics—imitating the general norms and expectations about the way to conduct ourselves in relationship with other people. This can be a good thing where the patterns we are imitating are healthy and loving. At a deeper level of observation, we note that we copy not only each other's behaviors and beliefs but also each other's *desires*. One example is a phenomenon that all parents will recognize. If there are two toddlers sitting in a room, there may be a particular toy sitting on the floor that is of no particular interest to either child. However, as soon as one child reaches for the toy, it suddenly becomes an object of intense fascination to the other child. Very quickly, we can have escalating conflict, as the second child *imitates* the desire of the first child.

The same principle operates through to adulthood. Advertising, particularly visual advertising, works because of mimetic desire. If an advertisement shows an image of a person whom we find attractive desiring a particular product, then our desire, with associated purchasing behavior, will be activated. Mimetic desire is activated more strongly when the person we are imitating is like ourselves. For example, my mimetic desire is more likely to be activated by my next-door neighbor's new Hyundai than by the Queen of England acquiring a new Rolls Royce. As another example, in one of the Marvel series of superhero movies, *Captain America: Civil War*, this mirroring of desire is portrayed in the escalating rivalry between Captain America and Iron Man.[4] They are like each other in the sense of both being superheroes. The title of the movie is also mirroring something about the highly divided nature of American society.

Girard's theories originated in his study of French novels. One of the literary phenomena that interested him was the commonly occurring theme of the love triangle. Many novels are based on this premise of shared desire of two men for one woman or vice versa. From this, among other things, Girard postulated that we learn what to desire from imitating the desire of others. He refers to this as "mimetic desire." We typically believe that what we desire is a personal choice, but it turns out that we

---

4. Russo and Russo, *Captain America*.

have less choice than we thought. Desire is often, if not largely, *caught* from other people at an unconscious level.

A colleague of mine who is a social psychologist has pointed out some parallels between Girard's theses about mimetic desire and the psychology of social influence, which studies the way in which humans compare themselves to each other.[5] As we get a flattening (social equalizing) of society, it's even more likely that mimetic desire will get activated on a broad scale, particularly when that society is highly interconnected through social media. The internet provides a mechanism by which contagious mimetic desire spreads like a highly infectious virus. Social media has given rise to the phenomenon of social influencers—often, younger people who have tens of thousands of social media friends/followers. Marketing companies now utilize social influencers to sell their products. Because the social influencer *likes* a product, their followers will also like it and buy it. The latter think they are making a free choice, but, largely, they are captives to unconscious mimetic desire.

When my desire for what another person desires is activated in the presence of scarcity (e.g., two toddlers but only one toy), then my neighbor is likely to become my *rival*. One of the interesting and potentially dangerous aspects of mimetic desire is that once a movement of mimetic desire starts to escalate in a crowd, it is highly contagious. It doesn't take long before the persons involved have forgotten the original object of their shared desire and now are just imitating each other's anxiously competitive emotions. The following are examples of mimetic rivalry that we may have observed in everyday life:

- A media interview with a politician close to an election, where an interviewer asks a question about policy, but the only response the politician gives is to attack the opposition, often in very personal terms. Policy gets buried under the weight of mimetic attack on one's political enemies, in which the shared object of desire is power.
- A special sale day, where people line up early outside the doors of department stores and then stampede over each other when the doors open.

---

5. The colleague told me that this is a reason electricity bills in some cities contain comparison data between household electricity use and use in the surrounding suburb. The electricity provider, in giving this comparison point, catalyzes an unconscious desire in people to match or beat their neighbors.

- Police treading carefully and strategically around emotionally charged groups of people. If we observe the way police operate in such situations, we notice that they tend to hang back wherever possible (thereby not contributing to rivalry and contagious escalation). Where possible, they try to carefully move the most emotionally charged individuals away from the main crowd.

- The economic free market, which relies for its success on mimetic desire on a huge scale. The free market has been spectacularly successful in delivering goods and services and in raising people out of poverty. It keeps mimetic conflict at bay, to a certain extent, through abundance of supply but has downstream consequences of environmental destruction.[6]

- Incivility/rudeness in general discourse. If we see other people being rude, or they treat us rudely, then we tend to imitate this in response. (I confess to having given another driver the finger when he beeped his horn at me. Fortunately, this did not mimetically escalate to a road rage incident.)

Girard notices how mimetic rivalry is a recurring theme in the Scriptures. We have already mentioned Adam and Eve, and Cain and Abel. Other examples include:

- Joseph's jealous brothers throwing Joseph into a pit and leaving him for dead (Gen 37:24)
- Two women coming to Solomon, arguing over who is the real mother of a baby (1 Kgs 3:16–28)
- King David's being attracted to Bathsheba, wife of Uriah, and arranging for Uriah's death (2 Sam 11)
- The parable of payments to vineyard workers (Matt 20:1–16)
- Jesus's disciples jockeying for position about who will be greatest in the kingdom of heaven (Matt 18:1–4)
- The hostility of the religious elders, scribes, and Pharisees towards Jesus (Matt 26:4)

---

6. Environmental destruction is often associated with what economists called "externalized costs." For example, if there is no cost to a company of dumping waste into a river, the company may do this rather than pass on costs of proper disposable to the customer. The environment bears this externalized cost.

- The hostility of Saul towards the early Christian communities (Acts 8:1; 1 Cor 15:9)
- The (implicit) rivalry between Peter and the beloved disciple (John 20:4–6; John 21:21–22)
- The stoning of Stephen (to which we could add the fate of nonviolent martyrs throughout the history of the church) (Acts 7:57)

(ii) Personal intrapsychic dimensions

So far, we have been reflecting on the nature of mimetic desire and how it can catalyze rivalry and violence. As Girard observes, the dynamics of mimetic desire are unconscious to us. We are frequently *unaware*, in the moment, of how our desires are being formed and then projected onto others. This is unsettling, because it suggests we are not as in control as we thought we were. We may be getting enmeshed in forms of desire that we do not recognize are problematic to relationships or from which we will find it hard to extract ourselves.

Mimetic rivalry can be compounded by adaptive strategies of the ego, as the ego tries to secure itself in the face of two deep primal fears. One is a fear of being *overwhelmed* by others (survival need). Another is that we will be *abandoned* by others (belonging need). Survival and belonging needs are part of our biological hardwiring. But they come with downsides, because they are both sensitive to threat. A perception that our survival is being threatened can lead to us placing rigid controls on our environment, including on other people, to help keep chaos at bay—thereby potentially doing violence to others. A perception that our belonging is being threatened can lead to ingratiating ourselves with others, so much so that we might lose a sense of our own identity (potentially doing violence to self).

Thomas Keating, a teacher of contemplative prayer, calls these defensive maneuvers "emotional programs for happiness."[7] Survival and belonging needs are a bit like a computer program running in the background, which, when threatened, launches an emotional program, occasionally accompanied by warnings of flashing red lights. Spending

---

7. What Keating calls "emotional programs for happiness" are thematically like what Nathanson, as a psychiatrist, describes as adaptive shame responses (Nathanson, *Shame and Pride*, 305–14).

our lives running emotional programs for happiness is not a great basis for peace for ourselves or for the people who surround us.[8]

The temptations of Jesus in the wilderness, immediately after his baptism, illustrate the following three commonly experienced emotional programs for happiness, all of which can be amplified through the mimetic dynamics of human interaction:[9]

- The desire to be *relevant or useful*—the temptation to turn stones into bread

- The desire to be *powerful over others*—the temptation to take political power over all the empires of the world

- The desire to be *spectacular or impressive*—the temptation to jump off the pinnacle of the temple and be carried safely down by angels

Theologically and spiritually, both survival and belonging needs are fears that stem from the deep wound of disconnection from the reality of our belovedness in the Christlike God (touchstone 1). Intense fears related to survival and belonging can be compounded by having been *sinned against* through poverty, violence, abuse, lack of education, or lack of primary nurturing love in childhood. If we have not had an experience of being loved by other people, it can be difficult to believe we could be loved by God. In the absence of an unconditional loving, healing, and forgiving encounter (with other people and with God), the resulting shame and grief can project inwards and outwards in destructive ways.

We will explore, in part 2, how we can constructively deal with the complexity of our own psyches and manage some of the powerful dynamics mentioned above. We will look at how the practice of contemplative prayer can help us to recognize and manage our own mimetic rivalries and emotional programs for happiness, so that they are less likely to undermine our relationships. For now, we need to look at something

---

8. I am not qualified to comment on psychiatric or psychological pathologies that can also contribute to violence towards others. As one example, I understand there is evidence emerging that paedophilia may have genetic or neurological origins (as with alcoholism), and such persons need to be managed, always with strict boundaries around children, to protect children from this kind of violence, rather than naïvely believing that therapy, a retreat, or transfer will address the problem. Regrettably, the church has failed dismally in this area. In fact, the church's efforts to cover up such crimes may, in part, be related to precisely the self-interested survival and belonging needs that I discuss.

9. These insights on Matt 4:1–11 come from Henri Nouwen.

else about ourselves, which Jesus has unveiled for us, which is the way *communities* deal with mimetic rivalry and violence.

PEACE THAT THE WORLD TRIES TO GIVE

All societies need mechanisms for limiting the violence that can arise from mimetic rivalry, reactive survival and belonging strategies, shame, and grief. These mechanisms have evolved from archaic societies through to our own time and have recognizable similarities. The mechanisms of *law, scapegoating, myth, and ritual* have proven to be somewhat effective in restraining external violence but also have shadow sides, which can mask and perpetuate violence.

(i) Peace through law

Girard points to the tenth commandment in the Decalogue (Ten Commandments) as an example of using law to limit mimetic rivalry. Note the potential triggers of mimetic rivalry in this commandment:

> *Neither shall you covet* your neighbor's wife. *Neither shall you desire* your neighbor's house, or field, or male or female slave, or ox, or donkey, or anything that belongs to your neighbor. (Deut 5:21)

The elaborate developments of law in the Scriptures serve to bind society together with norms of expected behavior that either *limit* mimetic rivalry or *inculcate* virtues of love and community. For example, the principle of an eye for an eye[10] was designed to limit escalating (mimetic) retaliation in response to a perceived harm.

Modern societies have developed their own legal mechanisms to *manage* the destructive dynamics of mimetic rivalry. For example, longstanding elements of legal and church systems that help deal with rivalry include:

- Applying law equally to all without fear or favor—to reduce the chance of jealousy being activated by some people being treated differently to others.

---

10. Exod 21:24.

- Strong separation of powers between legislators and enforcers—so that the law maker cannot benefit from giving themselves preferential treatment in relation to how a law is interpreted or applied.

- The law, at least in Australia, that deadly weapons can be carried only by specially authorized persons invested with signs of authority (police and army)—and limiting the number of weapons in circulation. The latter helps minimize contagious mimetic desire within society for the acquisition of weapons.

- Clergy and judges dressing in special robes,[11] and sitting in elevated benches, gives a slight sense of mystique—almost a divine authority. Because rivalrous relationships more easily ignite between people who are like each other, the establishment of a degree of *transcendent difference* (persons and roles that we all agree are not our rivals) serves to minimize rivalry. Strong contempt of court rules reinforce this point.

(ii) Peace through scapegoating and self-justifying myths

Girard proposes that when there is escalating anxiety in a community, there needs to be a circuit breaker to violence that could escalate to *all against all*. He proposes that if a group can find a person to blame for their internal conflict,[12] they can achieve (temporary) peace by uniting against a common enemy. The selection of the scapegoat is, by definition, irrational and arbitrary. So long as the scapegoat is sufficiently *different* from the conflicted parties, that can be enough to bring the parties together. Such differences could include distinguishing physical features or abnormalities.

Driving out (including killing) a scapegoat restores peace, because there is one thing on which the warring parties can agree: it is the

---

11. The Anglican Ordinal speaks of clergy being "set apart." While I am not a huge fan of this language, or its associated symbols like clerical collars, it can, at a purely practical level, help minimize rivalry in religious communities. It is notable that established churches with structured hierarchies tend to split less often than smaller Protestant churches. This may, in part, be attributable to the way in which hierarchies and formal roles help limit mimetic rivalry. However, hierarchies create their own shadow dynamics around power and control.

12. Girard argues that a community may also seek a scapegoat to blame for an internal sickness (plague). It is interesting to reflect on what scapegoats society is creating in the time of COVID.

scapegoat's fault! According to Girard, it is the unanimity of a group, which creates a shared agreement (story) that the scapegoat is morally guilty, that makes the scapegoating mechanism work in achieving a temporary cessation of hostilities. The following examples from Hebrew and Christian Testaments illustrate the scapegoating mechanism. In each case, note the unanimity of the community and the religious justification (myth) that is given:[13]

- Just then one of the Israelites came and brought a Midianite woman into his family, in the sight of Moses and in the sight of the whole congregation of the Israelites, while they were weeping at the entrance of the tent of meeting. When Phinehas son of Eleazar, son of Aaron the priest, saw it, he got up and left the congregation. Taking a spear in his hand, he went after the Israelite man into the tent, and pierced the two of them, the Israelite and the woman, through the belly. So *the plague was stopped* among the people of Israel. Nevertheless those that died by the plague were twenty-four thousand (Num 25:6–9).

- Joshua said, "Why have you brought this trouble on us? The LORD will bring trouble on you today." Then all Israel stoned him, and after they had stoned the rest, they burned them. Over Achan they heaped up a large pile of rocks, which remains to this day. Then the LORD *turned from his fierce anger*. Therefore that place has been called the Valley of Achor ever since (Josh 7:25–26).

- You do not understand that it is better for you to have *one man die for the people* than to have the whole nation destroyed (John 11:50).

- Indeed, an hour is coming when *those who kill you* will think that by doing so they are *offering worship to God* (John 16:2).

- The chief priests and the scribes stood by, vehemently accusing him. Even Herod with his soldiers treated him with contempt and mocked him; then he put an elegant robe on him and sent him back to Pilate. That same day *Herod and Pilate became friends with each other; before this they had been enemies* (Luke 23:12).

Lest we relegate the scapegoating mechanism to ancient history, Gil Bailie describes reports of the unifying effect in a crowd of hangings

---

13. Myth, for Girard, is a self-justifying story about the objective guilt of a victim that hides a murder that has brought cohesion to a community.

(UK), and the same applied for lynchings (USA) and beheadings (French Revolution).[14] A story that serves to justify communal violence is called a myth of sacred violence—what Walter Wink calls a "myth of redemptive violence."[15]

Although many societies have outlawed the death penalty, it may be that incarcerating people in prisons meets a similar need by society for vengeance (which gets renamed as just punishment). The state punishing people in this formal structured way reduces the likelihood that vigilante mobs may take the law (punishment) into their own hands. This kind of vicarious vengeance helps avoid unconstrained violence.[16]

Jesus preeminently reveals (unveils) sacred violence by willingly becoming the victim of both religion and state, as both try to establish peace through the unconscious mechanism of scapegoating.[17]

(iii) Peace through ritual

Through his study of literature and culture, Girard suggests that scapegoating worked so well in ancient communities that it had a transcendent quality to it, as if the gods had given the scapegoat to a community as a way of restoring peace. Scapegoats were, paradoxically, both demonized (for their perceived guilt) and divinized (for bringing peace to a community). Because of the transcendent peace-creating potential of scapegoating, Girard argues that primal acts of scapegoating lie at the root of all

---

14. Gil Bailie cites Coventry Patmore's sobering poem "A London Fête," describing the festive atmosphere surrounding a hanging (Bailie, *Violence Unveiled*, 86).

15. Neither Walter Wink nor René Girard absolutely equate every act of violence with myth or sacred violence. They acknowledge that most of us accept some limited use of force in our societies to restrain aggression towards vulnerable persons (such as in community policing). The issue is how community narratives evolve to justify demonization of identifiable groups as "the problem."

16. Vincent Lloyd discusses these dynamics in a radio interview on the *ABC* radio program *The Mine Field*. See Lloyd, "Should Prisons Be Abolished?"

17. In Christian liturgy, the Eucharist acts as an anti-myth by declaring the innocence, rather than the guilt, of the victim (Jesus), unmasking humanity's shared complicity in violence. Jesus is not unique in being the first person society has scapegoated. But the scapegoating mechanism is entirely transparent in Jesus, because God vindicates Jesus's innocence by raising him from the dead. In myths of crucified gods, the typical pattern is for the gods to throw off their temporary physical forms and return to their "true" forms as deeply vengeful characters intent on wreaking havoc on their former enemies. The difference between such myths and the resurrection of Jesus as forgiving victim is striking.

religions. The sacrificial rituals of religions served to reenact the death of sacred victims in safe and contained ways. This minimized regular outbreaks of scapegoating violence. The sacrifice of people gradually gave way to sacrificial animals. The word *religion* comes from *re-ligio*—re-ligament—to bind together.[18]

BIGGER THAN WE THINK: SWIMMING IN A SEA OF DISORIENTED DESIRE

These reflections about the unconscious roots of violence may seem abstract, so let's try to ground this in our own experience. If we are honest with ourselves, have we ever:

- conspired with a group, through our active or passive participation, to talk negatively about someone else rather than have a conversation with them?
- felt like we have been on the receiving end of a group's anxiety or fury and/or felt stripped of voice by a group?
- noticed ourselves creating a self-justifying fantasy about what someone else thinks and attributing malicious motives to them?

If you worship in a liturgical tradition, as I do as an Anglican, you will be familiar with the recitation of the general confession in every service. Have you ever had the experience of saying these words without really connecting them to your own experience? Perhaps you have had the experience, just before the confession, of trying to dredge up some unloving things that you did during the last week so that you can say the confession with integrity. One of the recommended spiritual practices of the church has been to examine our conscience before coming to worship,

---

18. It is on this point that Girard has been frequently challenged by scholars for not providing sufficient hard historic evidence that all religious rituals and myths originate in violent scapegoating. Critics point to myth and sacrifice having positive life-enhancing and community-building motives and origins rather than just restraining violence. Girard's response was that it is the very nature of scapegoating to hide the originating collective murder behind a veil of myth. Regardless of these debates about the foundations of religions, the observable dynamics of mimetic rivalry and scapegoating have sufficiently strong face validity in our own day to provide a useful diagnostic for exploring mimetic desire, rivalry, scapegoating, and contagious violence in our families, churches, local communities, commerce, government, and international politics.

so that we can bring our sins (unloving behaviors) to confession. Clearly, there is value in this honest self-examination. But the reflections above about the roots of violence in our disoriented desires may help us to see that sin is far bigger and more deeply entrenched in ourselves and in our communities than we might have imagined.

Suggesting to people that we are all caught up in violent systems can make people bristle with indignation. Most of us don't think that we are violent, because we associate the word violence with either verbally abusing someone or physically assaulting them. In her book on domestic violence in Australia, Jess Hill points out in disturbing and graphic detail how a great deal of violence does not involve actual physical contact. Very often, violence is expressed as threat, intimidation, control, deceit, and coercion. The first chapter of Hill's book begins with a quote from Evan Stark:

> Asking clients, "Is there someone in your life making you afraid?" or "Controlling what you do or say?" promises an even more profound awakening than asking women about violence.[19]

One of the challenges of dealing with violence is that the sources of violence are often unconscious, and violence can even be framed as having a good intent. For example, in a workplace, behaviors that are experienced as bullying (and frequently *are* bullying) might sometimes reveal relational incompetence rather than malicious intent. And yet the *impact* of the harm is no less. For these reasons, restorative practices, which we will explore later, apply a useful distinction between intent and impact. Regardless of what our *intent* was, we need to examine the actual *impact* of our behavior on other people.[20]

Many people will think that all this language about sin, scapegoats, victims, and myth is entirely antiquated. Surely, they may say, we have moved past all that mumbo jumbo, and we can find peace in the structures of a benevolent secular democracy? And yet, in the last hundred years, as people have turned away from religions in vast numbers, we

---

19. Hill, *See What You Made*, 11.

20. There can also be a hidden risk overly emphasizing impact. Girard observes that the sensitivity to the voice of the victim, under the cultural influence of Jesus, has resulted in victims making scapegoats (further victims) of their perceived persecutors, leading to an intractable cycle of violence. The shadow side of defining oneself as a victim can be an attempt to claim moral superiority through identifying as a victim. Some of these risks, which can include trying to shut down opposing voices, are explored in Haidt and Lukianoff, *Coddling of The American Mind*.

have experienced two world wars, several civil wars of ethnic cleansing, and a protracted "war against terror."

How do these ancient mechanisms of scapegoating, myth, and ritual show up in modern societies? In our modern (secular and religious) world, scapegoating and its self-justifying mythologies still exist, often in semi- or fully militaristic forms, bolstering communal narratives that *our tribe* is righteous and *your tribe* is evil. By dehumanizing and demonizing people, it makes it easier for us to treat others as less than human and even to kill them. The following are just a few examples of where we see this happening:

- The semi-religious nature of gatherings around dictators such as Hitler, Stalin, or Kim Jong-un, which are heavily underpinned by the rhetoric of constructing an enemy who is inherently evil (Jews, capitalists, America).

- In my own country, Australia, politicians and media organizations have frequently demonized asylum seekers as criminals by constructing a myth that they are *illegal queue jumpers*. This rhetorical move has served both political parties well as a vote winner.[21]

- The racism commonly reported by Aboriginal peoples. This has historic roots in a mindset during colonial expansion that certain groups of people were less civilized or less human than others and the legal fiction that the land was unoccupied.

- The "get tough on crime" rhetoric, which shows up in every political election and replaces evidence-based restorative approaches to dealing effectively with crime with mythologies that are demonstrably untrue (e.g., crime is out of control, and only locking people away will protect society from harm).

---

21. One well-known Australian broadcaster pointedly observed that if the asylum-seeking children being taken ashore from fishing boats had blue eyes and fair hair—in other words, that they looked more like white European Australians—that it could be inconceivable that they would be locked away in indefinite off-shore detention. Even though politicians can make a calm ethical case for an orderly border control system and for safety at sea, a giveaway that a scapegoating mechanism is at work in society is when a story is created about the corrupt moral character of an individual or group, in order to justify violence against them. To echo the high priest's observations about Jesus, "It is expedient that these criminal asylum seekers suffer for the sake of the nation."

- The capacity of social media to generate and rapidly circulate demonizing narratives and conspiracy theories about other people. This is frequently done with no basis in fact, no investigation, and no right of reply (no fairness or natural justice). Because there is no brake on such accusations, enormous numbers of people can get caught up in mimetic escalation. This phenomenon plays out at international political levels right through to online bullying in schools. In the university context in which I work, many conflicts escalate because students talk *about* other students in online chatrooms rather than have face-to-face conversations.

- The powerful ways in which our thinking is shaped by cultural stories. For example, from children watching cartoons like *Popeye* (I am showing my age!) through to almost every major crime and action movie, order can be restored in a community only by disposing of the enemy. The enemy has, of course, been thoroughly stripped of a meaningful history/story and is therefore reduced to a cardboard cutout of a human—reduced to being irredeemably evil (constituting a myth of redemptive violence).

- Evoking God in prayer that our "side" will experience victory in battle—whether that be on the battlefield of the board room or of war.

- The way in which we confidently identify with tribes: "I'm Protestant, not Catholic"; "I'm Shia, not Sunni"; "We are a Labor-voting house, not a Liberal-voting house"; "I'm spiritual, not religious."

- The violence we are doing to the planet through overconsumption and the use of fossil fuels.[22]

- The way in which pro and anti-vaccination groups project hostile and ungrounded accusations towards each other through social media, calling into question the integrity of the other as a class of people (the signal of the scapegoating mechanism is the use of dehumanizing language like "uncaring," "scum," "dogs," "corrupt").

---

22. It may be that the planet serves as a kind of scapegoat. For example, we ease our competitive rivalries by consuming more goods, and the sacrificial victim is the Earth itself. This sits as a blind spot for Australia because of our small population and our failure to acknowledge that we derive huge economic benefits through the export of fossil fuels.

Most of the time, the individual choices we make, even when we are unconsciously imitating the desire of others, are innocuous—like buying one brand of coffee over another. As a whole society, we are, in one sense, being carried along on a collective express train of unexamined desire, which has a whole raft of unintended consequences, including addiction, mental illness, violence, environmental destruction. The existence and trajectory of this express train transcend the morally neutral choices about whether I buy one type of coffee over another. On the express train, we are trapped—enslaved.

To survive as humans, we need to take sin and violence seriously. We cannot address a problem to which we are blind to or about which we are in denial. This is what Jesus was talking about when he said:

> Why do you see the speck in your neighbor's eye, but do not notice the log in your own eye? Or how can you say to your neighbor, "Let me take the speck out of your eye," while the log is in your own eye? You hypocrite, first take the log out of your own eye, and then you will see clearly to take the speck out of your neighbor's eye. (Matt 7:3–5)

Sin can be thought of as radical and destructive autonomy in which we become rivals with our neighbor to secure our own personalized needs. Sin is characterized by a mindset that "I exist independently of you. I need to win over you. I can use you (turn you into an object) to get my own needs met. You are disposable to me. You are not human." Sin whispers in Cain's ear, "You don't need your brother; you would be better off without him."[23] Sin whispers in the ear of political leaders, on all sides of a conflict, defending their country, "Hunt them down and kill them."[24]

Given the magnitude of sin and its consequences in disoriented relationships with God, the planet, and other people, well may we say, "Lord have mercy!" Given that God's promise is *life* (touchstone 1), how does God save us from this mess? How does God lift us out of this pit and bring us into communion with God's self and each other, when we are stuck in the matrix of sin, death, and violence?

---

23. My imagining about what might have gone through Cain's mind (Gen 4:9).

24. Following the death of American soldiers during the final evacuation of Kabul, US President Biden stated, "To those who carried out this attack, as well as anyone who wishes America harm, know this: We will not forgive. We will not forget. We will hunt you down and make you pay" (Shier, "President Biden Condemns"). This represents a mimetic mirroring of similar rhetoric by the enemy.

SUMMARY OF TOUCHTONE 2

1. Left to our own devices, we do not see as God sees. The gospel of peace not only unveils the character of God as love but also illuminates the nature of sin, to which we have been blind.

2. Violence is rooted in (disoriented) mimetic desire and rivalry—and both are inextricably linked with the negative outworking of deep survival and belonging needs, compounded by a sense of alienation from the truth of our belovedness in God.

3. Societies have developed ways of managing violence through scapegoating, law, myth, and ritual—all of which provide only temporary restraints on violence rather than a deep and lasting peace.

4. Sin is much deeper and violence more prolific than we may have first imagined. Alongside much that is good and beautiful as part of the good creation, humanity is soaking in a sea of disoriented desire and rivalrous relationships.

5. Scapegoating and self-justifying mythmaking manifests in multitudes of ways in contemporary society. Much of our violence is structural, and we derive tangible lifestyle benefits from it. Therefore, we avoid admitting our complicity and involvement in it.

REFLECT

1. Where do I notice scapegoating, blaming, and demonizing showing up in my life, family, workplace, or community?

2. When have I participated with a group in scapegoating someone?

3. Have I ever been on the receiving end of scapegoating?

4

Touchstone 3
Christ Gives a Peace That the World Cannot Give

LET'S RECAP WHAT WE'VE BEEN reflecting on so far. In touchstone 1, I grounded the gospel of peace in the revelation of God's Christlike nature. This revelation comes as grace and as an invitation to a freely chosen union with God.

In touchstone 2, I explored how Christ simultaneously unveils the character of God as love and the nature of sin, particularly how sin manifests itself in rivalry and violence, to which Jesus himself was subjected. If left unaddressed, violence can escalate to extremes, even to the destruction of the earth—a possibility that René Girard take to be a grim possibility. Girard proposes that societies limit violence (establish peace of a certain kind) through the mechanisms of law, scapegoating, ritual, and myth. This is the peacemaking that led to Jesus's crucifixion. Scapegoating can only ever result in a temporary peace (understood as absence of conflict), in which a community establishes solidarity by defining itself by what it is not—we are "not like them." Before long, mimetic rivalry will have kicked in again, and the community will be looking for another scapegoat.

Left to our own devices, we live our lives, unconsciously, within this matrix of disoriented desire, fear, and rivalry and, in doing so, fail to recognize that we are on an express train of destruction. Although not speaking in Girardian terms, Douglas Campbell illustrates the "invisible to self" nature of sin using the analogy of someone with an alcohol addiction. While in the grip of the addiction, the alcoholic is full of self-justifying reasons about how they do not have a problem, even though they may be leaving a trail of wreckage in their own lives and the lives of others. Only from the perspective of sobriety (freedom) can they look back and see the nature of their enslaved predicament and the impact of this on others.[1] In a similar vein, I invited us to consider the analogy of the movie *The Matrix*, suggesting that we, like the protagonist Neo, are trapped in a world where we are blind to the problems of disoriented desires.[2]

Because we take this world for granted, a *pattern-interruption*—a different kind of Logos—is needed to free us from the matrix. This is the focus of touchstone 3. We will reflect on how the Logos (Christ), the love that creates the world, is also the love that heals and transforms the world from death to life—from its lethal attraction to violence to the shalom of peaceful relationships. By grace, God can use the violence of the cross as the very *means* of loving the world, revealing God's love, triumphing over sin, and drawing us into a new peace-filled existence. As Jesus says in John's Gospel:

> Peace I leave with you; my peace I give to you. I do not give to you as the world gives. Do not let your hearts be troubled, and do not let them be afraid. (John 14:27)

As we reflect further, we will see that nothing is lost in the divine economy—even our sin and violence become the means of revelation, grace, forgiveness, and mercy.

THE HIDDEN SEED OF LIFE: DYING AND RISING

The Christlike God cannot combat our violence and our myths of redemptive violence with a violent logic of God's own. This would be ontologically impossible. As Martin Luther King Jr. put it, "Darkness cannot drive out darkness; only light can do that. Hate cannot drive out hate; only love can do that."[3]

God creates and saves by using a different kind of logic (Logos) to the human logic of rivalry and scapegoating. God liberates the world

---

1. Campbell, *Pauline Dogmatics*, 127.
2. Jer 6:14; John 9:41
3. King, *Strength to Love*, 37.

from sin and violence by voluntarily, lovingly, and fully entering our human condition. As an analogy, let us imagine a destructive conflict situation in which people are yelling and screaming at each other—completely enmeshed in a mimetic vortex. They cannot find their way out. They are trapped. The imagined situation could be anything from a family argument to a civil war. Now imagine Jesus entering this situation and quietly standing amid it. Because Jesus enters the space of conflict as a calm presence, not drawn into the mimetic frenzy, his very presence starts to change the dynamic. At one level, Jesus's presence creates a different *mimetic model* as he calmly holds a peaceful presence amid the anxiety and anger of a crowd.[4]

However, there is more to the work of Christ than being a model, as important as that is. Because Jesus stands in the space of non-rivalry, he immediately attracts attention as being different from the crowd and becomes an excellent candidate for being a scapegoat. The combined might of religious and state leadership turns on Jesus. He becomes a lightning rod for the rage that people were previously directing at each other. If Jesus is only a man, then all we have witnessed is another victim of human violence—a particularly good model of peace but also just another scapegoat (perhaps a pro-Jesus tribe would come along later and erect a shrine to Jesus and start killing his murderers—perish the thought that such a thing could happen!).

But as God, Jesus carries the violence of human wrath, as if through a lightning rod cable, into the ground of his death. By being raised as the forgiving victim, Christ reveals the reality of God's unconquerable life—a life that transcends our rivalries, forgives us for them, and will have no part in our death-dealing. Furthermore, by entering death (the only definitive thing that all humans share) and rising from it, Jesus reveals that physical death is not the final word.

Because we live in time (a feature of the created universe), we experience suffering, as our bodies inevitably wither and die. This is immensely painful and often imbues life with a sense of tragedy (this is explored at length in the book of Job in the Hebrew Scriptures). Jewish tradition, including Jesus himself, saw physical death as part of living in a created time-bound cosmos. This did not limit their faith in a good God. Saint Paul, particularly in Rom 5–6, portrays sin and death as being

---

4. This is observable in the story of the woman accused of adultery (John 8:1–11).

like a disease/contagion endemic to the human experience.[5] But what enslaves humanity is not so much the reality of physical dying but the *fear* of death:

> Since, therefore, the children share flesh and blood, he himself likewise shared the same things, so that through death he might destroy the one who has the power of death, that is, the devil, and free those who all their lives were *held in slavery by the fear of death*. (Heb 2:14–15)

The power that death has over people is *fear*. From a Girardian perspective, perceiving physical death as the complete extinction of life represents the ultimate scarcity to our ego, and we know that a perception of scarcity is one of the drivers of violence (touchstone 2). Perceiving life in this way drives us to secure our physical life using every means available to us and extract as much as possible from this short life, even if it means walking over other people. Such a life is a spiritual death. But Christ reveals that physical death is the door to a different and fuller life:

> Those who try to make their life secure will lose it, but those who lose their life will keep it. (Luke 17:22)

An analogy for what I am trying to describe can be found at the end of *The Matrix Revolutions* (the third of the *Matrix* series of movies).[6] Neo comes to a final confrontation with the violence of the machine world, embodied in the character of Agent Smith. Neo and Agent Smith fight each other in a confluence of escalating, mimetically charged rivalry. As mimetic doubles, neither can prevail. Neo suddenly comes to the insight that the only way to defeat Agent Smith's violence is by absorbing Smith's violence into himself. Neo cannot defeat the machine by playing by the machine's logic. Through his self-emptying, Neo implants a virus of peace into the computer program. This opens a doorway of reconciliation between the machine world and the human world. The penultimate scene shows Neo lying in the shape of a cross blazing with light.

The life, death, and resurrection of Christ is like a viral Trojan horse secretly planted into the dominant operating system of our world. I hesitate to use the word *virus* because we tend to associate viruses with the

---

5. Death, for St. Paul, means physical death. Paul also uses death in a metaphorical sense of that which is opposed to God's good purposes (i.e., life). Outside of a relationship with God, our physical lives can still be a form of death. Inside a relationship with God, physical death is a doorway to life!

6. Wachowski and Wachowski, *Matrix Revolutions*.

destruction of life. The word *seed* is better, because a seed, through its death, explodes with new life.[7]

Being present in the physical world and absorbing the worst of what we can throw at God (crucifixion) is the way God chooses to love the world from beginning to end. The Logos/love that creates the world is the same Logos/love that overcomes life-destroying sin/violence. The death and resurrection of Christ is not something God does as an afterthought, simply to mop up our messes, but is the revelation of God's eternal nature through which the cosmos is created.

God's creation and God's salvation are flip sides of the same coin. The cross and resurrection reveal the way God suffers with the world in the process of bringing the world to completion and ultimately to union with God's self. As an analogy, artists often speak of the suffering inherent in the creative process. The artist's suffering is not a morbid self-flagellation. It is a voluntarily chosen aspect of what creating beauty really involves. In a similar way, parents know before a child is born that bringing a child into the world and raising the child are going to involve pain as well as joy.[8] The Scriptures are saturated with the theme of the self-emptying, creating, and saving love of God in Christ, some examples of which follow:

- Let the same mind be in you that was in Christ Jesus,
  who, though he was in the form of God,
  did not regard equality with God
  as something to be exploited,
  but *emptied himself* [*kenosis*],
  taking the form of a slave,
  being born in human likeness.
  And being found in human form,
  he humbled himself
  and became obedient to the point of death—
  even death on a cross.
  Therefore God also highly exalted him
  and gave him the name
  that is above every name,
  so that at the name of Jesus
  every knee should bend,

7. John 12:24.
8. John 16:20–22.

    in heaven and on earth and under the earth,
    and every tongue should confess
    that Jesus Christ is Lord,
    to the glory of God the Father (Phil 2:5–11).

- He will *swallow up death* forever. Then the Lord God will *wipe away the tears* from all faces (Isa 25:8; cf. 1 Cor 15:54; Rev 21:4).

- John saw Jesus coming toward him and said, "Look, the *Lamb of God*, who *takes away the sin* of the world!"[9] (John 1:29).

- But it has now been revealed through the appearing of our Savior Christ Jesus, who *abolished death* and *brought life and immortality to light* through the gospel (2 Tim 1:10).

- He *disarmed the rulers and authorities* and made a public example of them, triumphing over them in it (Col 2:15).

- For God has done what the law, weakened by the flesh, could not do: by sending his own Son in the likeness of sinful flesh, and to deal with sin, he *condemned sin in the flesh*, so that the just requirement of the law might be fulfilled in us, *who walk* not according to the flesh but *according to the Spirit* (Rom 8:3–4).

- For I am convinced *that neither death*, nor life, nor angels, nor rulers, nor things present, nor things to come, nor powers, nor height, nor depth, nor anything else in all creation, *will be able to separate us from the love of God* in Christ Jesus our Lord (Rom 8:38–39).

- [He] *was handed over to death* for our trespasses and was *raised for our justification* (Rom 4:25; cf. Isa 53:4–5).

NOT JUST THEN BUT NOW: PARTICIPATION

If we think of the story of the death and resurrection of Christ as only a historical event to either believe in or not believe in, we miss the *present reality* of the saving work of God in our lives. God is saving the *present* world from sin, transitioning us into life through death, not only by a

---

9. The Lamb of God is an image of liberation. The Jewish listener would think back to the story of the Passover (Exod 12). When Jewish householders marked the blood of a lamb on their doors, death would see the blood as a sign that death had already visited and would "pass over" the house rather than enter it. In the Revelation of John, the slain lamb is the primary image of God (Rev 5:12–14, 8:17, 19:7); in his death, Jesus carries sin and violence into death and terminates them there.

peculiar event two thousand years ago but by grafting us onto the death and resurrection of Jesus *in this very moment.*

Through the Spirit, a seed of peace is placed in our hearts, drawing us *into* the peace of God now![10] Through the gift of the Spirit, we are enabled to embody a Christlike peace that the ego cannot do on its own (as we saw in touchstone 2, the ego is blind to many aspects of the complex, unconscious, psychological dynamics that lead to violence).

Through the Spirit, we are enabled to make our own voluntary consent to death (the symbolic death of submitting our egos to the call of Christocentric love—placing our egos at the foot of the cross). In doing this, we symbolically and spiritually pass through the same death through which Jesus passed to a new life that we experience (albeit partially) within this life on earth. We will explore more about what this is like in touchstone 4. Suffice to say that we begin to participate, *now*, in a new creation (life in God), which is untouched by the logic of sin and violence. St. Paul refers to this participation in the life of Christ as being "in Christ" (one of Paul's most used phrases).[11]

Jesus's prayer to his Abba (Father), "your will be done" (Lord's Prayer), becomes our prayer through the Spirit. God's Spirit draws us into the crucified and risen life of God. This life was previously hidden, like a tiny mustard seed . . . a smelly piece of yeast in dough . . . a treasure in a field.[12]

To say that we have died to sin means that sin (rivalrous relationships, ego-centeredness, individualism) is no longer the central logic of our lives. Our sin is nonviolently absorbed by God, and we are being transformed as our lives are formed by the new Logos (logic) of God in whom we are now living and who is living in us.

- So you also must consider yourselves dead to sin and alive to God in Christ Jesus (Rom 6:11).
- It is no longer I who live, but it is Christ who lives in me (Gal 2:20).
- Anyone united to the Lord becomes one spirit with him (1 Cor 6:17).

---

10. As we will discuss later, this seed *is* the Logos, through which the world is created, and who becomes fully visible in the life, death, and resurrection of Jesus.

11. See, e.g., Col 3:3.

12. Matt 13:31–50; Luke 13:20–21; Matt 13:44–46.

- As you, Father, are in me and I am in you, may they also be in us (John 17:21).

To be part of the new creation is to participate in the life of God *now* in *advance* of our physical death and to begin to appropriate resurrection life, specifically by being given a new mind[13] and the fruits of the Spirit[14] (touchstone 4). This initiative of God's love in Christ always *precedes* our response and is fanned into life *through* our response. As Brother Roger of Taizé reflects:

> Risen Christ, when we have the simple desire to welcome your life, little by little a flame is kindled in the depths of our being. Fueled by the Holy Spirit, it may be quite faint at first, but it keeps on burning. And when we realize that you love us, the trust of faith becomes our own song.[15]

A SOJOURN INTO TIME

To appreciate more deeply this mystery of *participating* in both the death and resurrection of Christ invites some mental flexibility around the nature of time. We (Westerners in particular) tend to think of time as running in a straight line. In our minds, we line up the events of history, such as Jesus of Nazareth being born at the time of King Herod, as points on the line. One of the consequences of this is that the significance of Jesus becomes something that happened in the *past*, which *superseded* earlier events on the timeline. In this mindset, the birth of Jesus would be a bit like God doing an operating system upgrade on our computer. If this were the case, then our understanding of God as Christlike would be contingent on history: God might choose to do another systems upgrade, as if the old were no longer any good.

In would be better, following the Gospel of John, to frame the significance of Christ in terms of meaning (Logos) rather than time. This is what John is doing at the beginning of his Gospel, where he writes, "In the *beginning* was the Word [Logos]" (John 1:1). The Greek word that English Bibles typically translate as "beginning" is *arche*. This is not a reference to temporal time but is more like the *originating principle*. God is

---

13. Phil 2:5; Rom 12:2.
14. Gal 5:22–26.
15. Brother Roger of Taizé, entry from July 13, 2021, in Frädrich, *Taizé Readings*.

the *origin*,[16] the originating logic (meaning/Logos/creative principle) of the universe. Just as the universe is physically constructed using eternal mathematical truths,[17] so those truths have their source in the Logos of God. The Logos is cruciform love. The Christian revelation is saying that this act of creating a universe, and saving it from sin and violence, is costly to God. God immerses God's self in the creative process. It seems that God cannot create a cosmos without getting God's hands pierced. This is what love is. Like a potter making a pot,[18] if there are glass fragments in the clay, then the potter is going to get cut. We know this, because God, the Logos, is made visible in the person of Jesus.

Even though we see the Logos in the shape of Jesus with our first-century eyes, the Logos (Word) is not limited in time to the first century CE. The Word, Christ, is eternally present to every time through the Spirit:

- God creates by Christlike (crucified and risen) Love
- God liberates by Christlike (crucified and risen) Love
- God remains present to us, through the Spirit, as Christlike (crucified and risen) love

One way of thinking about this could be to imagine time as a spiral, with the Christlike God located (metaphorically) at the center of the spiral. Christ's death and resurrection are equally present/imminent to *every* moment of history, through the Spirit.[19] Some pointers to this reality include:

- [The Word is the] Lamb slain from the foundation of the cosmos (Rev 13:8).

---

16. "Origin" is the English word used by David Bentley Hart in his translation of the New Testament.

17. Eternal, in the sense that mathematical truths do not rely on the human observer; they existed before people came along (this is an analogy for the existence of God not being a product of the human imagination).

18. Jer 18:4.

19. I have imagined a spiral rather than a circle to try to also reflect our experienced sense of learning and growing (rather than just going around in circles). The spiral provides some of this dynamism while also locating God at the center. We could potentially add to our imaginative exercise some of the mind-bending things that quantum physicists are now telling us about some of the mysteries of time/space, including how two particles can exist simultaneously in two places at once. Even in science, things are not as linear or predictable as we once thought.

- If you believed Moses, you would believe Me, for he wrote about Me (John 5:46).
- Before Abraham was, I am (John 8:58).
- They [the Israelites] drank from the spiritual rock that followed them, and the rock was Christ (1 Cor 3:4).

The Logos of God, made visible to us in the death and resurrection of Jesus, is present to us in the eternal *now*. When we *die to ourselves* through the symbolic act of baptism and prayer, our lives are united, in this very moment, to Christ's death and resurrection. We can only ever encounter the timeless God, and the timeless God can only ever encounter us, in this timeless instant—the moment in which I am writing these words and the moment in which you are reading them.

In every moment in which we say yes to God in prayer, or through a cruciform act of love (when we practice peace), we are participating in the death and resurrection of Christ. May this inspire us to live each moment in love towards others as if it is our last, because this moment *will*, one day, be our last! In this *participation* in the life of Christ, initiated by Christ in the Spirit, entirely by grace, God liberates us from sin and unites us to God (variously described as being reconciled to God, redeemed, saved, and delivered).

LITURGICAL REPRESENTATION

By dying, he has destroyed our death, and by rising, restored our life.
—Eucharistic Liturgy

In the Orthodox tradition, God's victory over sin and death, creating a pathway for humanity into life with God, is portrayed in the icon of the resurrection (sometimes called the harrowing of hell). This powerful image shows Jesus breaking down the doors of hell (symbolic of all that keeps people enslaved, including our own self-enslavement) and lifting out imprisoned humanity.

Eastern Orthodox scholar John Behr points out that the death and resurrection of Christ were represented liturgically and in art for several centuries as a single reality, rather than visually representing Good Friday and Easter Sunday as separate events.[20] The Pascha was a single representation of the love and victory of God over the forces of sin, death, and

---

20. Behr, *Mystery of Christ*, 98.

evil. It is not as if God has a really *bad* day on the Friday and then a *better* day on Sunday. Rather, the cross reveals the way God loves the world. On Easter Day, Jesus reveals himself to his disciples as alive (although it takes a good while still before they get it). It's not like God needed a three-day rest in the grave—but perhaps humans needed three days to accept that he had actually died! Over time, the church spread the originally unified Pascha liturgy over a three-day Easter Triduum, retelling the specific events of the three-day period from the Last Supper (and foot washing) through Good Friday to Easter Day.

FOUNDATIONS OF A CHRISTLIKE PEACE

There is a range of theological images and vocabulary that the Christian Testament deploys to articulate the fundamental significance of Christ's death, resurrection, and the gift of the Spirit. I will expand on these below. Each says something important about the way in which God deals with violence and invites us into God's alternative and enduring reality—the kingdom of God's peace. It is also important for us to note how certain theological concepts have absorbed accretions of violent human thinking over time. When this happens, we risk distorting the gospel of peace and reverting to the violence of human culture from which Jesus is delivering us. When we do this, we will inadvertently create a God made in our own image, rather than staying rigorously anchored in the Christlike God. The latter was the guiding lens for St. Paul:

> I decided to know nothing among you except Jesus Christ, and him crucified. (1 Cor 2:2)

(i) Deliverance

God as one who delivers the oppressed is consistent with images of a good Shepherd-King that we find in the Hebrew Scriptures and on which John draws in speaking of Jesus as the good Shepherd who lays down his life for his friends.[21] A king is good because of his *love and faithfulness* to his people demonstrated in the way he liberates them from their enemies. As the psalmist declares:

> The LORD has made known his *victory*;

---

21. John 10:1–18.

> he has revealed his vindication in the sight of the nations.
> He has remembered his *steadfast love and faithfulness* to the house of Israel.
> All the ends of the earth have seen the *victory* of our God. (Ps 98:2–3)

However, the victory of Christ the King does not come through military conquest. The *faithfulness* of Christ the King is seen in the way in which Christ delivers humanity from the enemy (slave master) of sin and death by nonviolently laying down his life. Hence, Christ the King is also *just*, because relationships can now be established in a new way, uncontaminated by rivalry and disoriented desire (the word *justice* means "setting relations right"). When St. Paul uses military language, he is not advocating military action by Christians against their enemies but pointing out that our fight is with the spiritual powers underlying human systems that enslave people:

> Our struggle is not against enemies of blood and flesh, but against the rulers, against the authorities, against the cosmic powers of this present darkness, against the spiritual forces of evil in the heavenly places. (Eph 6:12)

Killing people, whether through murder, capital punishment, or war, does not kill the underlying stories that people tell about each other—demonizing and scapegoating (touchstone 2). With great insight into his own shadow, born of harsh experience, Aleksandr Solzhenitsyn reflected:

> In the intoxication of youthful successes I had felt myself to be infallible, and I was therefore cruel. In the surfeit of power I was a murderer, and an oppressor. In my most evil moments I was convinced that I was doing good, and I was well supplied with systemic arguments. And it was only when I lay there on rotting prison straw that I sensed within myself the first stirrings of good. Gradually it was disclosed to me that the line separating good and evil passes not through states, nor between classes, nor between political parties either—but right through every human heart—and through all human hearts. This line shifts. Inside us, it oscillates with the years. And even within heart overwhelmed by evil, one small bridgehead of good is retained. And even in the best of all hearts there remains . . . an un-uprooted small corner of evil.[22]

---

22. Solzhenitsyn, *Gulag Archipelago 2*, 597.

This is a trap in understanding God's righteousness and justice primarily in terms of moral expectations, rather than in God's gift of steadfast love (relational fidelity). If the focus of our thinking about God is moral purity, we are only ever a hair's breadth from religious zeal, moral self-righteousness, and violence. St. Paul observed this reality in himself:

> You have heard, no doubt, of my earlier life in Judaism. I was violently persecuting the church of God and was trying to destroy it. I advanced in Judaism beyond many among my people of the same age, for I was far more zealous for the traditions of my ancestors. (Gal 1:13–14)

Pauline scholar Douglas Campbell captures the close connection between God's loving faithfulness and God's primary action as *deliverer* by showing how *dikaiosune* (the Greek word traditionally translated as either "justice" [NIV] or "righteousness" [NRSV]), is best understood as "deliverance." God can be said to be righteous and just precisely because God faithfully delivers God's people from oppression (sin, rivalry, violence) through the faith (faithfulness) *of* Christ[23] into resurrection life.

Through the death and resurrection of Christ, God delivers us, through God's Spirit, *in this present moment*, drawing us into communion with God. This new life, into which we begin to partially enter now, is realized fully after our physical death. In Christ, God is saving the human species. As in Adam (the state of humanity caught in the matrix of violently disoriented desire) *all* die, so in Christ are *all* alive!

The heart of the gospel is not about whether our goodness can get us to God. It is about God's goodness coming to us as gift. God doesn't save us because we are good/faithful. God saves us because God is good/faithful. We are relational beings, so our sin has ripple effects to others. Adam functions, symbolically, as a representative person: Adam is all of us trapped in mimetic rivalry. Saint Paul uses the word *flesh* to describe this state.[24] The grace of Christ has a ripple effect in relationships which *more* than undoes the sin of Adam:[25]

---

23. Often translated as "faith *in* Christ," which may have the unfortunate effect of suggesting that our deliverance is happening through *our* efforts rather than Christ's work. Our faith is only ever a consent (saying amen) to Christ's faithfulness—and even this is grace. See Rom 3:26 and Hab 2:4.

24. Regrettably, St. Paul's use of the word flesh has led to the mistaken idea that Paul hated the body. For Paul, the word flesh is very specifically a reference to the state of our life when mired in sin (violence, addiction, disoriented desire).

25. Rom 5:20–21.

- If, because of the one man's trespass, death exercised dominion through that one, *much more surely* will those who receive the abundance of grace and the free gift of righteousness exercise dominion in life through the one man, Jesus Christ. Therefore just as one man's trespass led to condemnation for all, so one man's act of righteousness leads to justification and *life for all*. For just as by the one man's disobedience the many were made sinners, so by the one man's obedience *the many* will be made righteous. But law came in, with the result that the trespass multiplied; but where sin increased, *grace abounded all the more*, so that, just as sin exercised dominion in death, so *grace might also exercise dominion* through justification [deliverance] leading to eternal life through Jesus Christ our Lord[26] (Rom 5:17–21).
- For since death came through a human being, the resurrection of the dead has also come through a human being; for as all die in Adam, so *all* will be made alive in Christ (1 Cor 15:21–22).

(ii) Healing

In the Synoptic Gospels, there is a clear association between Jesus announcing the reign of God and his ministry of healing. Jesus's healings take various forms, including delivering people from oppressive forces within (demons, in the language of the ancient world) and oppressive forces without (legalism, hypocrisy, hardness of heart, scapegoating). In the story of the healing of the Gerasene demoniac,[27] there is a clear link between the social isolation of the man held in chains at the outskirts of the town and his possession by demons. Is it possible that demonic possession is a way of describing the impact on the man of having been scapegoated; is he carrying the projected anxieties and fears of his village? After healing the man, Jesus sends him *back into* the village to proclaim what God has done. This healing involves reincorporation to community.

In Jesus's time, to be sick was sometimes perceived by people as associated with a person's moral failure,[28] and some forms of sickness ren-

---

26. Paul makes the same point five times in these few verses. Clearly, this is a key point!
27. Mark 5:1–20.
28. John 9:1–2.

dered a person socially isolated from the temple through being ritually unclean.[29] Jesus decisively breaks these linkages and, in so doing, demonstrates the unconditional love of God (articulated in touchstone 1). Such love has the potential to heal the deep-seated wounds of disconnection that underly personal shame, mimetic rivalry, grief, loss, and negative manifestations of survival and belonging needs (referred to in touchstone 2).

If we have grown up in a loving household/community that allowed us to develop a healthy individuation (a calm and firmly held sense of self in relationship to others), then we *may* be less prone to our identity being formed by imitating the desire of others. The stress associated with the latter can make us unwell.[30] To find a calm and secure identity in God is the beginning of being healed—saved from the stress of an identity that is externally, mimetically, shaped by others. I find it significant that Jesus resists the desert temptations (to fix, to be powerful, to be impressive) within the context of his baptism experience of being unconditionally loved by God his Abba (Father) who declares "this is my beloved Son [child]." Retaining this connection to his central identity occurs for Jesus in prayer. The Gospels say that one of Jesus's practices was to withdraw to deserted places to pray. As we will see in part 2, prayer is a form of *disengagement from* negative mimetic desire and *connection with* the desire of God. John's Gospel makes this explicit, where Jesus says,

> Very truly, I tell you, the Son can do nothing on his own, but only what he sees the Father doing; for whatever the Father does, the Son does likewise. (John 5:19)

(iii) Forgiveness and reconciliation

Jesus teaches us to ask for forgiveness as part of his teaching on prayer: "Forgive us our sins as we forgive those who sin against us" (Luke 11:4). I have heard preachers reduce this to something like, "We are very bad, but God is good and forgives us and, in doing so, saves us from being

---

29. Luke 8:43–48.

30. It is notable that the first generation of young people to have never known life without a smart phone is now entering university, with record levels of anxiety and depression presenting to psychologists. Admittedly, this is only a correlation, but there is research already emerging of a causative relationship. See Crenna-Jennings, "Young People's Mental and Emotional Health."

punished by God." If we frame forgiveness as a transactional exchange and release from the fear of punishment from an angry parent, then we miss the point and are making God in our own image—the image of violently distorted human relationships. The point of forgiveness is not to save us from an angry God. The point of forgiveness is that it flows directly from God's character as deliverer.

> I baptize you with water for repentance, but one who is more powerful than I is coming after me [the Christ]; I am not worthy to carry his sandals. *He will baptize you with the Holy Spirit and fire.* (Matt 3:11)

Forgiveness is part of God's *liberating* activity through the Spirit. God's forgiveness is a form of deliverance from the slave master of unforgiveness. To receive the forgiveness of God and to pass that forgiveness to others is not only to be set free but also to set others free from the accusatory, legalistic, finger-pointing gesture. Saint Paul, following Jesus, makes this clear:[31]

- When you were buried with him in baptism, you were also raised with him through faith in the power of God, who raised him from the dead. And when you were dead in trespasses and the uncircumcision of your flesh, God made you alive together with him, when he *forgave* us all our trespasses, erasing the record that stood against us *with its legal demands.* He set this aside, nailing it to the cross (Col. 2:12–14).

- If you *forgive* the sins of any, they are *forgiven* them; if you retain the sins of any, they are retained (John 20:23).

In this latter verse, Jesus is inviting us to consider the consequences of retaining sins against others. When we do this, we risk unforgiveness eating us internally like a cancer. Jesus's teaching on forgiveness is an extravagant overturning of vengeance and any implied *need* for blood sacrifice in the human/divine relationship:

---

31. One understanding of the *Satan* in the Hebrew Scriptures is a role within the heavenly court that accuses, like a prosecuting attorney (Job 1:6–12). The *Advocate* (Holy Spirit) in John's Gospel acts as a comforter—a defence attorney (John 14:16). I was fascinated to learn from a Muslim colleague about the close conceptual link in Islam between being set free (*àfa*) and having one's sins wiped out.

- Whereas the vengeance of Lamech would be "seventy-seven-fold" (Gen 4:24), Jesus commanded his follows to "forgive seventy-seven-fold" (Matt 18:22).
- Whereas Abel's blood cried out from the ground for vengeance (Gen 4:10), Christ's death and resurrection speaks a "better word than the blood of Abel" (Heb 12:24—this is the word of forgiveness).
- Whereas the Torah had linked forgiveness to blood sacrifice, Christ reminded people that God did not require sacrifice and offerings (Heb 9:22, 10:5; Matt 9:13; Ps 40:6, 50:13).[32]

The consequences of withholding forgiveness can be catastrophic when expanded to the level of whole societies, one manifestation of which is genocide. The process of forgiveness at individual levels and at the level of whole societies is part of the extremely demanding work of nonviolent peacemaking. We will expand on the practicalities of this in part 3. The main thing to note at this point is that the practice of forgiveness, as a core practice of peace, is theologically anchored in the fact that we are already forgiven by God and liberated from the devastating slavery of unforgiveness.

(iv) Non-retaliatory loving solidarity

The practice of nonviolence, which includes the work of forgiveness, is a deep, sometimes painful, and ultimately transformative process for us and for the communities in which we live. The prophet Isaiah reflected on this kind of transformation in a series of passages commonly referred to as the suffering servant passages.[33] Jesus frequently quoted Isaiah, and I imagine that Jesus had the suffering servant in mind as he reflected on his own journey to Jerusalem. I can also imagine the apostolic witnesses

---

32. It is a caricature that temple Jews offered the blood of animals to appease God. Rather, because Jews considered the blood to contain life, the offering of blood was symbolic of offering one's own life to God as an act of worship. Sacrifice was to enable people to *experience* forgiveness rather than *achieve* forgiveness. However, later Jewish prophets, and Jesus himself, advocated doing away with even animal sacrifice. The great reversal was that God, in Christ, was sacrificing God's self to humans rather than humans to God.

33. Isa 42:1–4; 49:1–6; 50:4–9; 52:13—53:12.

reflecting on the suffering servant as they came to an understanding of the significance of Jesus's death.[34]

The last of the suffering servant passages, from Isa 53, is particularly intricate. It reveals how the suffering servant (which may be referring to an individual or to the nation of Israel) innocently (unjustly) and nonviolently bears the violence of other human beings in a way that is redemptive. Paraphrasing the essence of some of the key verses:

- The suffering servant is crushed (by us) for our iniquities (Isa 53:5).
- The servant goes silently like a lamb to the slaughter (Isa 53:7)—note Jesus's silence before Pilate (Mark 14:61).
- The treatment of the servant is a perversion of justice (Isa 53:8).
- There is no violence in the servant (Isa 53:9).
- The servant pours himself out to death (Isa 53:12) without reciprocal violence (note Jesus self-emptying in Phil 2:8).
- Through the servant's nonviolence, there is a profound education for us—a correction to our thinking (Isa 53:5).[35]
- Through the servant, the will of the Lord will prosper (Isa 53:10).
- Through the servant, the will of the Lord will shed light (open our eyes) to our own violence (Isa 53:11).

A crucial question is the attitude and role of God in the suffering of the servant. Is God playing an active or passive role, or any role at all? The suffering servant passage mentioned above includes these disturbing words in most English translations of the Bible:

- The Lord has laid on him the iniquity of us all (Isa 53:6).
- It was the will of the Lord to crush him with pain (Isa 53:10).[36]

---

34. Acts 8:32–33.

35. The NRSV translates Isa 53:5b as "upon him was the punishment that made us whole." Tony Bartlett argues that the word translated as "punishment" is better translated as "education." Consistent with this, see Isa 53:1, "Out of his anguish we shall see light, he shall find satisfaction through this *knowledge*. The righteous one, my servant, shall make many righteous" (Bartlett, as cited in Hardin, *Jesus Driven Life*, 199–201).

36. Jersak points out that the LXX (Greek version of the Hebrew Scriptures, used as a source by the Greek authors of the Christian Testament), translates this verse as "The Lord wishes to cleanse Him of His wound." The same Greek word, *katharisai*, is used in reference to Jesus's ministry of healing (Jersak, *More Christlike Word*, 103). Humans do violence; God heals us from violence.

Consistent with touchstone 1, we need to read these verses christologically—through the lens of Jesus. When Jesus prays to God in the garden of Gethsemane "not my will but yours be done" (Luke 22:42), the *will of God* is not found in the infliction of pain on Jesus but in Jesus (God's own self) loving to the end. Regrettably and horribly, this will mean being crucified. The violence and the infliction of pain belongs to humanity. Jesus bears our violence in himself rather than mirroring, replicating, or vengefully returning violence upon us.

Through Christ's death, resurrection, and ascension, God reveals God's glory as self-giving love. This is a glory that is revealed only through the path of humble love, even to death. To say that God *wills* pain can be properly understood only in the sense of a voluntary choice to suffer pain oneself rather than impose pain on someone else. This now leads us to explore some more nuances of what we understand by Christ's 'sacrifice.'

(v) Sacrificial love—the movement of the heart towards another

The Christian Testament portrays God's love using a shocking and counter intuitive image of God giving up their own child. Drawing on the story of Abraham's willingness to sacrifice his son, Isaac, St. Paul reflects:

> He [God the Father] who did not withhold his own Son, but gave him up for all of us, will he not with him also give us everything else? (Rom 8:32)

Applying a twenty-first-century lens to this story, we know that any father who acted as Abraham did towards Isaac would be arrested and have their children removed from them. But even within the context of its day, this story functions as *revelation* precisely because it evokes horror in the mind of the reader and especially readers who are parents. The act of killing one's own child or that God would require this to happen is repugnant.

How are we to make sense of this through a christological lens? If we deploy the language of sacrifice in a way that originates from conceptions of God that are not, in the first instance, shaped by Christ, then we can distort the gospel *and* do real damage to people's faith (trust) in God.

One of the ways our thinking about sacrifice can be distorted is when we project our own human justice frameworks onto God. This can easily happen if we *begin* with a premise that we can, through our own reason, recognize our own sinful predicament *independent* of, and *before*, the revelation of God in Christ. Using a contractual paradigm,[37] we make God in the image of a human judge who, to be internally consistent, *must* dispense a punishment. In this paradigm, the sacrifice of Jesus means that Jesus takes God's violent punishment on our behalf. By starting with a conception of justice that starts other than with Christ, we have made God in the violent image of the state.[38]

The above legal/contractual paradigm misdiagnosis the human problem. The human problem is not a legal justice challenge. As we saw in touchstone 2, we are, prior to revelation, blind to our own predicament as sinful and violent people. As Girard observes, as does St. Paul, prior to revelation, we are *not* actually free agents (free in the way in which we know freedom after revelation). Our human predicament is a spiritual sickness (disoriented desire) that needs to be illuminated and healed.

If we start with a proposition that God *must* violently punish in order to be just and to have any kind of relationship with us (because of God's purity), then we have built violence into the very heart of God (albeit an internalized violence), and Christ's sacrifice has become the appeasement of violence. God will have become subject to our myths of redemptive violence (no redemption without the guilty being killed). On the contrary, in Christ, we find God stepping right into the mess of our sin and violence, taking the initiative to relate to us *despite* our violence, in order to restore us to relationship. *This* is what Christlike sacrifice means.

When we establish all our thinking about God on Christ and the inner relationships of the Trinity, there can be no division between the Father and the Son. The Son is not saving us from an angry Father. Jesus is always and only ever doing what he sees the Father doing.[39] The Hebrew Scriptures and the Christian Testament both make it clear that God does not *require* sacrifice (sacrifice in terms of punishment, spilling blood in worship, or making scapegoats in community life):

---

37. A key aspect of contractual thinking is that a person is a free agent, and if they knowingly break the law, then society and/or God should punish them.

38. This is the logic of the penal substitutionary theory of the atonement (PSA). This theory has become dominant in Western Protestantism. It is a relatively late development in Christian thought. PSA resonates with a human desire to balance the scales of justice through punishment. The PSA theory is not universally held, particularly in the Eastern Orthodox traditions, and in significant parts of Roman Catholicism and Anglicanism.

39. John 5:19.

- If I were hungry, I would not tell you,
  for the world and all that is in it is mine.
  Do I eat the flesh of bulls,
  or drink the blood of goats? (Ps 50:12–13).

- I [God] desire mercy, not sacrifice (Hos 6:6).

- Go and learn what this means, "I desire mercy, not sacrifice." For I have come to call not the righteous but sinners (Matt 9:13).

From a Christian perspective, we need to understand sacrifice in Trinitarian terms where the will of the Son is simultaneously the will of the Father and vice versa. A positive and redemptive notion of sacrifice makes sense only in light of gratuitous self-giving:

> I lay down my life in order to take it up again. No one takes it from me, but I lay it down of my own accord. I have power to lay it down, and I have power to take it up again. I have received this command from my Father. (John 10:17–18)

In this sense, John's Gospel extends the insight of the Synoptic Gospels (Matthew, Mark, Luke) in relation to the death of Jesus. The passion narratives of the Synoptic Gospels portray Jesus as a sacrificial lamb, because Jesus is crucified at the Passover Festival—an image that connects liberation from slavery to sin with liberation from slavery in Egypt. John's Gospel adds the important insight that Jesus is an active agent in his death. Jesus's life was not *taken from him* as if he were a passive and helpless victim.[40]

Through Christ's sacrifice (self-giving love for the benefit of another), God opens a new mode of existence for humanity. Cognizant of Christ's active mode of being, we will not passively accept a false identity as a victim in the struggles of our lives. We actively receive and celebrate our dignity as a beloved child of God—and through this adoption, God opens the possibility of us loving self and neighbor in the way that Jesus loves.

We see an experiential analogy of sacrifice in the sacrifices that parents make for their children, even to the point of suffering violence for them. For example, a parent may willingly stand in the doorway of their home in the face of someone trying to break in.[41] This in no way

---

40. John 10:18.
41. John 10:1–15.

justifies the violence but acknowledges the possibility that, in some cases, carefully chosen and strategic suffering of violence on behalf of another is Christlike. Another analogy might be if a child breaks a priceless vase: when the parent forgives the child rather than punishing them, the parent can be said to have paid a price. The cost of forgiveness is paid by the one doing the forgiving. This way of understanding sacrifice does not imply any punitive violence on the part of the parent.

Self-giving love for another is frequently articulated by the biblical authors when they utilize ancient images of sacrifice as a *redemptive payment*:

- For the Lord has *ransomed* Jacob and has redeemed him from hands too strong for him (Jer 31:11)

- Shall I *ransom* them from the power of Sheol? Shall I *redeem* them from Death? (Hos 13:13).

- For the Son of Man came not to be served but to serve, and to give his life a *ransom* for many (Mark 10:45).

- Keep watch over yourselves and over all the flock, of which the Holy Spirit has made you overseers, to shepherd the church of God that he *obtained with the blood* of his own Son (Acts 20: 28).

- You were *bought with a price*; do not become slaves of human masters (1 Cor 7:23).

- Christ *redeemed us* from the curse of the law by becoming a curse for us—for it is written, "Cursed is everyone who hangs on a tree"[42] (Gal 3:1).

- For all have sinned and fall short of God's glory, being made upright as a gift by his grace, through the *manumission fee*[43] paid in the Anointed One, Jesus: Whom God set forth as a [*hilasterion*] place of atonement[44] through faith in his blood, as a demonstration of his

---

42. The religious and state authorities weaponize the law to justify the killing of Jesus. Notably, in referencing Deut 21:22–23, St. Paul removes any suggestion that it is God doing the cursing.

43. A manumission fee is an amount paid to free a slave.

44. A lot of ink has been spilled over the translation of *hilasterion*. Some translations have "expiation" or "propitiation." NRSV has "sacrifice of atonement" (main text) or "place of atonement" (footnote). James Alison draws attention to 2 Sam 21:1–6 where the seven sons of Saul are handed over by David to the Gibeonites to "expiate" their wrath—a convenient scapegoat for an incoming king (Alison, *Jesus the Forgiving*

justice[45] through the dismissal of past sins (Rom 3:23–25, Hart, *New Testament*).

Metaphors of redemptive payment speak into a world that was very familiar with slavery, where a payment would be made to free a slave from their slave master. You can imagine, if you were a slave, how happy you would be if someone made a payment of a kind that you could never, in your wildest dreams, achieve for yourself. This might raise the question "How much would I be willing to pay/give to free someone I love?" Perhaps if one of your own children were in slavery, you might give up your own life to free your child. The language of "ransom" and "redemption by blood" is trying to capture this kind of self-giving.

Where theology has bolted down very unhelpful tracks is when the language of redemptive payment gets pushed too far by specifying *to whom* the payment is made, when this is not actually stated in the text. One false trail has been to say that the payment is being made to the Satan/devil (a slave master). The disturbing problem with this is that it assumes that divine love needs to do deals with the devil—a thought that would be inconceivable to Jews.[46] Another false trail has been to say that the death of Christ was a payment being made to God the Father, on behalf of humanity, to appease God's wrath. Some of the difficulties of this view have already been mentioned above.

To summarize, the metaphor of redemption by blood sacrifice is a powerful one. It speaks to the depth of God's love for the world, as deep as a parent giving up their life for their child to deliver them from slavery—provided we do not push the metaphor beyond what it is meant to do.

Out of this understanding of the work of God, I understand sacrifice as a *movement of the heart towards another, for their benefit*. René Girard

---

Victim, 3:259–70). In a footnote to his translation of the New Testament, David Bentley Hart says, "[*Hilasterion* is] technically: a word that could mean either 'expiation' or something 'expiatory,' but in the standard Greek rendering of Hebrew scripture had the special meaning of the Mercy Seat covering the Ark of the Covenant [Exod 25:17–22]" (Hart, *New Testament*, 292). Consistent with this, NRSV footnote has "place of atonement." In summary, God opens the doorway to union (at-one-ment), which has been blocked on the human side of the relationship by sin and violence. The work of Christ is delivering/liberating us from that sin.

45. NRSV has "righteousness" rather than "justice." Either way, following Douglas Campbell, the work of Christ is all about God setting relations right through delivering us from the slavery of sin.

46. Another ancient theory of the atonement, called Christus Victor, proposed very disturbingly that God tricked the devil by using Jesus like bait on a fishhook.

acknowledges that the Scriptures open up this understanding of sacrifice as self-giving love—a gospel counternarrative to sacrifice as scapegoating. As a specific example, Girard points to the story of two women who bring a child to King Solomon, both claiming to be the child's mother.[47] The real mother was revealed by her willingness to sacrifice her own claim on the child for the child's benefit. Girard sees this as a powerful prefiguring of the love of Christ.

Christ's sacrifice is a self-offering to end all human sacrifices. This sacrifice of "at-one-ment" creates one reconciled humanity. S. Mark Heim articulates much of what I have been saying like this:

> Christ became a curse for us. Jesus suffered for our sins. We are washed in the blood of the lamb, redeemed by his death. Behold the Lamb of God who takes away the sins of the world. These and many other formulations are variations on this same dynamic. They refer both to the sacrificial practice that claimed Jesus and to the redemptive purpose that worked against it. Christ became cursed and accused as all scapegoats do, for the sake of the unity his accusers sought. That is according to the fallen wisdom of sacrifice. But it is according to the wisdom of God that Christ was willing to be treated so, to become a curse for us in order to liberate victims and sacrificers alike from this changeless cycle.[48]

In the next touchstone, we will explore what our lives look like as we begin to participate in this new realm of existence. This participation in Christ is a gift of the Spirit; it is the gift of a new mind. This is a mind that has the same kenotic (humble, self-emptying) character as Jesus. It is associated with the fruits of the Spirit, all of which express a Christlike peace.

SUMMARY OF TOUCHSTONE 3

1. To save us from the matrix of sin, death, and violence, God uses a different kind of logic (Logos) from the self-reinforcing and self-justifying violent ways in which humans try to establish peace. This logic is Christ himself—God's kenotic (humble, self-emptying) life, death, and resurrection. Through his resurrection, Jesus reveals the

---

47. 1 Kgs 3:16–28
48. Heim, *Saved from Sacrifice*, 308.

triumph of God's love over death; *deliverance* from sin, violence, and death; *healing*; *forgiveness*; *non-retaliatory solidarity*; *and sacrificial love.*

2. Through the Spirit, we are grafted onto the kenotic pattern of Christ's death and resurrection. In this process, God is freeing us from the disoriented and grasping desires of mimetic rivalry. Our desire is remade in the pattern of the non-rivalrous relationships of the Trinity (resurrection life).

REFLECT

1. In what ways are the death and resurrection of Christ and God's healing, forgiveness, and nonviolent reconciliation significant to me?

2. Have I ever found it difficult to forgive someone and even weaponized that against that person by withdrawing from them or intentionally withholding forgiveness as a way to punish them? What did that feel like? Have I ever had someone withhold the forgiveness that I so desperately craved from them? What did that feel like? Have I ever worried that God would not forgive something that I have done? What did that feel like?

3. Have I ever had someone suffer for me—in a healthy and loving way? What was that like? Have I ever given my life for someone in this way?

5

Touchstone 4
Christ Enables Us to Practice Peace

BECOMING HUMAN

It can be a huge release to realize that this whole journey of being loved into a new life is not about us or our personal ticket into a place called heaven. We cannot earn a relationship with God or build the kingdom of God through right actions or right beliefs. I have heard many sermons that implored congregations to "build the kingdom of God." Regrettably, this can just load people up with guilt about their inadequacies. Jesus never talked about us *building* the kingdom. Jesus spoke of the kingdom as a vision of God,[1] which we are invited to enter.[2]

The kingdom is what the world looks like when God's love is manifested on earth. Through the alternative logic (Logos) of the cross, God breaks through the matrix of our disoriented, rivalrous desires. The Holy Spirit grafts us onto God's own dying and rising in Christ.[3] This is life

---

1. Jesus's parables typically begin with "The kingdom of God/heaven is like . . ."
2. Matt 18:3, 19:23.
3. There has been debate through the centuries about whether humans can resist grace. For the sake of psychological and spiritual health, free consent to God is important. God is not spiritually dominating us. And yet, when I recall my own journey, all the experiences I had which led me to say yes to Christ were, when I think about it, total grace. Grace is hugely attractive when we encounter it. Saul had no control over

for us and for the earth. We refer to this good initiative of God with all kinds of theological words: salvation, healing, reconciliation, redemption, atonement, righteousness, justice.

To respond to God's invitation (repentance) certainly contains transformational power, so long as we remember that we were loved before we repented and loved equally afterwards. Repentance has power, because confessing *Christ* as Lord expresses a willingness to move with the grain of God's love. It is like opening a gift and discovering the joy of it. In this discovery, we recognize the Word (Christ) loving us. This is abundant life. Our yes to God involves placing our ego in God's service, consciously, day by day. This means giving up our compulsive needs to fix, be powerful, be right, and be liked—which all fuel mimetic rivalry and violence (touchstone 2). This is good news for ourselves and others. Through God's grace, we come to the insight that we are part of the problem (violence), and, by God's grace, we start to become part of the solution (peace).

As we gaze on Jesus, God reorders our disoriented desire. We move from a mindset of scarcity/mimetic rivalry to knowing ourselves, as with all creation, as abundantly loved. God draws us, by the Spirit, into communion with all of life, and, therefore, our lives become inherently nonviolent. We may find ourselves singing joyfully with all creation, Yes! Thank you! Alleluia! God strengthens us in prayer, in the company of the ecclesia (church)—a group of fellow travelers, called into a communion of peace. In this communion, we can admit we are fallible, failing daily, dying, and being raised.

This is what we mean by baptism. We are, with the company and support of others, saying no to the illusions and lies of the world. The death and new life of baptism is like Neo taking the red pill in the movie *The Matrix*. There is a moment in the film where Neo is given a choice by Morpheus (who will become Neo's mentor) whether Neo wants to discover what the matrix is and, by extension, to be freed from slavery. Morpheus says to Neo, "There is no turning back. You take the blue pill, the story ends, you wake up in your bed and believe whatever you want to believe. You take the red pill, you stay in wonderland, and I show you how deep the rabbit hole goes. Remember . . . all I'm offering is the truth, nothing more."[4]

Christ revealing himself on the Damascus road but, in the end, St. Paul said yes to God through one difficult circumstance after another.

4. Wachowski and Wachowski, *Matrix*, in scene 25:45—29:50.

Spoiler alert . . . when Neo takes the red pill, he is flushed out of the matrix in one of the best metaphors for baptism ever devised by contemporary cinema. This is death to Neo's old life, and yet it is also a kind of birth (matrix means 'womb', and Neo means 'new'). It does not make Neo's life easier. In many ways, his life just got a whole lot harder. But now he is truly alive. An echo of St. Paul can be heard:

> Do you not know that all of us who have been baptized into Christ Jesus were baptized into his death? Therefore, we have been buried with him by baptism into death, so that, just as Christ was raised from the dead by the glory of the Father, so we too might walk in newness of life. (Rom 6:3–4)

John Behr speaks of the process of dying with Christ as *becoming human*,[5] being made in the image of the true human, Jesus. God's declaration "Let us make a human" (Gen 1:26) reaches its culmination in Jesus's last words on the cross, "It is finished" (John 19:30). As Pilate so ironically and truthfully declared to the crowd, "Behold the *anthropos* (human)" (John 19:5). Jesus, the completed human, is human precisely because he expresses the full depth of God's love for the cosmos in his voluntarily chosen self-giving.[6] It is in this *particular* way—fully immersing himself in the worst that humans can do to each other and to God, the brutality and injustice of the cross, that God reveals his glory as infinite love.[7] When we voluntarily die to (egoic) self by consciously placing ourselves in the service of Christ, we are embracing what it means to be a full human being. In doing so, God is making us into God's own image. This means loving as Jesus loves. Centrally, this includes being a people of peace.

Our participation in Christ is enacted in the Eucharist where we *eat* the one we have slain, in order to face our violence rather than deny it. In this liturgy, we honesty admit our complicity in the violence of the world and open ourselves to God's forgiveness and ongoing gift of the Spirit. The Eucharist symbolizes a vision of one universal humanity.[8] It is a sign of God including and gathering us together (re-member-ing us) in contrast to the mimetic rivalries that separate, divide, and kill.

---

5. Behr, *Becoming Human*, 71.

6. John 3:16.

7. "When I am lifted up" (on the cross) is a recurring phrase (in various forms) in John's Gospel.

8. Isa 25:6.

THE MIND OF CHRIST AND GIFTS OF THE SPIRIT

This participation in the death of Christ, in advance of our physical death, is accompanied by the gifts of a new mind[9] and the fruits of the Spirit.[10] We now look at some of the tangible ways in which these gifts manifest in our lives as we pray "thy kingdom come on earth," as the mind of Christ shapes us and as our lives take on a cruciform shape:

(i) Courage: the fear of death is dispelled

Someone told me once that the phrase "Be not afraid" occurs around 365 times in the Hebrew and Christian Testaments, once for each day of the year. I have not verified this, but I like the idea. One of the major seeds for nonviolence in the early church, inspired by the resurrection of Christ, was a fearlessness towards death.

As I observed in touchstone 1, God intends the reconciliation of everything in God. Since God stands outside time (time is a created condition of the physical universe) and death occurs within time (people get old and die), it is inconceivable that physical death exists within the actual life of God. Hence St. Paul can say, "The last enemy that will be destroyed is death" (1 Cor 15:26). But within this limited time/space universe, we can still say, in faith, that death is not the end, because, through Christ, death becomes a doorway to the timeless life of God.

In the absence of Christ (an entirely speculative thought), we would physically die, and that would be it—kaput—silence—gone. Nothing else. A meaningless universe would chug along and eventually fizzle out and perhaps crank up again through another big bang. In the meantime, the death of innocents would be a painful and meaningless casualty of the entire process. But because God *is* involved, we can conceive of a life that transcends physical death. The death and resurrection of Christ speaks into the fear of death that lurks in the unconscious of us all, driving much of the disoriented desire that we named in touchstone 2. The cross and resurrection:

- Mitigate[11] our acquisitive desires for power, prestige, and reputation, which psychologically underly much of our anxious striving,

---

9. 1 Cor 2:16; Phil 2:5–8; Rom 12:2.
10. Gal 5:22.
11. I say "mitigate" rather than "eliminate," because most people, in my experience,

summarized in the statement "Eat, drink and be merry, for tomorrow we die"[12]

- Mitigate our archaic survival and belonging strategies in which we turn our neighbor into an object of personal instrumental value—a thing to secure our own well-being. Christ dying for everyone, without exception, means that everyone has an inconceivably unique and intrinsic value. As such, we treat everyone, as Martin Buber says, as a 'sacred thou.'

Because of Christ's resurrection and Christians' participation in this new life, many Jesus-followers through history have found the strength to willingly became nonviolent martyrs rather than worship an idolatrous emperor or kill other people in an emperor's wars. In his short work *On the Incarnation*, Athanasius, who was one of the intellectual architects of the Nicene Creed, says:

> For of old, before the divine sojourn of the Savior took place, even to the saints death was terrible, and all wept for the dead as though they perished. But now that the Savior has raised His body, death is no longer terrible; for all who believe in Christ tread him under as naught and choose rather to die than to deny their faith in Christ. For they verily know that when they die, they are not destroyed, but actually [begin to] live, and become incorruptible through the resurrection.[13]

Another dramatic example is Ignatius of Antioch's Letter to the Romans. Ignatius, a late second-century bishop, was a disciple of Polycarp, who was a disciple of John (the author of the fourth Gospel), so we are hearing a very early Christian testimony. Ignatius wrote his Letter to the Romans while being marched off by the army to be killed (martyred). He appeals to the Christians in Rome not to save him from his impending death, because, through his voluntarily chosen nonviolent witness to Christ, he will be *born* into his true life. For St. Ignatius, to be born into the life of God, through his nonviolent testimony to the love of Christ, was to *become* a human being:

---

carry a fear of death, particularly when we are young. As we grow in faith (trust) and experience of the life of Christ, this often reduces.

12. The mindset of the wealthy farmer in Jesus's parable. See Luke 12:13–21.
13. Athanasius, "On the Incarnation," §27.

> I have no use for the delights of this world and all its kingdoms. I would prefer dying in Jesus Christ to ruling over all the earth. I seek him who died for us; I desire him who rose for our sake. I am about to be born again. Understand me, my brothers; do not hinder me from coming to life [by dying], do not wish me to die [by remaining in this world]. I desire to belong to God, not to the world. Do not seduce me with perishable things. Let me see the pure light; when I am there, I shall be truly a man [human] at last. Allow me to imitate the sufferings of my God.[14]

When I was a theological student in the early 1990s, I met a Uniting Church minister, Neville Watson, who told me about his travels with a group of peacemakers into Iraq during the first Gulf War. Their purpose was to express solidarity with Iraqi people during the intensive bombing of Baghdad. They put their own lives at risk alongside their fellow humans, inspired by the example of Jesus. Neville taught me about the courage required in nonviolence, where a person must be willing to die but not to kill.

The movie *Hacksaw Ridge* tells another true story of nonviolence in war by a young Christian named Desmond Doss, who went to war as a medico because he was a Christian conscientious objector to bearing arms.[15] He was the only noncombatant to win the Congressional Medal of Honor after rescuing dozens of wounded men from the battlefield. Hauerwas speaks of how the gospel becomes present in the world through the transformed lives of followers of Jesus:

> [Jesus] proclaims that the kingdom is present in so far as his life reveals the effective power of God to create a transformed people capable of living peacefully in a violent world.[16]

Whenever we make a conscious attempt to live and lead nonviolently, we are making an act of courageous trust in which there is no certainty of the outcome. Nonviolence may not get us the result we want. We might suffer violence ourselves. We might not achieve the kind of peace we hope for. In the Synoptic Gospels, Jesus walks into the place of death, trusting his heavenly Father amid extreme violence and brutality. Yet Jesus does this, because it is what he feels love is calling him to. This is

---

14. Ignatius of Antioch, "Letter to the Romans." I am grateful to John Behr, a patristics scholar, for this insight.
15. Gibson, *Hacksaw Ridge*.
16. Hauerwas, *Peaceable Kingdom*, 129.

the mindset we are invited to bring into our nonviolent living and leadership. It has its own inherent integrity as an act of love—as an expression of the mind of Christ.

(ii) Peace and joy

Jesus says he gives a peace that the world cannot give (John 14:27). Luke's Gospel puts this right at the beginning as a summarizing theme for his Gospel:

> By the tender mercy of our God, the dawn from on high will break upon us, to give light to those who sit in darkness and in the shadow of death, to guide our feet into the way of *peace*. (Luke 1:78–79)

We have seen that this is a peace rooted in God overcoming the power of sin (mimetic violence) and gifting us with new life. This life flows out of the non-rivalrous relationships within God's inner life, between the Father and Son, and the extension of unconditional grace towards us who have been incorporated into that divine life. God is not our rival!

Saint Paul begins nearly all his letters with a greeting of "grace and peace" and puts peace as one of the fruits of the Spirit:

> the fruit of the Spirit is love, joy, *peace*, patience, kindness, generosity, faithfulness, gentleness, and self-control. (Gal 5:22–23)

Under the overarching umbrella of love,[17] all the fruits of the Spirit contribute to peace. Just do a quick face validity check on that. Think about our own relationships and then ask, is it not true that if we are patient, kind, generous, faithful, gentle, and self-controlled, that we are much more likely to contribute to peace in our relationships?

Once again, the Jesus story reminds us that peace is not something that we heroically achieve by force of will but is the fruit of remaining connected to the vine of Christ. This is what helps us know whether, in any relationship, I am being shaped by the mind of Christ or my own ego. If it is the former, there will be a sense of grace/gift/surprise about it, but when I am under the control of the old mind/flesh, I tend to get anxious, grumpy, controlling, and inordinately attached to getting my own way. Peace is a gift that is associated with the renewal of our minds in Christ:

---

17. 1 Cor 13:1–12.

- Though I was blind, now I see (John 9:25).
- To set the *mind* on the flesh is death, but to set the mind on the Spirit is life and peace (Rom 8:6).
- Do not be conformed to this world, but be transformed by the renewing of your *minds* (Rom 12:2).
- Since, then, you have been raised with Christ, set your *minds* on things above (Col 3:2).
- From now on, therefore, *we regard no one from a human point of view*; even though we once knew Christ from a human point of view, we know him no longer in that way. So if anyone is in Christ, there is a new creation: everything old has passed away; see, *everything has become new*! All this is from God, who *reconciled us* to himself through Christ, and has *given us the ministry of reconciliation*; that is, in Christ God was *reconciling* the world to himself, *not counting their trespasses against them*, and entrusting the message of *reconciliation* to us. So we are ambassadors for Christ, since God is making his appeal through us; we entreat you on behalf of Christ, *be reconciled* to God. For our sake he made him to be sin who knew no sin, so that in him we might become the righteousness of God (2 Cor 5:16–21).

(iii) Kenotic space-making

In his Letter to the Philippians, cited earlier, St. Paul says, "In your relationships with one another, have the same mind as Christ Jesus" (Phil 2:5).

Having the *mind* of Christ is not just about having loving thoughts towards other people. It includes embodied action. As we saw in touchstone 1, the *being* of God cannot be separated from God's *work* in the life and death of Jesus. God's love is love in action.

Therefore, a vital expression of the mind of Christ is the *practice* of creating space for others through our own self-emptying, just as God "emptied himself, taking the form of a servant" (Phil 2:7). How we do this in one-to-one conversations and create conditions for making space for others in groups will be the focus of part 3. We will also see in part 2 how opening space for others is linked to opening space within ourselves.

Kenosis, rather than being miserable self-denial, creates room for the abundant life that God is offering. Theologian Ben Myers puts it like this:

> [The holy life is not a self-negation] but a joyous intensification- a generous and reckless enlargement of the self, as one particular human life is placed wholly at the disposal of others. . . . The amplification of the self is at the same time its displacement: the self becomes freer and more expansive only when it ceases to see itself as the center of things. The ego is both enlarged and deposed.[18]

A word of caution needs to be sounded about the *displacement* of self, in light of many people's experience of violence. Jesus is not modeling a passivity that is complicit in the unjust violence towards him. Jesus's death is inherently unjust and violent. Jesus chooses, carefully and strategically, to respond nonviolently to the violent powers of religion and state. Jesus's death is an inevitable consequence of him speaking truth to power. Jesus chooses what will happen and when, on his own terms. He submits himself to the inevitable and ghastly logic of the Pax Romana (peace of Rome). He absorbs the ferocity of human violence on the cross, carrying it all into his death where it is ended (rather than perpetuated through vengeance). Jesus's nonviolence comes from a position of loving power. Jesus in John's Gospel says:

> I lay down my life in order to take it up again. No one takes it from me, but I lay it down of my own accord. I have power to lay it down, and I have power to take it up again. (John 10:18)

(iv) Prototypes of peace: catalyzing positive mimesis

I proposed in touchstone 2 that one of the main social manifestations of sin is mimetic rivalry, leading to violence. However, it is also true that the mimetic desire that underpins rivalry can be positive. Imitation of others is a simple fact of being human. St. Paul not only acknowledges this reality but invites a positive manifestation of imitation:

> Be imitators of me, as I am of Christ. (1 Cor 11:1)

A notable example of positive mimesis can be seen in Martin Luther King Jr.'s teaching about nonviolence during the American civil rights

---

18. Myers, *Christ the Stranger*, 77.

movement. Inspired by Christ, protestors learned how to strategically expose themselves to violence without retaliating. The courage and skills to do this did not happen automatically; they required prayer, discipline, and training. Another example is Nelson Mandela, whose twenty-seven years of imprisonment and ultimate commitment to forgiveness and non-violence transformed the hearts of millions and helped avoid a bloodbath of retaliatory violence in the immediate aftermath of apartheid.

In his reflection on the suffering servant passage in Isa 53 (referred to in touchstone 3), a passage that the Christian tradition has always seen as a prefiguring of Christ, Bartlett observes the mimetic effect of the suffering servant's non-retaliation in the face of hostility:

> Contempt is a mimetic transfer, discharging a steady collective violence on another; but then if that mimesis meets a free space filled with peace, trust, and non-retaliation then inevitably—by almost a law of mechanics—that transfer will begin to mutate into those very opposite emotions.[19]

This mimetic movement is not simply a heroic humanism. The transformational power of this kind of mimesis is a gift of the Spirit. It typically has a cruciform character. St. Paul's insight is that Christ, through his healing/delivering power, has unleashed God's divine life into the universe, through God's Spirit, in a way that *more* than overcomes the virus of mimetic rivalry:

> The free gift is not like the trespass. For if the many died through the one man's trespass, *much more surely* have the grace of God and the free gift in the grace of the one man, Jesus Christ, abounded for the many. And the free gift is not like the effect of the one man's sin. For the judgment following one trespass brought condemnation, but the free gift following many trespasses brings justification. If, because of the one man's trespass, death exercised dominion through that one, *much more surely* will those who receive the abundance of grace and the free gift of righteousness exercise dominion in life through the one man, Jesus Christ. Therefore just as one man's trespass led to condemnation for all, so one man's act of righteousness leads to justification and life for all. For just as by the one man's disobedience the many were made sinners, so by the one man's obedience the many will be made righteous. (Rom 5:15–19)[20]

---

19. Tony Bartlett, as cited in Hardin, *Jesus Driven Life*, 197.
20. The "one man" here does not require us to read Genesis as literal history. We

Paul's reflection can sound esoteric, and we might find it hard to get our heads around the metaphysics of it. So, I will try to ground what I understand Paul is meaning in terms of everyday relationships.

We have seen that Jesus saves us (humanity) from slavery to sin by revealing the substrata of all reality as kenotic love and through embodying that love in his life and death. Jesus is the image of the invisible God. Because we are *formed* by images, to gaze at Christ is to be *(re)made* in his image. St. Paul talks about this transformational power of the divine image:

> And all of us, with unveiled faces, seeing the glory of the Lord as though reflected in a mirror, *are being transformed* into the same image from one degree of glory to another; for this comes from the Lord, the Spirit. (2 Cor 3:18)

The primary ways that Christians gaze at Jesus is through the Scriptures, prayer, and the church community. This gazing transforms us not by heroic effort but by a receptivity to the Holy Spirit. The risk of us heroically trying to imitate Jesus is reduced when we remember that when we gaze at Jesus, we are not so much imitating the specifics of the life of Jesus of Nazareth. What we are imitating is the *pattern* of Jesus's kenotic life and his desire to listen only to the desire of his Abba. This is why the early Christians were called "people of the way" (Acts 9:2)—the way of the cross.

If we are getting heroic about imitating Jesus of Nazareth, then it is likely that our ego is getting inflated. This would invite careful discernment. Jesus saves us from the tyranny of the self-referential ego that is always trying to secure itself. God gives us an alternative reference point, the inner witness of the Holy Spirit and the outer witness of the saints. Jesus delivers us from the egotistical attachment typically associated with mimetic rivalry.

Through the grace and gift of the Holy Spirit, we can choose to let go/participate in the dying and rising of Christ. This occurs in practice whenever we take a stance of active nonviolence, as an agent of reconciliation, when attacked. In participating in the Trinitarian divine life, we are drawn into communion with our neighbor who is also held in the love of God, whether they know it or not. In this sense, the Holy Spirit is the maker of community. The Holy Spirit is bringing order/communion

---

can understand Adam to be the human who represents all humans in their state of entrapment in sin/rivalry.

(the new creation) out of chaos. In this communion, we can perceive and cooperate with the new age of the kingdom of God, which is God's resurrection action on earth/in creation. It is all gift. We cannot and don't need to save ourselves.

The Spirit (internal) and liturgy (external expression) create a realignment with God. Our inner compass is dragged back into alignment with the Logos—the enfleshed Word. In the Eucharist, we recall and participate in this holy communion, becoming signs and heralds of the kingdom of God, which is God's desire for the world—the reconciliation of all life for the common good.

When we in the church are living the resurrection life, what does it look like? What are we doing? How are people treating each other? Are we observing Spirit-inspired relational (therefore situational) ethics? Rather than being slaves to black-letter law and legalism, are we discerning the law of love written on our hearts, rooted in the imitation of Christ's kenotic love?[21] Are we standing in humility before others or in prideful attachment to our own truth? Are we concerned about the impact on the whole community and not just individuals/myself? Ben Myers, referring to the work of Rowan Williams, says, "The church is not one interest group alongside others but a community whose only interest is the interest of all . . . any purely individual freedom is pathological."[22]

The church, as a people imitating the kenotic pattern of Christ's life, is a radical new social construction—a universal humanity. This requires living in the pain and tragedy of human difference. In learning to embrace difference, we neither collapse our own God-given identity nor do we try to control others. The *other* always remains a mystery to us, and truth emerges out of the space between us, through dialogue. In part 3, we will explore the *how-to* of dialogue that transcends the mere interest-based negotiation into which we sometimes fall in church decision-making.

My contention is that this is challenging work and that churches have the wonderful potential to apply themselves to this work by becoming communities of practice. The early church communities, which contained both Jews and gentiles, were prototypes of peace, bringing together people who may previously have been in enmity. Saint Paul may have known, or even broken bread, with the family members of those he had once been persecuting. The church has the potential to be a school

---

21. Jer 31: 33; Heb 10:16.
22. Myers, *Christ the Stranger*, 61.

in which we learn to live without (or with less) rivalry, seeking always to imitate only the desire of Jesus as he imitates the desire of his Abba. The litmus test of our work is whether such imitation shows up as loving service, generosity to the poor, welcoming the stranger, and caring for the earth, while recognizing that the specifics will be unique to each person.

This work of peace in Christian communities can be gritty. St. Paul talks about the body of Christ as a communion of different gifts. But it is also a communion of differing politics, strong options for things about which people care deeply, and diverse cultural backgrounds and assumptions. Rabbi Jonathon Sacks reminds us that God has gifted us with the *dignity of difference*. I'm sure sometimes we wish it were not so. If only people thought like me! But this is not going to happen. Hence, even more so, the church has the potential to practice the difficult and challenging work of peace. If we are not discerning Jesus in the midst of our differences and embodying his mind, then what do we really have to offer the world? Not much, probably. Paul speaks of the connection between the humility of Christ and humility in our relationships:

- . . . *with all humility and gentleness, with patience, bearing with one another in love*, making every effort to maintain the unity of the *Spirit* in *the bond of peace*. There is one body and one Spirit, just as you were called to the one hope of your calling, *one Lord*, one faith, one baptism, *one God and Father* of all, who is above all and through all and in all. But each of us was given grace according to the measure of Christ's gift (Eph 2:4–7).

- Therefore be imitators of God, as beloved children, and *live in love*, as *Christ loved us* and gave himself up for us, a fragrant offering and sacrifice to God (Eph 5:1–2).

- Husbands, *love your wives, just as Christ loved the church* and gave himself up for her, in order to make her holy by cleansing her with the washing of water by the word, so as to present the church to himself in splendor, without a spot or wrinkle or anything of the kind—yes, so that she may be holy and without blemish. In the same way, *husbands should love their wives* as they do their own bodies. He who loves his wife loves himself. For no one ever hates his own body, but he nourishes and tenderly cares for it, just as Christ does for the church, because we are members of his body. "For this reason a man will leave his father and mother and be joined to his wife, and the two will become one flesh." This is a great mystery, and I am applying it to Christ and the church[23] (Eph 5:25–32).

(v) Justice means setting relations right

In touchstone 3, I mentioned the strong conceptual association between the words *justice, righteousness,* and *deliverance.* I said that the word often translated as righteousness means God's covenant faithfulness (relational fidelity) seen in God's action to save/deliver people from the power of sin, violence, and death (the matrix of disoriented desire). Through this act of deliverance, God gifts us with the possibility of relationships with God, and between persons, that are not bound up in rivalry and violence. We are gifted with peace and joy. Justice is best defined as *God's action to set relations right.*

Imagine for a moment that someone has does something bad (unjust) to us. It could be something simple, like a person aggressively cutting us off on the road. Or it could be something serious, like theft or assault. In such situations, it is natural for us to want to lash out and pay back, even if that payback is done on our behalf by the force of the state. This is another example of mimesis: if you hurt me, then I will hurt you. The notion of justice as setting relations right may be a long way from our mind. If we feel like this, then we may want to reach out for the punitive systems of the state. Such situations might include situations where there is:

- A need to restrain a violent person to stop an offence against someone else

- A felt need by a harmed person to have someone punished for what they did

- Frustration caused by repeated behaviors and/or where things are just not getting better

- An actual or perceived cover-up or denial by a person or organization that has no evident interest in relational repair. In a situation like this, a person may feel they have no alternative but to enlist coercive power to have their concerns heard and remedied.

---

23. Note the reversal of traditional culture, where it was typical for the woman to leave her home and join the man's household. The theological allusion is Christ humbly leaving his heavenly home to dwell with humans and unite himself to us. John's Gospel and the Revelation of John develop in detail this image of betrothal.

However, if we conceive of justice primarily in terms of punishment done *by* the state *to* someone, then we typically fail to address the deep needs that many people have for the effects of crime to be acknowledged and healed at a relational level. The gospel of peace offers us a different lens on the meaning and implementation of justice—what is now broadly called restorative justice.[24] Restorative justice seeks to address the relational needs to which harm or crime gives rise. In many situations, what survivors of crime want includes:

- For one's pain to be heard and vindicated (particularly by the offender but also by organizations and society) and, as part of this, to receive a genuine apology
- To see evidence of the genuineness of that apology through restitution
- To understand why something happened—particularly, why did this happen to *me*
- To feel safe—to ensure that the same thing does not happen to me or to anyone else again
- To see evidence that the system is changing—to help prevent recurrence

Regrettably, legal systems are not well designed to deal with these relational needs, because, structurally, formal investigation and legal systems take control out of the hands of the people most able to deliver on these needs and hence to *set relations right*. The people most able to set relations right are victims, offenders, and their supporting communities. Jesus is touching precisely on this point when he says:

> So when you are offering your gift at the altar, if you remember that your brother or sister has something against you, leave your gift there before the altar and go; first be reconciled to your brother or sister, and then come and offer your gift. Come to terms quickly with your accuser while you are on the way to court with him, or your accuser may hand you over to the judge,

---

24. Restorative justice (RJ) processes are common in traditional Aboriginal approaches to justice. In Western justice systems, the growth of RJ emerged from experiments in community/family justice initiated by Mennonite communities, drawing specifically on the biblical conception of justice as setting relations right. In Australia and New Zealand, the work began to be formally trialled in youth community justice conferencing from 1989.

and the judge to the guard, and you will be thrown into prison. (Matt 5:23–25)

George MacDonald, in his sermon on justice,[25] frames justice in terms of fairness. If a person has hurt us, then the *just* outcome we are really seeking is for the other person to treat us fairly. This may include apologizing and searching for what is needed to set things right. If there is any kind of punishment in the process, it must be in the passive and temporary sense of allowing a situation to play out in a way that creates conditions for genuine reconciliation to occur. For example, a person might need a coercive restraint to protect society for a period until the offender and/or harmed person are ready to engage in a restorative process.[26]

Restorative justice, the practice of which will be outlined further in part 3, requires holding people to account by asking them to admit and take responsibility for their actions. As George MacDonald observes in his essay on justice, it could never be just or fair to ask an innocent person to be punished for a guilty one. When St. Paul says "While we were sinners Christ died for us," he is not saying that God is taking a punishment on himself that rightly belongs to us. That would be unjust and unfair. We are all accountable for our own behavior. However, Jesus *is* willing to die as a victim of injustice rather than violently retaliating. This opens a pathway for healing and *true* justice—setting relations right through healing and forgiveness. To achieve true justice, understood as *setting relations right*, requires much more than punishing a guilty person. It requires processes that deliver on people's deeper needs as outlined above.

For those of us who live in a colonizing country, an important part of restorative justice will be acknowledging how Christian mission was piggybacked onto colonization.[27] In Christian missions, to become

---

25. MacDonald, *Unspoken Sermons*, 268–89.

26. The Australian Royal Commission into Institutional Responses to Child Sexual Abuse found it to be important that organizations should make financial restitution to victims prior to any restorative conversation. Then if the harmed person was willing, a voluntary restorative engagement might occur later—in which a senior member of the offending organization could listen to the harmed person share their story and offer a face-to-face apology. The latter is not always the sequence in restorative practices but has advantages in a situation of significant power imbalance, so that a more powerful party does not put a survivor in a position of having to tell their story and be judged on whether they "deserve" restitution.

27. At a recent conference I attended, several Aboriginal Christian leaders talked about how they integrate their Christian faith with their traditional cultural beliefs and

Christian was frequently accompanied by a requirement to dress like a European and to speak English.[28] In Australia, the *Uluru Statement from the Heart* can be thought of as a national call for restorative justice.[29]

Being one in Christ[30] does not mean the annihilation of cultural differences that all contain unique beauty and insight. Saint Paul did not expect Messianic Jews to stop being Jews. But Paul also had to deal fiercely with missionaries who wanted Jesus-followers to adopt Jewish practices.[31]

REALITY CHECKING

In this fourth touchstone, we have been exploring some of the characteristics of having the mind of Christ. Before we go any further, let us do a little reality checking. It is a self-evident reality that just because we think practicing peace is a good idea doesn't mean we consistently do it. Despite God being good, loving us, and calling us to abundant life, we know that we do not always see ourselves and others as God does. We know that we sometimes dump on ourselves and on other people. Despite knowing, in a cognitive sense, about God's goodness and love, we also know we can be cruel, violent, and deceitful. Despite our good desires, our actions do not align with our good intentions. With great self-insight, St. Paul summarizes the dilemma like this:

> For I do not do the good I want, but the evil I do not want is what I do. Now if I do what I do not want, it is no longer I that do it, but sin that dwells within me. So I find it to be a law that when I want to do what is good, evil lies close at hand. For I delight

---

practices. Their challenge to the Australian Church is how to take the gospel out of the pot of European culture and replant it in the pot of the ancient and evolving Australian context. The Māori Anglican priest Jay Ruka makes similar observations in the New Zealand context.

28. In Australia, we have only recently begun to come to terms with the devastating impact on Aboriginal people flowing from the policy of removing Aboriginal children from their families. Stories from individual Christian missions in Australia are mixed and frequently came down to the cultural sensitivity and basic humanity of individual missionaries. One Noongar man recounted to me how some Christian missions served to protect language and culture from the most destructive aspects of colonization. Other missions were guilty of systemic child sexual abuse over decades.

29. Uluru Dialogue, "Uluru Statement."

30. Gal 3:28.

31. Gal 1:6–7.

in the law of God in my inmost self, but I see in my members another law at war with the law of my mind, making me captive to the law of sin that dwells in my members. Wretched man that I am! Who will rescue me from this body of death? (Rom 7:19–24)[32]

In our better moments, we let the Holy Spirit get a hold on us, and the fruits of the Spirit show up (sometimes I have found myself being uncharacteristically generous). At other times, we get caught up in the mimetic vortexes of daily life. Considering our self-evident hypocrisy, we might find ourselves wondering, what does it really mean to say that we have received the mind of Christ?

The experienced reality seems to be that we live in two dimensions simultaneously. Through the gift of the Spirit, we have a foot in the new creation, through the mind of Christ, and yet we also experience the tugs and pulls of rivalry and competition. One way this reality has been illustrated in popular culture is the picture of an angel sitting on one shoulder and a devil sitting on the other, each whispering in an ear and competing for our attention. But all this does is make us feel like we are in living in a spiritual war zone. Douglas Campbell gives a more helpful metaphor. He invites us to imagine ourselves sitting in a room with two pieces of music playing at the same time. One sound system is playing a beautiful piece of music that inspires peace and joy. Another sound system is playing a piece of music that inspires fear, anxiety, and fantasies of violence. This presents an invitation not to fight against the negative but to consciously keep coming back to the positive.[33]

> Not that I have already obtained this or have already reached the goal; but I press on to make it my own, because Christ Jesus has made me his own. Beloved, I do not consider that I have made it my own; but this one thing I do: forgetting what lies behind and straining forward to what lies ahead I press on toward the goal for the prize of the heavenly call of God in Christ Jesus. Let those of us then who are mature be of the same mind; and if you think differently about anything, this too God will reveal to you. Only let us hold fast to what we have attained. (Phil 3:12–16)

---

32. There is scholarly debate whether St. Paul is drawing a contrast between pre- and post conversion states or whether this type of struggle is an ongoing part of the human experience even as a Christian. The overall thrust of Paul's arguments suggests the former, but my experience resonates with the latter.

33. Campbell, *Pauline Dogmatics*, 143–47.

Another reality check we could explore is the one of *credibility*. Would our theological proposition about Christ's defeat of evil pass the "pub test"?[34] We can find plenty of examples of how the world is screwed up, and evil seems to have the upper hand.[35] The metaphysics of God defeating sin is beyond us. Earlier, I suggested some contemporary metaphors that might help us to connect the cross with our own experiences of violence. Despite their continued experience of violence under various emperors, the first Christians had the sense of having been set free from appalling tyrannies of oppression. For St. Paul, this meant God liberating St. Paul (Saul) from his previous legalism and hate. St. Paul concluded, based on his own experience and the love of other witnesses to Christ whom he met, that something indeed had shifted in the spiritual powers in the universe.

While rivalry and death continue on earth, we will finally see the triumph of love when united to God in the life to come, which lies beyond our physical death (touchstone 1). In our life on earth, we just get a foretaste of the age to come, and, when we do, it is stunningly beautiful. Each day we may experience ourselves being shaped by a new piece of music—the music of the new creation. The significance of the encounter with Christ is not that "it happened to someone else historically, and so I believe it on the weight of evidence" (which did not work, even for the disciples) but that a breakthrough (unveiling) of a deeper reality is occurring to us in this present moment, and we are being invited to participate in it.

The crucifixion was an evil act, and yet God makes use of it to defeat the violent powers of the world in a way that is difficult to comprehend metaphysically. However, we can point to its reality psychologically (freedom from addiction), sociologically (freedom from mimetic rivalry), and practically (nonviolence works better for establishing peace than violence). I recently had a conversation with an American friend about the intense economic and racial fragmentation within her country and whether the political situation had made this worse. Her observation was that certain politicians had raised the already-existing shadow side of America to consciousness (by which she meant the shadows of racism and poverty). We may remember how René Girard talked about how Jesus has illuminated the scapegoating mechanisms in all its ugliness. Such things must be named so we can deal with them.

This is what St. Paul is getting at when he says that "all things work for good" (Rom 8:28). Even when circumstances are at their ugliest, the gospel

---

34. *Pub* is an Australian colloquialism for hotel/bar.
35. Job had the same observation (Job 21).

invites us to consider not "how is God *in* this" but "what can God's love bring *out* of this?" I have sometimes thought that God's grace operates like Siri, the digital voice in an Apple iPhone, which helps us find our way across a city. Regardless of the wrong turns we make, Siri recalculates the route and *invites* us back on track. How could we understand what scapegoating is unless we had experienced it and Christ had revealed it to us? Nothing is lost, even violence, in the divine economy. God makes use even of our sin.

Anthony De Mello tells a parable that reminds us not to be presumptive about assuming God is a causative agent in physical events:

> An old farmer had an old horse for tilling his fields. One day the horse escaped into the hills and when all the farmer's neighbors sympathized with the old man over his bad luck, the farmer replied, "Bad luck? good luck? who knows?" A week later the horse returned with a herd of wild horses from the hills and this time the neighbors congratulated the farmer on his good luck. His reply was, "Good luck? Bad luck? Who knows?" Then when the farmer's son was attempting to tame one of the wild horses, he fell off its back and broke his leg. Everyone thought this very bad luck. Not the farmer whose only reaction was "Bad luck? good luck? who knows?" Some weeks later the army marched into the village and conscripted every able-bodied youth they found there. When they saw the father's son with his broken leg they let him off. Was that good luck? Bad luck? Who knows.[36]

SUMMARY OF TOUCHSTONE 4

1. In grafting us to the vine of Jesus, the pattern of his life, the indwelling Spirit gives us a new mind (the mind of Christ) and the gifts and fruits of the Spirit.

2. We are becoming part of God's purpose to *make* humans. We grow into our humanity by freely choosing death (giving our lives in love), symbolized in baptism, in advance of our physical death.

3. Our new mind is characterized by courage, peace, and joy.

4. Our new mind is characterized by kenosis (self-emptying), which, in practical terms, means making internal and external space for others.

---

36. De Mello, *Sadhana*, 150–51.

5. Mimetic desire can be positive when it is Christlike—the desire for the will of the Abba. A church that desires in this way will be a living prototype of peace, the kingdom of God on earth. This is symbolically expressed in the Eucharist and enacted in our relationships.

6. Christlike justice is restorative justice.

7. As well as conceiving of justice as repairing harm and resetting relationships in family, community, organizations, and legal systems, Australians are being invited by Aboriginal people to a national restorative justice conversation about colonization (there may be parallels for readers in other countries).

8. We are all works in progress. We live in two simultaneous realities—the sin and violence of the old world (Adam/flesh) and the new creation (with the gift of the mind of Christ). It is like having two pieces of music playing simultaneously. The metaphysics is beyond us but not the experienced reality. We are hypocrites. We will fail in our aspirations for peace. And we are forgiven by God for doing so.

REFLECT

1. To what extent and in what circumstance does my faith show up in courage, peace, and joy?

2. Where do I experience kenosis (self-emptying) in myself or others? What does this feel like?

3. In what ways would I see my church (or other community) being a prototype of Christlike peace? How well do I and my community deal with conflict and harm?

4. Does justice in my experience of family, church, community, or workplace lean towards punishment or restoration of relationships? In what ways?

5. In what ways do the cries of Aboriginal communities (in Australia or parallels in other countries) for truth telling and restoration speak to me? How am I responding?

6. Where in my life do I notice/hear the music of the new creation?

6

Nonviolence and Scripture

GIVEN HOW GOD HAS DEALT, and is dealing, nonviolently with our violence, we must, for the sake of theological coherence and missional credibility, grapple with violence in Scripture and Christian vocabulary.

READING VIOLENT SCRIPTURE

The Scriptures are full of stories of violence, and this violence is frequently attributed directly or indirectly to God. The most disturbing of this material relates to the violent invasion of the promised land by the Israelites. A Wiradjuri man[1] with whom I once I spoke pointed out that many Australian Aboriginal people hear the biblical stories about people being dispossessed of their land in a way that is quite different from Christians of European descent. The latter will typically hear the story from the perspective of the invader and the former from the perspective of the invaded.[2]

---

1. Aboriginal people of the area now known as New South Wales in Australia.
2. Australian historian Henry Reynolds provides extensive evidence that the Australian continent was recognized as officially occupied under the relevant definitions of international law at the time of Captain Cook's arrival. However, key politicians and commercial interests systematically ignored and fought against these legal realities.

- If you will diligently observe this entire commandment that I am commanding you, loving the LORD your God, walking in all his ways, and holding fast to him, then the LORD will drive out all these nations before you, and you will dispossess nations larger and mightier than yourselves. Every place on which you set foot shall be yours; your territory shall extend from the wilderness to the Lebanon and from the River, the river Euphrates, to the Western Sea. No one will be able to stand against you; the LORD your God will put the fear and dread of you on all the land on which you set foot, as he promised you[3] (Deut 11:22–25).

- Every place that the sole of your foot will tread upon I have given to you, as I promised to Moses. From the wilderness and the Lebanon as far as the great river, the river Euphrates, all the land of the Hittites, to the Great Sea in the west shall be your territory. No one shall be able to stand against you all the days of your life (Josh 1:3–5).

- Samuel said to Saul, "The LORD sent me to anoint you king over his people Israel; now therefore listen to the words of the LORD. Thus says the LORD of hosts, 'I will punish the Amalekites for what they did in opposing the Israelites when they came up out of Egypt. Now go and attack Amalek, and utterly destroy all that they have; do not spare them, but kill both man and woman, child and infant, ox and sheep, camel and donkey." (1 Sam 15:1–3).

These stories are traumatizing and scandalous for many readers. How do we reconcile this kind of violence with a Christlike God who gives his life for his enemies rather than destroying them and teaches us to do the same? Furthermore, in what sense, if any, can be it said that God inspires such texts? Trusting one's own discomfort can be a useful starting point. God has given us hearts of flesh so that we *feel* the discomfort of violence rather than try to rationalize it away with a heart of stone. It is appropriate to feel deeply disturbed when we read these texts, to the extent of asking, "What the hell is going on here?"

Navigating this territory requires us to remain firmly grounded in our foundation of the Christlike God. We need to read Scripture in the light of Christ—we could say, with the *mind of Christ*. We are on solid hermeneutical grounds in taking the approach of reading all the

---

3. Amongst other texts of terror involving divinely sanctioned violent overthrow of land and people, see Deut 20:1–18; Num 31:1–18.

Scriptures (Hebrew and Christian Testaments) through the lens of Jesus. Jesus himself teaches us how he is the lens, or interpretive key, to Scripture. The most striking example is the story of the resurrected Jesus meeting two disciples on the road to Emmaus.[4] Even though the disciples had spent three years with Jesus and had heard him preach on the Scriptures, they still did not comprehend him (the Synoptic Gospels all paint the disciples as constantly failing to understand Jesus). Jesus needs to spend a day walking with them on the road to Emmaus, opening their eyes to read the Scriptures as pointing to himself.

Both St. Paul and John adopt this hermeneutical principle: the Scriptures need to be interpreted in the light of Christ. For example, Paul discovered that reading the Scriptures with the mindset of zeal (an allusion to the violent zeal of Phineas[5]) made Paul a hateful person. Paul found he needed to rethink the way he read his own Scriptures and tradition. Paul says later that Scripture had previously been veiled for him.[6] He had to reorient his hermeneutic lens from zeal to faith:[7]

> . . .as to zeal, a persecutor of the church; as to righteousness under the law, blameless. Yet whatever gains I had, these I have come to regard as loss[8] because of Christ. More than that, I regard everything as loss because of the surpassing value of knowing Christ Jesus my Lord. For his sake I have suffered the loss of all things, and I regard them as rubbish, in order that I may gain Christ. (Phil 3:6–8)

In John's Gospel, we note Jesus's observation about how reading the Scriptures in a way that is inconsistent with Jesus leads to death, and, in fact, to Jesus's own death:

- You search the scriptures because you think that in them you have eternal life; and it is they that testify on my behalf. Yet you refuse to come to me to have life (John 5:39–40).

---

4. Luke 24:13–35.
5. Num 25:6–13.
6. 2 Cor 3:14.
7. Green, *Sanctifying Interpretation*, 158. See also Rom 4:1–3.
8. The Greek is stronger. It is more like "regard as excrement" (Hart, *New Testament*, 394).

- The Jews answered him, "We have a law, and according to that law he ought to die because he has claimed to be the Son of God"[9] (John 19:7).

All of this is alerting us to something important. We cannot just read the Scriptures straight off the page, as a historian or anthropologist might do, and think that this will illuminate our hearts and minds about *who* God really is. Rather, God is only known through an experienced *encounter* with God. The latter comes through an *unveiling* of the kind that occurred to the two disciples on the road to Emmaus, as Jesus opened the Scriptures as pointing to him, accompanied by a physical enacting of this reality in the breaking of bread.[10] Hearing a secondhand story *about* someone is different to *knowing* them directly. To really know a person, we need a direct encounter.

How then should we approach violence in the Scriptures? It will all depend on the hermeneutical approach we take.[11] I outline, below, some common approaches:

(i) Historical-literalist

One hermeneutical approach is the *historical-literalist* approach. This is simply to take the text on face value. If we went back in a time machine, we would see precisely what the text said happened. If the text says that God says something, then God said it; if the text says that God ordered the slaughter of men, women, and children, then that is what God said. People who take this approach justify it using the argument that God wrote the Bible (guiding the hands of the human author), because there is no reason to think that God would not make God's self transparently clear.[12] Even though the reader may still be very discomforted by God's apparent violence, sometimes our internal discomfort may be rationalized by saying "God is in control—God is doing something in this

---

9. A caution against anti-Semitism: the emphasis here is not on Jews in a racial sense but in a particular way that certain opponents of Jesus read the Scriptures in a way that led them to reject Jesus violently and seek his death.

10. Luke 24:13–35.

11. For a neat and readable summary of the main hermeneutical approaches, see Green, *Sanctifying Interpretation*.

12. There is a self-reinforcing circularity to this position: "We know that God wrote the Bible because it says in the Bible that God wrote the Bible."

violence that I can't quite understand, and, even though it looks brutal, God must have God's own good reasons."

This approach to reading carries a range of inherent difficulties. At the simplest level, there are variations between the most ancient source manuscripts; the Bible we buy in a bookshop is based on the best estimate of scholars (which is why we frequently see footnotes in the Bible related to textual variants). Then there are the multitudes of internal differences within the Bible itself, most notably the fact that we have four Gospels rather than one.[13] A claim that the text of the Bible should be unambiguously clear and plain in every detail is no more than a rhetorical hermeneutical claim. If anything, Jesus loves teaching in parables specifically to make us think beyond the obvious.[14] The fact that faithful Christians diverge significantly in their interpretation of texts is evidence that texts are frequently neither plain nor obvious.[15]

In addition, it concerns me that the historical-literalist approach does not give sufficient heed to our own deep sense of discomfort about God's apparent brutality. The Holy Spirit, testifying to the Christlike God, surely helps us to trust our discomfort at the self-justifying violence that resulted in Jesus's crucifixion. By extension, we should be discomforted with violence everywhere in the Bible. I recall my relief, as a theological student, when I came across the writings of Walter Wink, in which Wink says that depicting God as one who needed to be placated by blood sacrifice, particularly that of his own Son, served to make atheism eminently sensible.[16]

(ii) Discard the Old Testament

A second approach involves ignoring the parts of the Scriptures that we do not like. This is happening when people say they reject the God of the Old Testament but like the God of the New Testament. A second-century theologian, Marcion, took this approach. It simply doesn't work, when we remember that:

---

13. See Jersak, *More Christlike Word*, for a list of examples.

14. Matt 13:3.

15. Some of the positions that I make in this book will not be accepted by all Christians. A key question then becomes how we have nonviolent conversations about our different perspectives.

16. Wink, *Engaging the Powers*, 149.

- The Christian Testament is saturated with allusions to the Hebrew Scriptures.

- Jesus in his teaching, and the authors of the Christian Testament, draw heavily on the Hebrew Scriptures; we can understand Jesus as Christ only in light of the Hebrew Scriptures.

- Violence is not unique to the Hebrew Scriptures; there is also plenty of violent and threatening language in the Christian Testament, culminating in the extreme violence of the cross.

(iii) Progressive revelation

A third approach is called *progressive revelation*. This proposes that God reveals God's self progressively in accordance with humanity's growing capacity to understand God and the conceptual frames of reference available to people at various times. This might include God portraying God's self as warlike at historic moments when it was inconceivable for gods to *not* be perceived as warlike. This approach to revelation assumes that God reveals God's self slowly, until humanity is developmentally ready to perceive the full revelation of God in Jesus. I reject this hermeneutic primarily on the grounds of my foundational assertion that God is, was, and always has been Christlike, and that it would be contrary to God's character to reveal God's self as anything other than Christlike. Another difficulty with the idea of progressive revelation is that it can tend towards Christian or modernist arrogance.[17] It seems to imply that Christians have more insight than Jews or that modern people are smarter or more enlightened than the ancients when it comes to matters of the Spirit.

(iv) Progressive discernment

A fourth approach is known as *progressive discernment*. This assumes that the Christlike God has consistently been revealing God's character, but humans are not always very attuned to this revelation. Sometimes

---

17. I am fully aware that even my foundational statement that "God is Christlike" could be seen as an example of claiming that Christianity is superseding or superior to Judaism. The risk of this makes it even more important to remember that Jesus was a Jewish man who was interpreting his own tradition, not rejecting it (Matt 13:52). Jesus, paradoxically, interprets his own tradition and the character of God in a Christlike way (Luke 24:13–35).

humanity hears clearly and sometimes badly, but, regardless of how well we are listening, the Spirit will bring good out of how we respond. This approach accepts, even embraces, the observable reality that people hear (discern) the voice of God differently over time, even when viewing the same events or reading the same texts.

An example of this evolving discernment can be observed in the early church. In light of the revelation of God in Christ, the church commonly applied four main lenses in interpreting the words of the biblical text:[18]

- *Literal*—this was not the same as what I referred to above as a historical-literalist reading (what we would see if we went back in a time machine). A literal reading meant discerning the actual words on the page. In ancient Greek texts, the individual letters were not separated from each other. All the letters ran together, so the first job of the reader was to discern the words from the mass of individual leaders and, therefore, whether this structuring of words was what the writers intended.[19]

- *Anagogic/Eschatological*—taking a story as pointing to people's destiny in God (eschaton, new creation, new heaven and new earth)

- *Allegorical*—where events in the Hebrew Scriptures are read symbolically as illustrating an aspect of Christ. For example, the violent invasions of the promised land may be read as an allegory of God destroying the enemy (evil desires) within. Saint Paul takes an allegorical approach when he talks about Christ as the *type* of the true human and Adam as the *type* of the old.[20]

- *Moral*—drawing out principles in the text for how people should live ethically

---

18. We see multiple examples of this in the early church teachers, commonly referred to as the church fathers and the desert father and mothers. This is sometimes called the Patristic Era (first to eighth centuries), which provides vital insights into how early Christians thought and prayed.

19. Modern historical-critical analysis of texts includes (amongst other things) research at the *literal* level into the best available manuscripts, their possible historical sources, and what certain words may have meant in the context of their day. But this literal analysis does not exhaust the spiritual meaning of the text for the contemporary reader.

20. Rom 5:14.

One obvious implication of this approach is that the Christian reader is invited to trust the Spirit of truth to teach us in new ways in every age.[21] We would need to acknowledge that the voice of God may have been discerned in a particular way in the original context in which it was written (the intent of the original author), then a different way in the first century, and then a different way again in the twenty-first century. This seems to be precisely what Jesus does as a Jewish rabbi, as do the biblical authors, as they take older scriptural traditions and adapt them to new contexts in ways that would have seemed quite alien to the original authors.

(v) Discernment in travail

A fifth approach to reading the text is one that I find compelling in relation to the insights of René Girard and my foundation, in touchstone 1, of the Christlike God. This is a variation of progressive discernment. It approaches the text as a living example of the perpetual human struggle between discerning the Christlike God (three steps forward) and being drawn into the mimetic vortexes of human violence (two steps back). René Girard refers to the Scriptures as a "text in travail," reflecting the travail of humans in coming to know God.[22]

Michael Hardin, a theologian who reads through christological, Girardian-influenced lenses, proposes that there are two hermeneutics discernable in the Bible:

- The sacrificial hermeneutic—which we can observe wherever a community is trying to establish peace by expelling a sacrificial victim (scapegoat) (we touched on this in touchstone 2).
- The non-sacrificial hermeneutic—which we see preeminently in Jesus as the "forgiving victim" who ends the cycle of vengeance and victim-making by declaring the forgiveness of sins for those who killed him.

This is not a steady trajectory of development, as if humans are getting smarter or more enlightened. Rather, it reflects a struggle within humans from the beginning of time until today. It reflects the process of the Christlike God pressing in on people of every age.

21. John 16:13.
22. Girard, as cited by Hamerton-Kelly, *Violent Origins*, 141.

The theological travails of people in the Genesis stories are not hugely different to our own when it comes to making victims or experiencing ourselves as victims. We find reversions to victim-making within the Christian Testament as well as the Hebrew Scriptures. When we read the text in this way, all aspects of the text, both violent and nonviolent, can serve to reveal the pattern of Christ's death and resurrection. For example, when Achan is killed,[23] when Phineas is running a copulating couple through with a spear,[24] when the children of the Amalekites are being slaughtered,[25] and when the Levite's concubine is being dismembered,[26] we can see an anticipation of Christ's (God's) suffering on the cross.

René Girard, and other Christian scholars who have been influenced by his work, sees the fingerprints of the Christlike God throughout the Hebrew Scriptures—illuminating, critiquing, and progressively overturning violence:

- God marking Cain to prevent vengeful attacks (Gen 4:15)
- Joseph's forgiveness of his brothers (Gen 50)
- The sensitivity in the Scriptures to the collective victims of society—women, children, orphans, nonresident aliens, and refugees (Lev 19:33–34)
- The forgiveness of debts in the Year of Jubilee, to prevent an inordinate accumulation of wealth into the hands of a few with its associated production of debt slavery (Deut 14:28–29)
- The rejection of human sacrifice and particularly the "detestable practice of child-sacrifice" (Deut 18:9–11)
- The eschatological vision of a banquet in which traditional enemies dine together (Isa 11:55)
- The story of Elijah hearing the voice of God in "sheer silence" rather than in the fire and whirlwinds of his passion, which had resulted in him trying to prove himself right and justify God by slaughtering the prophets of Baal (1 Kgs 19:12).

23. Josh 7.
24. Num 25:1–13.
25. 1 Sam 15.
26. Judg 19. Note that, as a kind of scapegoat, the storyteller strips the concubine of her identity. Yet the fact that the story is recorded at all serves as a revelation of the killing of an innocent victim and, in light of Christ, functions as a story that reveals and subverts human violence.

- The move in the Hebrew Scriptures against temple sacrifice (1 Sam 15:22; Ps 50:8–15, Isa 1:1–10, Jer 7:21–26, Hos 6:6)
- The voice of victims throughout the psalms crying for vindication against unjust mobs (only occasionally does the cry move from a cry of vindication to a cry for vengeance)
- The voice of Job proclaiming his innocence and his unjust suffering against the accusations of his so-called friends (Job 29)

These biblical witnesses recall us to our own struggles with violence and our progressive deliverance by the Christlike God. In this way, there is a sense in which we can understand violent texts as inspired, provided we recognize the function the text is performing. The text is God's word to the extent that it bears witness to the Word (Logos—Christ). The text is inspired in the sense that it gets under our radar and acts as a comfort when we are aligned with Christ and a discomfort when we are moving away from Christ.[27] We might find ourselves saying, "Oh my goodness—I have been violent just like that person, *and* I have used God to try to rationalize my behavior." This kind of revelation leads to lament and repentance.

This makes sense when we consider that a nonviolent God acts on humans only by persuasion and invitation rather than coercion. Revelation in Scripture is always going to reflect a subtle dance between God's address to us (through reading, teaching, preaching, prayer, Eucharist, community) and our openness of heart to the Spirit. The Scriptures, through the Spirit, are gently inviting us into a humble (kenotic) and trusting communion with God and with each other. Our arrogant certainties are constantly being deconstructed (except the ceaseless comfort of knowing that God loves us and that God can even do something useful with our failings). As John's Gospel puts it:

> When the Spirit of truth comes, he will guide you into all the truth; for he will not speak on his own, but will speak whatever he hears, and he will declare to you the things that are to come. (John 16:13)

For the Christian disciple, Scripture is not acting as a historical textbook, even though historical events lie, to a greater and lesser extent,

---

27. St. Ignatius of Loyola developed his teachings on the discernment of spirits around this insight. When we are moving *towards* God, we will experience consolation; and when we are moving *away* from God, we will experience desolation.

behind the text. Rather, the text points to the travail of every age between gospel and violence. All Scripture is useful (even God-breathed[28]) to the extent that is helps us to see the pattern of God's dying and rising and lead us, through Christ, to peace. Origen, in his commentary on John's Gospel, says that anything that helps us to perceive the pattern of Christ and God's call on our lives can be called gospel (good news):

> But if the writings of Paul were gospel, it is consistent with that to say that Peter's writings also were gospel and, in general, those [writings] which present the sojourn of Christ and prepare for his coming and produce it [his coming] in the souls of those who are willing to receive the Word of God who stands at the door and knocks and wishes to enter our soul.[29]

Even violent passages of Scripture are performing a revelatory function. The stories of violent scapegoating in the name of God may shock us into thinking, "That is me; I have done that." The text refuses to allow us to become self-righteous, even self-righteously nonviolent! Jesus challenges the blind spots of our inner scribe and Pharisee:

> Woe to you, scribes and Pharisees, hypocrites! For you build the tombs of the prophets and decorate the graves of the righteous, and you say, "If we had lived in the days of our ancestors, we would not have taken part with them in shedding the blood of the prophets." (Matt 25:29–30)

Whenever we read dark and violent texts of terror in the Scriptures, they may well make us say, "Lord, have mercy; we need you." As much as historical events lie behind the biblical stories, the spiritual power of Scripture is not in history per se but in the way in which God can *get to us* through the stories. By reading the Scriptures as only providing interesting historical data about God (to be believed or not believed), we keep God at a safe distance and subject to our criteria of historicity. However, through the Bible (and in other ways), God is addressing us with an *apocalypse now*—drawing us under the cross and, only from the humility (kenosis) of that place, to perceive the Christlike God. This address is a word of peace. The mind of Christ enables us to hear Christ speaking through the Scriptures and therefore also enables us to discern how we can so easily weaponize the Scriptures against ourselves or others. Saint Paul calls this kind of religious zeal the "ministry of death" (2 Cor 3:7).

---

28. 2 Tim 3:16.
29. Origen, *Commentary on John's Gospel*, ch. 1, para. 26.

The story of Jesus invites us to rigorous self-reflection. Will our lives be ones of being or making victims, or of active self-giving in which the vicissitudes of life both soften our hearts but also give us the courage to nonviolently address our own violence and that of others? When we go into a conflict situation, will we perceive other people as problems to be fixed, or could we perceive the situation as pregnant with the possibility and activity of God's divine life? Our hope is for the latter.

Our next task is to revisit some of the gnarly manifestations of violence that lurk within our Christian vocabulary. The unexamined use of these common Christian concepts, some of which are an integral part of our worship, can have extremely negative pastoral impacts and may contribute to creating violent (un-Christlike) conceptions of God, with a consequential risk of increasing violence between people. In particular, let's now have a closer look at the concepts of *judgment, wrath, and hell*.

SUMMARY

1. The Scriptures are the word of God to the extent that they bear witness to the Word (Christ) behind and in the Scriptures. In this process of spiritual reading, Christ is transforming our hearts into hearts of flesh. Sometimes this will provoke an outrage in us, as God's name is evoked to justify violence, and this very outrage may be a sign of how Scripture is inspired.

2. The Scriptures reflect the travail of people in every age, a travail that we share with them, between discerning the Christlike God speaking in and through the Scriptures (three steps forward) and becoming enmeshed ourselves in mimetic rivalry and self-justifying violence (two steps back).

REFLECT

1. What aspects of violence in the Bible or Christian vocabulary discomfort me? In what ways can I reconcile such violence with the person of Jesus?

2. What would I say to someone who says, "I like Jesus, but I don't believe in the God of the Old Testament"?

7

Nonviolence, Judgment, and Wrath

A CONSISTENT POSITION IN THIS BOOK is that God is nonviolent in the way that Christ is nonviolent. Therefore, we must try to make sense of violent language in the Christian Testament under the intersecting themes of judgment, wrath, and hell. I'm grouping these as related themes, because one or more of them frequently shows up in very unhelpful ways in terms of:

- Undermining our primary foundation of knowing God as Christlike
- Undermining confidence in our relationship with God
- Undermining our confidence to talk about the goodness of God with others (healthy evangelism) or being weaponized to threaten and intimidate others

An example may help here. I have a friend who works as a hospital chaplain. She has told me that it is common to hear people who are experiencing difficult times, such as major illness, say something like, "What have I done to deserve this?" or "Why is God doing this to me?" Such statements suggest that people see life and faith as a kind of transaction. If I am good, then God will reward me; and if I am suffering, then God must be judging/punishing me. This kind of narrative, which is regrettably very prevalent in the church, is a testimony to the failure to anchor our theology, teaching, and preaching in the Christlike God.

As mentioned earlier, I live in the Anglican Church tradition. Every Sunday in our eucharistic liturgy, we say a prayer of confession that begins with the words,

> *Merciful God*, our maker, and our *judge*,
> we have sinned against you in thought, word, and deed,
> and in what we have failed to do:
> we have not loved you with our whole heart;
> we have not loved our neighbors as ourselves;
> we repent, and are sorry for all our sins.
> *Father, forgive us.*
> Strengthen us to love and obey you in newness of life;
> through Jesus Christ our Lord. Amen.

This prayer is immediately followed by the declaration of absolution from the priest, which assures us that we are forgiven by God. For those who have a solid trust in the Christlike goodness of God, forgiveness and absolution are a comfort. We are reassured in the liturgy that to be human is to be fallible and hence to make mistakes. We can face up to the fact that we hurt ourselves and others and be assured that God remains steadfastly faithful and present to us as one who forgives. What concerns me, however, is how liturgy shapes our thinking about God and our images of God in subtle ways that the author of prayer books did not intend. How might this happen?

In many places in the Scriptures, God's righteous judgment and/or wrath is directed at Israel itself and thereby constitutes an honest self-critique by Israel for idolatry, arrogant nationalistic self-assertion, and "detestable practices" like child sacrifice and exploitation of the poor.[1] The nation becomes the recipient of God's judgment, apparently in the form of being overthrown violently, the most significant examples being the Assyrian and Babylonian conquests. At other times, God's judgment and wrath are directed at Israel's enemies. In two of the most famous hymns of praise in the Bible, God is said to "bring the mighty down from their throne" (Hannah's prayer,[2] which is a model for Mary's great hymn of praise—the Magnificat[3]).

We might, on the face of it, think that all this is a good thing. It might assure us that God has a strong sense of justice. As the psalmist says,

---

1. 2 Kgs 17:9–18; Isa 57.
2. 1 Sam 2:1–10.
3. Luke 1:50–55.

"Righteousness and justice are the foundation of your throne; love and faithfulness go before you" (Ps 89:14). The positive side of the language of divine judgment and wrath is that it conveys God's passion for fairness and God's firm and categorical no to anything that dehumanizes people. At its best, judgment involves clear and compassionate truth-speaking and a desire to actively work against dehumanizing forces.

I was talking to a group of students once who were particularly angry about an injustice in the world.[4] Someone had told these students that they should not be so angry. What this meant was, "Your anger scares me." We were able to have a conversation about how anger is a feeling activated deep in the body that tells us that something is not right. Anger is intricately linked to our sense of justice as fairness. Our sense of justice is intricately linked to narratives we have absorbed about "the way things should be around here." We all carry around our own sense of what is *right*, but, regrettably, it does not take much for our internalized self-righteous Pharisee to get wound up and start yelling for the guilty to be punished.

Despite making a strong link between judgment and punishment, the biblical authors were also confident that God's wrath would not last forever. God would eventually turn away God's "justified" fury and wrath, forgive the people's sins (after, of course, a suitable period of punishment, like seventy years in exile), followed by restoring God's people to the land. This sequence of sin, judgment (often violent), forgiveness, and restoration permeates the Scriptures. And yet there is an unsettling threatening dynamic in this cycle in the way it equates divine judgment with divine violence.

- *If you do not* diligently observe all the words of this law that are written in this book, fearing this glorious and awesome name, the LORD your God, *then* the LORD will overwhelm both you and your offspring with severe and lasting afflictions and grievous and lasting maladies (Deut 28:58–59; see vv. 58–68 for a full and colorful elaboration).

- Surely his salvation is at hand *for those who fear him*, that his glory may dwell in our land (Ps 85:9).

---

4. This was a time when students were particularly involved in the Black Lives Matter and Me Too movements.

- His mercy *is for those who fear him* from generation to generation (Luke 1:50).

If the people are not faithful, then God's violent judgment (wrath) can turn on them in an instant. A contemporary parallel of the application of this cause-effect logic was when some conservative Christians announced that the destruction of the World Trade Center in New York was God's judgment and punishment on their perception of the decadent morals of America.

The pattern of wrath, violent punishment, forgiveness, and temporary peace equates exactly to patterns we find in domestic violence. Because our human experiences of being judged have sometimes been associated with anger/wrath, sometimes violently, it is very easy to project this onto God. It is easy to make God into the image of violent persons in our lives. Being on the receiving end of violent anger/wrath is one of the most terrifying things humans can experience, particularly if the other person is bigger, stronger, richer, or more well-armed than ourselves. For this reason, we need to treat passages that refer to God's wrath with particular care.

One example of where we need to listen carefully is St. Paul's Letter to the Romans. In his letter, Paul is tackling a legalistic adversary who is using the threat of the wrath of God as a weapon against gentile members of the church in Rome to get them to adopt Jewish cultural practices.[5] Paul, as we have seen, is hypersensitive to the weaponization of law. Paul will not accept turning God into a wrathful law-wielder. Paul knows that the grace of God saved him from being precisely such a wrathful person. Because God has "abolished the law with its commandments and ordinances [in order to] create in himself one new humanity in place of the two, thus making peace" (Eph 2:15), we do not need to be afraid of God. Paul sees the law as having a positive function, but he recognizes that it was *zeal* for the law that had activated destructive anger within him, on behalf of God. Paul is not going to go down that track anymore. He says, "For the law brings wrath; but where there is no law, neither is there

---

5. I am following Campbell's contention that St. Paul in Rom 1–12 makes use of the ancient literary tool of diatribe. In Rom 1:18–32, we are hearing the voice of Paul's adversary who is drawing on and deploying Wis 13:1–9, 14:8–14, 14:22–28 as a piece of anti-gentile rhetoric.

violation" (Rom 4:15). For Paul, the law is not a bad thing in itself but is potentially hugely destructive in activating violent judgmental zeal.[6]

Judgment is problematic whenever it is located outside the context of a loving covenantal relationship. Those who have worked in large organizations may have experienced some of the potentially dark side of judgment in the dreaded[7] annual performance review. Depending on the level of trust in the employer/employee relationships, such processes can become a form of structural violence in which persons we do not trust can judge us in quite mechanistic, non-relational ways.[8]

How can we redeem the important concept of judgment in the light of the Christlike God and hear language about wrath in a constructive way? Judgment is important. We make judgments all the time. We judge whether one course of action is better than another. Therefore, judgment does not have to be linked automatically to wrath or violence. Understanding the judgment of the Christlike God requires us to reconceptualize judgment in nonviolent terms within the context of the loving relationships of the Trinity and a God who is irrevocably committed to humanity. These relationships are, as we explored earlier, the pattern and template for all loving human relationships between persons.

Three metaphors for God, all informed by God as Christlike, may help to get a sense of how God's nonviolent judgment is a manifestation of covenantal love—the metaphors of physician, parent, and teacher.

(i) Physician

The early church frequently used the image of God as a physician. This is not surprising, because in the Synoptic Gospels we find a cyclical pattern of Jesus preaching the gospel of the kingdom of God and Jesus healing people. The two things are closely associated with each other. Salvation

---

6. Someone said to me once, "If you have a car called Sin and you want to make it go really fast, pump it full of law." I can't recall who said this, but it seems like a useful metaphor. See 1 Cor 15:56.

7. I used "dreaded" advisedly. Having spent seven years working in human resources management, I have never met someone who looked forward to performance reviews.

8. Trust is a product of three things. Trusting another involves believing that another person is fair (intends my well-being); is capable (of delivering on what they say); and is dependable (will fulfill their commitments). In all three of these factors, we can trust God, and, hopefully, we will have at least some experiences of this trustworthiness being mediated through covenantal human relationships.

comes from the word "to heal" (salve). When we go to a doctor, he/she may make a *judgment* about an unhealthy aspect of our lifestyle. A classic and powerful example of this is the risen Christ's words to Saul of Tarsus on the Damascus road, which results in Saul's conversion:

> When we had all fallen to the ground, I heard a voice saying to me in the Hebrew language, "Saul, Saul, why are you persecuting me? It *hurts you* to kick against the goads." (Acts 26:14)

Perhaps it was this firsthand experience that led St. Paul to later reflect, "For the wages of sin is death, but the free gift of God is eternal life in Christ Jesus our Lord."[9] This kind of judgment is offered in our best interests. We can either hear this judgment and act on it or we can reject it. When John's Gospel speaks of judgment, such judgment is invariably framed in terms of God helping people to see themselves more clearly and honestly:

> This is the judgment, that the light has come into the world, and people loved darkness rather than light because their deeds were evil. (John 3:19)

Here, God's judgment is oriented to life rather than to condemnation:

> God did not send the Son into the world to condemn [judge] the world, but in order that the world might be saved [healed/delivered] through him. (John 3:17)

We could think of a physician's laser beam that burns out a cancer in the body as an analogy for God's refining fire,[10] an image used regularly in the scriptures to illustrate purification. In the Christian Testament, we see a reworking of prior scriptural images of the fire of punitive judgment. Consider the following passage in which Jesus firmly distances himself from the example of Elijah who had called down fire on the prophets of Baal:

> When the days drew near for him to be taken up, he set his face to go to Jerusalem. And he sent messengers ahead of him. On their way they entered a village of the Samaritans to make ready for him; but they did not receive him, because his face was set toward Jerusalem. When his disciples James and John saw it, they said, "Lord, do you want us to command fire to come down

---

9. Rom 6:23. That is, sin brings its own consequences (wages) rather than God dispensing violent punishment.

10. Mal 3:1–4.

from heaven and consume them?" [Other ancient authorities add *as Elijah did.*] But he turned and rebuked them. [Other ancient authorities read *rebuked them, and said, "You do not know what spirit you are of, for the Son of Man has not come to destroy the lives of human beings but to save them."* (Luke 9: 51–55)

The following passage from Luke's Gospel portrays fire as linked with the work of the Holy Spirit. In the story of John baptizing people by the Jordan River, John says:

> I baptize you with water. But one who is more powerful than I will come, the straps of whose sandals I am not worthy to untie. He will baptize you with the Holy Spirit *and fire*. (Luke 3:16)

Here, the fire of the Holy Spirit illuminates and reveals both the truth about Christ's love and the truth of our human condition, and therefore "judges" sin. But this judgment does not involve God destroying people. As St. Paul puts it, "All [without exception] have sinned and fall short of the glory of God . . . [and are] justified by his grace" (Rom 3:23–24). Rather than projecting wrathful fire onto unfaithful or evil people (typically those whom we classify as unfaithful or evil), Christ absorbs human wrath on himself. As we saw in touchstone 3, Christ's nonviolent self-offering is how God defeats sin and death.

In the Christian Testament, the fire of judgment *is* a fire of truth, forgiveness, and mercy. In the book of Revelation, which often disturbs the reader with its images of fiery judgment, Babylon is not some evil other (person, group, or nation). Babylon represents us all in our human systems of manipulative and coercive power (mimetic rivalry, violence, and death).[11] Fire represents the transformational process of purification God through which takes us in reconciling us to himself. But this is not something God does *to us* in a punitive way from a detached distance, but *with us* through the cross. Another way of making this important hermeneutical point is to say that all language of judgment in the Bible (and the book of Revelation in particular) must be subject to the literal control of the "lamb slain before the foundation of the world."[12]

---

11. It is true that Revelation is speaking into the situation of a persecuted first-century church, with strong imagery of Rome and the Roman emperor. But as Scripture, it speaks to the universals of the human condition and God's final victory over evil by the "reverse power" of the Lamb. See Llewellyn, *Lamb Power*.

12. Rev 5:13–14; 13:8.

(ii) Loving Parent

One of Jesus's favorite terms for God is Abba/Father. The prayer that Jesus taught his disciples begins "Our Father." The prophet Hosea conveys this lovely image of parenthood, in which God says

> When Israel was a child, I loved him, and out of Egypt I called my son. But the more they were called, the more they went away from me. They sacrificed to the Baals and they burned incense to images. It was I who taught Ephraim to walk, taking them by the arms; but they did not realize it was I who healed them. I led them with cords of human kindness, with ties of love. To them I was like one who lifts a little child to the cheek, and I bent down to feed them. (Hos 11:1–4)

Anyone who has been a parent knows that part of parenthood includes making judgments about a child's behavior in the interests of raising the child into a loving human being. We do not always do this well, because we don't have the wisdom, or the patience, of God. But, through grace, we find it is possible to judge in a way that is characterized by the fruits of the Spirit (peace, patience, kindness, generosity, self-control).

In a similar vein, parents sometimes need to allow the consequences of a child's decisions to play out. This can also be a type of judgment. This becomes more important as children move into young adulthood. Provided it is not directly life-threatening, parents will often need to allow teenagers to make their own decisions and live with the consequences rather than stepping in to protect them. Jesus's parable of the father and two sons is an example of this.[13] One way of thinking about wrath spiritually is in terms of natural consequences for actions. As a young man in the merchant navy, there were times when I drank too much and ended up with an awful hangover. Suffering this physical effect and being expected by the boss to show up to work on time the next day could be considered a type of *wrath* (consequence) that I brought on myself, even though no one was yelling angrily at me (except my sore head). As Ps 7:16 puts it, "Their mischief returns upon their own heads, and on their own heads their violence descends"; or as Jesus said, "Put your sword back into its place; for all who take the sword will perish by the sword" (Matt 26:52).

---

13. Luke 15:11–32.

(iii) Honest and Discerning Teacher

God's loving judgment can also be mediated to us through teaching. Jesus is frequently referred to as teacher (rabbi), and St. Paul lists teaching as one of the gifts of the Spirit[14] and vital ministries in the church. I know that useful teaching has occurred when another member of the church has lovingly helped me to see myself more clearly. This could come from preaching, a Bible study, or a pastoral conversation. On the other hand, a shadow side of teaching has been the misuse of power and coercive control by teachers in positions of structural authority.

I have been trying to show how essential it is to frame judgment and wrath within our foundational image of God as Christlike. When we start with Jesus—when we know that our relationship with God is secure within a loving covenantal relationship (touchstones 1 and 3)—then we can read texts of judgment and wrath as rhetorical teaching tools to make us pay attention to our own sin and violence (touchstone 2).

Unfortunately, in relation to wrath, some major translations of the Bible work against a nuanced understanding. For example, in most translations of Rom 5:9, where the Greek text is "*saved from the wrath*," the translators of the English version add the words "*of God*," because they *assume* this is what St. Paul meant. It is a big assumption. Brad Jersak draws attention to the Wisdom of Solomon 18:22–23 where "the wrath" is another name for "the destroyer," which, by the time Wisdom was written, Jews no longer associated with God but with Satan.

Jesus saves us not from an angry Father but from *the wrath, the destroyer, the Satan*.[15] Now it is certainly true that, in some texts, St. Paul speaks of the wrath of God. Douglas Campbell suggests that such texts need to be read with the overall trajectory of Paul's thought in mind, which is a rock-solid conviction about God's unconditional grace. Whatever Paul means by the wrath of God, it is a distinctive reconceptualization of how we experience human wrath. It is perfectly reasonable to hear Paul's occasional usage of the wrath of God as meaning God's strong no to relationship-destroying behaviors, rather than equating wrath with a divine violence that breaches God's declared unconditional loving commitment to humanity.[16]

---

14. Eph 4:11; Rom 12:7.
15. Richard Murray, as cited by Jersak, *More Christlike Word*, 109.
16. Speaking to a church under persecution, St. Paul draws on classical apocalyptic

NONVIOLENT JUDGMENT

God's nonviolent judgment is something that is *mediated* to us through loving, committed (covenant) relationships. The most powerful experience in my own life of this kind of loving judgment was when I was a child. I was about six years of age and my brother about four. My father owned a slug gun (a gun that fires small pellets). The gun was sitting in the corner of a room. One day, I picked the gun up and pointed it at my brother as a kind of childish play. Clearly, this disturbed my brother, who reported the incident to my father. Sometime later, my father came to me, carrying the gun, bent down to my eye level, and, with great seriousness (and, I perceived, a good deal of restrained anger), said, "Did you point this gun at your brother?" I admitted that I had, at which point my father stood up and left the room and hid the gun. He never said another word to me about this event. Looking back, I felt like my father had judged me with a fervent and loving concern. I don't even recall him yelling at me, and yet I had been *judged* by the truth. I believe that my father had also judged himself for having left the gun in an accessible location. This is the closest personal analogy I can find to how the judgment of God works—a penetrating and corrective truth within the context of a committed covenantal relationship.[17]

I count myself incredibly fortunate that I had such a wise and loving father, who in turn, I am sure, has made it possible for me to imagine and trust the loving God whom Jesus names as his Abba. I now know that if a suffering person is asking the question "Why is God punishing (judging) me?," a useful pastoral response is to carefully explore the origin of such thoughts about God. People typically have little insight into how their internal images of God have been formed. A gentle conversation may help the person to see that they have unconsciously projected onto God the experience of internalized voices of self-judgment, which they absorbed through abusive human relationships. These internalized dialogues frequently manifest as feelings of deep unworthiness (toxic shame).

---

language of God destroying God's enemies (2 Thess 1:5–9). Such rhetorical devices were common in antiquity and would have been recognized as such by listeners rather than used to construct a violently punitive image of God. It may also be that Paul occasionally reverts to some of his old pre-conversion religious zeal. No one is entirely consistent, including Paul.

17. The story of my father would be an example of what Campbell describes as "evaluative judgment" in contrast to "punitive judgment" (Campbell, *Pauline Dogmatics*, 420–21).

Questions like "Why is God punishing me?" or "Why is this happening to me?" (to which any answers we produce are likely to be speculative or plain wrong) may be better reframed as "What can I learn from this? How could God be bringing some good out of this (bad) situation?" It may be that after reflecting for a time on a particularly nasty experience, we say, "Wow—I learned a huge amount from that." We may have learned so much that we indeed say, "God was in that experience." But the statement that "God was in that" should not be expanded to mean "God made that happen." The fact that so much good can come out of catastrophe (COVID is a big example) is a testimony to God's goodness and grace rather than an argument that God introduced the catastrophe for a punitive or corrective reason. Jesus makes this point explicitly when people try to give negative events a theological justification.[18] The crucifixion was simultaneously a moral catastrophe in terms of its violence and a manifestation of ultimate love in terms of what God did with it.

Understanding judgment and wrath in the terms elaborated above helps us to avoid:

- Equating justice, judgment, and anger with violence—especially a violent parent
- Driving a wedge between God's mercy and God's judgment
- Becoming moralistically judgmental towards others

One of the most beautiful literary examples of the integration of God's *mercy* and *nonviolent* judgment is explored by Isak Dinesen (Karen Blixen) in the novel *Babette's Feast* (also made into a movie). The story is set in a tiny Danish village amongst a small and aging congregation of Pietistic Lutherans, each of whom carries long-standing loss and grief. After many years of service in this austere environment, the main character, Babette, offers to cook a magnificent dinner for her host family and members of the small church. Babette had shown up at their door fourteen years earlier, fleeing the revolution in Paris, and had become the housekeeper in return for accommodation and very simple food. The special dinner turns out to be extremely lavish, and only later does the reader discover that Babette had in fact won the French lottery and had decided to expend the entire winnings on the meal, in thanks for the villagers' hospitality (the overtones of Eucharist are unmistakable).

---

18. John 9:2.

At the dinner, one of the guests, a military general, makes a speech that includes the text below, which draws on Ps 85:10. In this verse, truth (which illuminates sin) and mercy (God's compassionate setting relations right) are integrated like flip sides of the same coin. The members of the church see themselves in new ways and experience reconciliation through Babette's extravagant gift. Their previous hard-heartedness is *judged* (illuminated) and healed, not through condemnation but through Babette's kindness and overflowing generosity. We may recall the parable of the father and two sons, where the father's first response to his returning son is to provide a feast and where his words to his older, resentfully obedient son are "All that I have is yours."[19] In *Babette's Feast*, the general testifies to his sense of God's mercy:

> 'Mercy and truth are met together.
> Righteousness and peace have kissed each other.'
> Man (sic), in his weakness and short sightedness, believes he must make choices in this life. He trembles at the risks he must take. We know that fear.
> But no. Our choice is of no importance. There comes a time when our eyes are opened. And we come to realize at last that mercy is infinite. We need only await it with confidence and receive it with gratitude. Mercy imposes no conditions.
> And see! Everything we have chosen has been granted to us, and everything we renounced has also been granted. Yes, we even get back what we threw away.
> For 'mercy and truth are met together; and righteousness and peace have kissed each other.'[20]

SUMMARY

1. The nonviolent deliverance of God through Christ teaches us how to frame judgment and wrath in terms of clear correction of all in us that stands against love.

2. Judgment is merciful when set within the context of a loving covenantal relationship, such as we have in the Christlike God.

---

19. Matt 21:28–32.
20 Axel, *Babette's Feast*, 1:26:53—1:28:36.

REFLECT

Have I experienced a time when I was judged within the context of a loving relationship? What was that like? To what extent did it help me grow?

8

Nonviolence and Hell

HELL IS ANOTHER CONCEPT THAT has frequently been used in Christian tradition to try to terrorize people into right action or right belief. For some strange reason, we thought that people needed to be manipulated into making decisions rather than relying on the goodness of God to attract people and the inherent goodness of a moral action to be its own motivation. In a way, this is not surprising. Psychological studies have shown that people are, in fact, motivated to act by fear-based messaging.[1]

Some of the most effective public evangelistic campaigns (successful in terms of getting "converts") have involved laying out a clear choice, roughly summarized in the phrase "turn or burn (in hell)." It never worked for me, because it always struck me that it portrayed God as either uncaring (abandoning multitudes of people to the fate of their own disoriented desire) or pathologically violent (actively committing people to either extinction or eternal suffering). If God were either, then I simply wasn't interested. As a university chaplain, I have had more than one student (and one would be too many) in my office in tears because they were attracted by Jesus but were told by a fellow Christian student that their unbelieving family members were all destined for eternal torment because they did not believe in Jesus. Abusive theology shows up quickly as abusive psychology. Let us briefly trace where these conceptions of hell

---

1. A spectacular example of this was during the AIDS crisis of the 1980s. A public advertising campaign in Australia involving the image of a grim reaper was demonstrably effective in raising awareness of the seriousness of AIDS and what people should do to protect themselves.

come from and whether the concept of hell can be redeemed in light of the Christlike God.

The concept of hell as a place of death and/or suffering comes late in the development of the Bible. For much of their history, the Jews did not have any shared belief around an afterlife or a concept of hell such as is portrayed in popular mythology of a fiery place of torment. The closest we come to an underworld is the Hebrew term *Sheol*, which means the "place of the dead." Sometimes, the Bible refers to this place as a pit. When people died, they were buried, and that was the end of it.

- But you are brought down to Sheol, to the depths of the *pit* (Isa 14:15).
- Remember that my life is a breath;
  my eye will never again see good.
  The eye that beholds me will see me no more;
  while your eyes are upon me, I shall be gone.
  As the cloud fades and vanishes,
  so those who *go down to Sheol* do not come up;
  they return no more to their houses,
  nor do their places know them any more (Job 7:7–10).

In the intertestamental period, when the Hebrew Scriptures were translated into Greek, the term Sheol was translated as Hades. It was also during this period that distinct groups, even within Judaism itself, started to speculate more about the resurrection of the dead. One line of thought was that everyone who died went down into Sheol in a passive state of death (like falling asleep) before everyone was raised for judgment on a future day of the Lord. This judgment would sort people into categories of either evil (who go to either final annihilation or eternal, conscious torment in fire) or good (who go to paradise). A variation involved two different holding places (the unrighteous going to sleep in Sheol and the righteous going to paradise) prior to the general resurrection and judgment. The latter would inevitably involve, for the bad, either annihilation or eternal suffering.[2]

The historical context for the development of this thinking was, for the Jews, five hundred years of foreign oppression under the Babylonian, Persian, Greek, and Roman empires. Even though the people had

---

2. For a more extensive description of the various conceptions of hell, see Jersak, *Her Gates*.

returned from exile in Babylon and had reconstructed the Jerusalem temple,[3] there was always the looming background threat or reality of foreign occupation. Many had started to speculate that justice on earth could occur only when God dramatically intervened in this world to declare the *old age* to be ended and the *new age* of the kingdom inaugurated under God's Messiah. This expected kingdom forms the theological and psychological backdrop to the life of Jesus. In Jesus, God would make things right by bringing political justice on earth.[4]

As we can see, the language of a *final judgment* involving the destruction of the wicked is an extension to extremes of the theme of judgment and wrath, which we explored earlier. It has an intense sense of ethics in the sense of pointing out that the way we live is important. It also speaks to an instinct in most people that "bad" people should not get away with cruel behavior that violates others. The word that is commonly translated as "hell" in the Gospels is *Gehenna*. This draws on imagery of an actual place in Israelite history—the Valley of Gehenna, which was previously a place of child sacrifice.[5] At the time of Jesus, it was a stinking garbage dump with smoldering fires that never went out. The story is saying, "Think of the worst possible place imaginable, like the Valley of Gehenna: that is what God will do to the wicked." The huge challenge that the latter has presented to Christians is how to reconcile this imagery with a God who looks like Jesus and who teaches us to "love your enemies."[6] How can God teach us to love our enemies unless God is first and always doing the same? How could a good God treat God's own children, even badly behaved children, in such a savage way? Could we imagine sending our own children to a place of torment called hell?

In my experience, people cling to a doctrine of hell as an actual place/reality based on a perceived moral necessity. That is, human freedom and the meaning of justice itself make sense only if God finally punishes bad or unfaithful people. Such an understanding of justice stands in contrast to a conception of justice as *setting relations right* through healing and restoration (see reference to restorative justice in touchstone 4 and again in pt. 3).

---

3. The Second Temple, the remains of which still constitute the spiritual center of Jerusalem for Jews.
4. Isa 25:6–10; Mark 10:37.
5. Mark 9:47–48, Isa 66:24.
6. Matt 5:43–47.

The Eastern Orthodox scholar David Bentley Hart resists any suggestion that hell could be an enduring reality.[7] Firstly, he argues that a truly free person will not, ultimately, choose to reject divine love. To reject such love would indicate that we are not in our *right mind* (the younger son in the parable returns to his father once he comes to his *right mind*). God will either patiently wait for us[8] or actively seek us out,[9] as long as it takes, even beyond physical death. Hence, the *freedom to choose* argument fails. Secondly, there are so many unequivocally universalist passages in the Bible that we must leave open the most obvious conclusion that a God who is love will succeed in God's loving goal of bringing all the lost sheep home.[10] Categorically, this does *not* mean that God can or will tolerate evil. Nor does it remove the reality of judgment. Nor does it remove God's freedom. But it is a legitimate statement of hope based on the goodness of God we see in Christ. A universalist hope means that, in the end, God is triumphant in love only when God deals with the sin that keeps us separated from God and brings union and reconciliation to the cosmos.[11] I believe the latter is what St. Paul is referring to when he says:

> No one can lay any foundation other than the one that has been laid; that foundation is Jesus Christ. Now if anyone builds on the foundation with gold, silver, precious stones, wood, hay, straw—the work of each builder will become visible, for the Day [of judgment] will disclose it, because it will be revealed with fire, and the fire will test what sort of work each has done. If what has been built on the foundation survives, the builder will receive a reward. If the work is burned up, the builder will suffer loss; *the builder will be saved, but only as through [purifying] fire.* (1 Cor 3:11–15)

The way we think about what the Bible variously calls hell, Hades, underworld, place of the dead is a logical extension of the way we think about judgment. If our image of God is primarily legal/juridical, and we believe that justice and judgment have no meaning apart from a *necessary* punishment by God, then we will need to extend judgment to its logical extremity through the necessary existence of hell for the persistently unrepentant.

7. Hart, *That All Shall Be Saved*, 200–9.
8. Luke 15:11–32.
9. Luke 15:3–7.
10. Luke 15:4.
11. 1 Cor 15:28.

But if our conception of judgment is located within a covenant relationship with the Christlike God which is more like a physician, parent, or teacher, then we can and should think of language of hell as a teaching and pastoral intervention, as a warning, a wake-up call, a radical surgery, or a purifying fire. One of the passages in the Gospels that seems the most categorical and decisive about final judgment and punishment is Matt 25:31–46. The NRSV translates the last verse as:

> These [those who failed to recognize Jesus in the poor] will go away into eternal punishment, but the righteous into eternal life.

David Bentley Hart's more accurate and literal translation is:

> These will go to the chastening of that Age, but the just to the life of that Age.

The age being referred to is the new age that God inaugurates—in which God invites us to participate now, in advance of our physical death (as mentioned in touchstone 3). Referring to the Greek word *kolasis* ("chastening"), which is frequently rendered in English translations as "punishment," Hart says in a footnote:

> The word, kolasis, originally meant "pruning" or "docking" or "obviating the growth" of trees or other plants, and then came to mean "confinement," "being held in check," "punishment" or "chastisement," chiefly with the connotation of "correction."[12]

All this language is consistent with the way judgment in framed in the Christian Testament, as illumination, forgiveness, and purification. One thing that church tradition has definitively said about the place of the dead is that Christ has entered it to preach good news. The earliest baptismal creed of the church, the Apostles' Creed, says "he [Jesus] descended into hell."

> For this is the reason *the gospel was proclaimed even to the dead*, so that, though they had been judged in the flesh as everyone is judged, *they might live in the spirit as God does*. (1 Pet 4:6)

It seems inconceivable to me that Jesus would go into hell to make people miserable about themselves—a kind of rubbing people's noses in their failures. It would seem more in the nature of the Christlike God that Christ would visit hell to finally heal people's grief, pain, and trauma

---

12. Hart, *New Testament*, 53. See also Jersak's extensive exploration in *More Christlike God* and *Her Gates*.

sufficiently for them to reach out to him and be raised with him. We can believe that that no one is beyond the love of God, even in death/hell. As St. Paul puts it:

> I am convinced that *neither death*, nor life, nor angels, nor rulers, nor things present, nor things to come, nor powers, nor height, nor depth, nor anything else in all creation, *will be able to separate us from the love of God in Christ Jesus our Lord*. (Rom 8:38)

The Russian Orthodox theologian Olivier Clément tells a story of meeting a great contemporary mystic, Father Sophrony (1896–1993) of Mount Athos:

> I asked him what would happen if a human being refused to open their heart and welcome the love which was offered to them, and this is the answer he gave: "Be sure," he said, "that as long as there is someone in hell, Christ will be there with them." And in that same tradition, all those who have written commentaries on Isaac the Syrian have reminded us that God stays at the door of every heart, even the hearts that remain closed to him, and that, if necessary, he will wait for all eternity until they open to him.[13]

In the last two chapters, I have been inviting us to imagine what the universe, and our world, is really like at the deepest level of being, sometimes drawing on metaphysical and metaphorical language to describe the indescribable. This is a world conceived, narrated, and made comprehensible by the life, death, and resurrection of Christ and Christ's ongoing presence through the Spirit. To pick up Douglas Campbell's metaphor again, this is like a beautiful piece of music that is shaping our perception of life. Are we listening to the music of the new creation, characterized by the peace of Christ, or are we listening to the music of the old world, which frequently makes peace by violence and which is passing away?

We live in an in-between space and time where the forces of violence are strong, but the emerging reign of God's peace is a present reality and a certain hope. James Alison says that the world's violence is no more than fireworks in the lee of the erupting volcano, the latter being the peace of God.[14] We ought not get overly fascinated by the fireworks but pay attention to the eruption of divine life. This resurrection life is one

---

13. Clément, *Taizé*, 80.
14. Alison, *On Being Liked*, 13.

which we can know and experience more deeply through the practices of contemplation, to which we now turn our attention.

SUMMARY

1. In light of the nonviolence of God in Christ, we can understand hell as a rhetorical image related to the cry of the human heart for justice, in the light of immense human injustice and suffering. It is a statement of God's no to our violence, while never closing the door of divine love from God's side.

2. God's judgment includes the reality that all that is destructive of love within us will be finally healed by God. Imagery of fire speaks of purification and refinement rather than destruction, because God's covenant commitment is irrevocable. God does not wish to lose anything that God has made.

3. We can also think of hell in terms of the hells that we create on earth, particularly in the form of the violence we do to each other. God is not the instigator of violence, but God can bring good out of it.

REFLECT

1. How, in the past or now, have I thought about hell?
2. To what extent is language about hell useful and relevant to today's world?
3. It is comforting or discomforting (true or heretical) to consider the possibility that hell could be a rhetorical device rather than a final annihilation of life or an eternal torment? If the latter, can you reconcile this with God as Christlike?

Part 2

CONTEMPLATION

Contemplation is very far from being just one kind of thing that Christians do: it is the key to prayer, liturgy, art and ethics, the key to the essence of a renewed humanity that is capable of seeing the world and other subjects in the world with freedom—freedom from self-oriented, acquisitive habits and the distorted understanding that comes from them. To put it boldly, contemplation is the only ultimate answer to the unreal and insane world that our financial systems and our advertising culture and our chaotic and unexamined emotions encourage us to inhabit. To learn contemplative practice is to learn what we need so as to live truthfully and honestly and lovingly. It is a deeply revolutionary matter.
—Rowan Williams (Archbishop's address to the Synod of Bishops in Rome, 2012)

9

Integrating Perception
Affect, Emotions, and Story

WE HAVE SEEN THAT THE practice of peace flows out of the theological premise that God is Christlike and calls all creation into loving union with God. God reveals this by grace rather than something we figure out by our own insight or gain through any personal virtue. This revelation also illuminates the predicament of our entrapment in sin (mimetic rivalry, competition, and violence) and the degradation of relationships. God delivers us from this enmeshment by drawing us into the cruciform pattern of God's life—involving a radical reorientation of our desire. God gifts us with a transformed mind and the fruits of the Spirit, which are foretastes of the new creation and our ultimate union with God.

Even though we are receiving these gifts, we continue to live simultaneously in two realities. Just because we are beginning to see our predicament, we are not entirely free from violent and disoriented desire. Just because we know we should be nonviolent does not mean that we always are. We can think of the simultaneous realities of freedom and mimetic entrapment as like two pieces of music playing at the same time in the same room. We are always attending, consciously, to one or another. This process of listening and discerning is an invitation of love, which Jesus summarizes in the two great commandments.

> One of the scribes came near and heard them disputing with one another, and seeing that he answered them well, he asked him, "Which commandment is the first of all?" Jesus answered,

"The first is, 'Hear, O Israel: the Lord our God, the Lord is one; you shall love the Lord your God with all your heart, and with all your soul, and with all your mind, and with all your strength.' The second is this, 'You shall love your neighbor as yourself.' There is no other commandment greater than these." (Mark 12:28–31)

God gifting us with a new mind is not just about being given a new cognitive or intellectual sense of things, the new mind not just having *right ideas* about God, as if we are saved from violence by knowledge. Even the structuring of this book into categories of theology, contemplation, and action risks giving the impression that our perception flicks neatly between thinking at one moment and feeling at another. In fact, our perception is much more complex. Being given a new mind means that our whole perceptual apparatus—the way we perceive and interact with the world—is being transformed.

We may be helped here by Donald Nathanson's work, building on Silvan Tomkins's previous work, on the interrelationship between the body, emotions, and thoughts.[1] Donaldson illustrates how our first perceptions of the world occur at a visceral level through the body when we are babies. Humans (as with many animals) are born with several hard-wired physiological responses, which are designed to either optimize or minimize stimuli in our environment in order to enhance physical and emotional flourishing. These physiological responses are called *affects*, and each of them provides a motivational direction. For example, the affect of *interest* and *enjoyment* draws us towards something, whereas the affect of *fear* is the body starting to prime itself against risk. In this framework, there are seven basic affects:[2]

Basic Affect	Motivational Direction
Interest—Excitement	Engage
Enjoyment—Joy	Affiliate
Surprise—Startle	Stop, look, listen
Fear—Terror	Self-protect
Distress—Anguish	Seek and provide comfort
Anger—Rage	Attack!

---

1. Nathanson, *Shame and Pride*.
2. Chart from Abramson and Moore, "Promoting Positive Peace," 133.

Dissmell	Avoid
Disgust	Get rid of it
Shame—Humiliation	Seek to restore

The affect system is preverbal and helps the baby to negotiate their needs with the environment (initially through caregivers) well before the baby forms mental words. As we develop verbal language, we begin to use words to describe what we are experiencing in our bodies. Emotions are verbal articulations of what the child has already experienced and articulated (through facial expression) as a bodily affect. The child can now say, "I *feel* hungry." The child also starts to construct stories (scripts) in connection with affects and emotions. For example, assuming I am in a loving/caring relationship with primary caregivers, when my body expresses *distress* by crying because I am hungry, I discover I will be fed. This bodily experience forms the foundation for a script (an internal narrative about the way relationships work) about whether I can rely on other people when I am in need. It is reasonable to assume, for example, that Jesus's deeply trusting relationship with the Abba was shaped by deeply nurturing primary relationships with his earthly parents, Mary and Joseph.

The direction of meaning-making between affect (body), emotions, and scripts can, of course, run in all kinds of directions. For example, we may have found ourselves telling a story (script) about a person or situation in our lives, which just keeps getting repeated, even though it is not serving us or our relationships very well. Some examples could be:

- That person hates me.
- I don't trust that person.
- I'll never amount to much.
- Life is a meritocracy, and I have earned everything I have.
- I am a victim of the world's injustice.

We tell stories as if they were objective truth, when, in fact, they are just stories, told from one angle (every viewpoint is a view from a point). When we tell negative stories about others, they can become self-fulfilling prophecies (sometimes called a vicious cycle). For example, I might say, "I don't trust that person." As a result, I start to withdraw from the person or treat them with suspicion. That may lead to the other person unconsciously imitating my closed way of being. Their behavior then reinforces my internalized story that I can't trust the other person. In such ways, our internal narratives/stories shape our external realities. Fortunately, we can change our scripts and our behaviors. Even though I might not trust a person, I might, as an experiment, decide to *behave* as if I trust them and then see what happens. In doing this, we can act our way into new ways of thinking.

I have found in coaching situations that people find it easier to try new *actions* towards someone rather than to try to change their *feelings* towards that person. For example, in restorative justice conferences (ch. 16), we cannot expect people to always like each other. All we can ask them to do is to tell their stories (an action) truthfully. When everyone does this, feelings between people will frequently change.

Affect theory demonstrates that we cannot neatly silo our perceptual and meaning-making systems into head, heart, and hands. Rather, all three domains are constantly interacting with each other. We are making a distinction between the domains in this book (i.e., between theology, contemplation, and action) only for the sake of exploring the complexity of our sense of self—teasing things apart, so that we can put them back together again. To have the mind of Christ (touchstone 4) does not mean we get a mind-transplant, as if Jesus's thoughts become our thoughts. Rather, it means that our mental-emotional-bodily perceptual system, through the gift of the Spirit, starts to adopt a more loving (cruciform) orientation to the world, manifested as loving God and loving our neighbor as ourselves.[3] This is how God is making us into a people of peace. In the next two chapters, we will explore more deeply the inner work of loving God and loving neighbor.

SUMMARY

Being given a new mind is a way of saying that our whole perceptual apparatus—the way we perceive and interact with the world—is being transformed. Our language, emotions, and bodies are an integrated linguistic perceptual system.

---

3. Alan Sieler explores in detail how language, emotions, and body interact in communications in his three volumes on ontological coaching.

REFLECT

Have I ever noticed myself constructing an inner story about someone with whom I am in conflict? If I am doing this now, is there a risk this could be a self-fulfilling prophecy (vicious circle)? Could I try adapting my *behavior/actions* towards the person and see what effect this has on the relationship?

10

Loving God
Contemplative Prayer

More than ever the word about Jesus spread abroad; many crowds would gather to hear him and to be cured of their diseases. But he would withdraw to deserted places and pray. (Luke 5:15–16)

To love God does not just mean to have warm fuzzy spiritual experiences about God, even though we may occasionally have such an experience (which we can welcome as a form of consolation). God's love is not defined by our emotional landscape. God's love is revealed in the covenant faithfulness of God in Christ. For Christians, part of our loving (faithful) response to God's faithfulness is prayer.

There are many ways to pray, including thanksgiving, petition, intercession, and confession. In liturgy, we pray in words, Scripture, symbols, visual images, and actions. Another less well-known type of prayer is called contemplative prayer (sometimes called meditation).[1] Contemplative prayer originated in the Christian tradition of the desert monks of the third and fourth centuries in Egypt and was a significant influence

---

1. In the World Community for Christian Meditation (WCCM). The word *meditation* can be confusing because in the Benedictine tradition of Lectio Divina, meditation includes thinking about a scriptural text. The WCCM uses the word meditation as a practice of prayer that moves us into contemplation—the prayer of silence, which is beyond words and images.

on St. Benedict (sixth century) in the creation of his Rule (principles/instructions) for the monastic communities he established.[2] Contemplative prayer has found a resurgence in the twentieth century, particularly through the teachings of Thomas Merton, Thomas Keating, and John Main, and is now promoted and practiced widely across many Christian denominations. Former Archbishop of Canterbury Rowan Williams frequently spoke of the importance of contemplative prayer, as have Anglican theologians Sarah Coakley and Sarah Bachelard.[3]

Contemplative prayer is not a replacement for other forms of prayer but a practice that deepens prayer by moving prayer from words (head) to silence (heart). It cultivates a particular quality of deep attention, typically through the repeated and gentle repetition of a word or phrase of Scripture, as well as attention to the breath. For example, the World Community for Christian Meditation suggests using the word *maranatha* (divided into four equally stressed syllables of *ma-ra-na-tha*), an Aramaic word that means "Come, Lord."[4] Whenever the mind wanders, even to good and holy thoughts, we resume the repetition of the prayer-word.

Contemplative prayer is a significant *practice of peace*, because it enables an experiential connection to each of the theological touchstones articulated in part 1. For example:

- Contemplative prayer is an expression of a fundamental trust in God's grace and covenant promises. Each time we return to saying the prayer-word, after noticing our mind wondering, we are implicitly saying to God something like "I trust that you are working in me and delivering me and healing me, even when I cannot believe it, feel it, or see it." We realize that even being able to return to the prayer-word is a manifestation of grace (just in case we get full of

---

2. See Cassian (born c. 360) for an early detailed account of this form of prayer drawn from his own experience of visiting the desert fathers and mothers (Cassian, *Conferences* §10, 125–40).

3. For various contemporary examples, see the websites for Contemplative Outreach, The World Community for Christian Meditation, The Centre for Action and Contemplation, and the Taizé community.

4. Saint Paul uses this word at 1 Cor 16:22. An example of another focus for prayer in early church use was "Come to my help, O God; Lord, hurry to my rescue" (Ps 69:2) (Cassian, *Conferences* §10, 132). The Taizé community in France has become well known for the way in which it sets such short phrases to music, which the congregation sings in communal prayer.

our own success in praying, which would be just another preoccupation of the ego [touchstone 1]).

- Contemplative prayer helps to reorient our desire towards God and away from all the mimetic images that are trying to captivate our attention, like the desert temptations of relevance, power, and impressiveness. It is a practice of "dying with Christ" (Rom 6:8) and can sometimes even feel like parts of the ego are passing away (touchstone 2).[5]

- Contemplative prayer is a form of kenotic *participation* in Christ. We develop a practical capacity for *letting go* of the immediate concerns of the ego. As we shall see in the next chapter, being able to identify and release physical affects, thoughts, and emotions, rather than being hijacked by them, is a particularly useful capability when it comes to maintaining a nonviolent presence in highly conflictual situations (touchstone 3).

- Contemplative prayer contributes to being a better listener in everyday conversations and is therefore a way of loving our neighbor. As Sarah Bachelard, a teacher of contemplative prayer, puts it, contemplative prayer develops "mental muscle memory" for suspending our own agenda, invasive thoughts, and feelings in the interests of attending to another. Developing a capacity for inner silence increases our capacity to listen deeply to others (touchstone 4).[6]

Contemplative prayer develops a felt trust that the spaciousness of silence is nothing to be afraid of and, in fact, is full of the presence of God. I have found this to be particularly useful in the facilitation of circles, which I will talk about in part 3. Whether a circle has five people or five hundred, the empty circle turns out not be empty at all but is pregnant with the Spirit. However, the empty space of a circle can catalyze anxiety among participants who are carrying multiple agendas into the room and wondering what is going to happen in the space between them. For the facilitator to model that *this circle is a safe place to be*, through their own

---

5. We need to exercise care in our language. In Christian spirituality, the ego is not *bad* and we don't need to "kill" it, which is clearly an act of violence to self. Rather, God invites us to put the desires of the ego into the service of God—just as Jesus says of this own experience: "Very truly, I tell you, the Son can do nothing on his own, but only what he sees the Father doing; for whatever the Father does, the Son does likewise" (John 5:19).

6. See also St. Benedict's ninth degree of humility in his *Rule*, ch. 7.

calmly held presence, is important to the well-being of participants and the usefulness of the dialogic process. Harrison Owen, who devised the Open Space Technology process, has said that the most important formation for Open Space facilitators is to learn to meditate!

The practice of physical retreat into nature is frequently associated with contemplative prayer, and it not surprising that the contemplative prayer tradition was forged in the deserts of Egypt. Aboriginal peoples in Australia have known this for millennia, experientially and intuitively, and have much to teach new Australians. Senior Australian of the Year (2021) Dr. Miriam-Rose Ungunmerr Baumann speaks of the aboriginal practice of *dadirri*, which means "inner, deep listening and quiet, still awareness."[7]

Retreating to the desert (the unbuilt environment) provides space to recognize the ways, internally and externally, in which we have become enmeshed in the vortexes of mimetic desire. The desert is like a decompression chamber. I once took a group of university students to Koora Retreat in the Great Western Woodlands of Western Australia where we asked the students to turn off their mobile phones for four days. Sitting around the campfire at the end of the first full day, two students from Europe observed, "We've realized today that we don't actually need a lot of *stuff* to be happy."[8] It is our compulsive acquisitive desires, activated by all the desires of people around us, that fuel our competitive rivalry with each other. Reflecting on "fleeing" (retreating), Rowan Williams says:

> What you are ultimately "running" from is just this, your compulsions; you are making a break for freedom. So it isn't a matter of trying to run away from yourself . . . but, we might almost say, running away to yourself, to the identity you are not allowed to recognize or nurture or grow so long as you are stuck in the habits of anxious comparison, status-seeking and chatter. As so often in these considerations, we have to think of this as a discovery of space, room to breathe.[9]

People sometimes ask what the difference is between contemplative prayer (Christian meditation) and what is popularly known as mindfulness meditation. The short answer is that the focus of meditation is God

---

7. "Australian of the Year Awards."

8. Baird writes beautifully about how direct contact with nature is helpful for well-being, citing much research to support this assertion (Baird, *Phosphorescence*, 33–42).

9. Williams, *Silence and Honey Cakes*, 79.

and that it does not seek any particular outcome. The only goal of contemplative prayer is God. We pray in this way because God is our end and our good. I recall walking through an abandoned railway tunnel in a national park near my home. During the walk, I remembered a joke that took my fancy when I was a child: "The light at the end of the tunnel is an oncoming express train." But an alternative way of thinking about it is that the light at the end of the tunnel is *resurrection life*, towards which the Spirit is drawing us. On the sides of the tunnel are multitudes of mimetic distractions, rivals for our attention. The repetition of the prayer-word develops a muscle of attentiveness to God.

As the Benedictine monk Bede Griffiths put it, "The object of Christian meditation is to encounter Christ in the depths of one's being, not mediated by words and thoughts, but known by his presence in the Spirit. . . . . Jesus did not leave us the New Testament. That came after. He left us the Holy Spirit"[10] (touchstones 1 and 4). Every time we return to saying the prayer-word after a period of distraction, we are saying, "At this moment, God, my attention to you is more important than my thoughts and feelings about you or anything else." The ego finds it difficult to not be the center of attention, which is why contemplative prayer can feel difficult, requiring all our heart, soul, mind, and strength.

Even though, in contemplative prayer, we are not aiming at achieving any particular outcome, the paradox is that this kind of prayer does, in fact, contribute to our practice of peace. This is unsurprising when we remember that the Holy Spirit is the spirit of peace. In this sense, contemplative prayer shares similar psychological benefits with mindfulness meditation. Contemplative prayer can help us become more aware of the inner dynamics of our own psyche, which can either help or hinder communication with others. We now turn to exploring this aspect of how prayer contributes in a practical way to love of self and love of neighbor by developing a greater awareness of what is going on within.

SUMMARY

1. Faith means to *trust* God. Contemplative prayer is an embodied form of trusting that God's healing Spirit is at work in the depths of our being, even when we are not specifically thinking *about* God.

---

10. Griffiths, *New Creation in Christ*, 63.

2. Contemplative prayer is a response to Jesus's first commandment to love God with all our heart and is a kenotic participation in the life of Christ.

REFLECT

1. What has been my experience of contemplative prayer? Is this a practice I would consider doing? If so, go to the website of the World Community for Christian Meditation and read the paragraph on how to meditate and begin.
2. Begin each day with a commitment to a *doable* amount of time. If I can do only five minutes, then I commit to five minutes every day. If I can commit to ten minutes, I do that. Could I work up to twenty minutes? Could I then work up to twenty minutes twice a day?

11

Loving Neighbor
Conversation and the Inner Village

WHEN I WAS IN MY twenties, I worked for several years as a human resources (HR) manager in the shipping and banking industries. I was blessed to have some wise supervisors at mentors. One senior HR manager—let's call him Peter—had a turn of phrase that has proved to be one of the most useful things I have learned. My work would often take me into situations where people in the organization were in conflict. This included managers having problems with staff members or staff members having conflicts with each other. People would ask me, as an HR manager, for advice on what to do or to intervene to sort such things out. Sometimes, I had no idea what to offer, and I would take these thorny scenarios to Peter for advice. Peter would listen carefully, lean back in his chair, put his hands behind his head, look off to the middle distance for a few moments, and finally look at me and say, "Have they talked with the other person?" This was nearly always the question Peter asked, so I learned to ask the question myself. If someone were complaining about something or someone, I would say, "Have you talked with them about it?" Most of the time the answer was no. Even if the answer was yes, it would frequently turn out that people had not talked *with* each other but had just talked *at* each other (argued). At the risk of oversimplification, a significant aspect of practicing peace is about having *effective loving conversations*. Just about everything that happens in this world happens through conversation.

CONVERSATION SHAPES PERSONS

In touchstone 1, I observed that our personhood is constituted and formed in relationship with other people. The idea of an autonomous individual is an illusion. Every conversation we have shapes us in either small or significant ways. Similarly, every conversation we have has a formational effect on others. The contemplative mind cultivates an attentiveness to the quality, or absence, of Christlike love in our conversations.

I remember an encounter (it was not a conversation—it was more of a rant) I once had with a young person, which illustrates this point. I was standing in the front yard of our house when a boy about twelve years of age roared past me at full speed on a miniature motorbike on the footpath. I was furious because my wife and I had developed a bond with two little twin boys next door who were of toddler age and would often play in the front yard of their home. My mind generated a scenario of one of these toddlers wandering onto the footpath and being hit by the boy on the motorbike, which would certainly have resulted in severe injury, if not death. A few minutes later, I heard the boy on the motorbike returning along the footpath from the other direction again at full speed. As he approached, I stepped out onto the footpath and put out my hand like a traffic policeman, ordered him to stop, and then proceeded to angrily chastise him.

I have since reflected on this encounter in terms of how it has shaped my personhood and might have shaped the personhood of that boy. In relation to my own personhood, I have felt a range of emotions from self-justification; to guilt; to shame; and, ultimately, to humility. I was struck that, despite all my good aspirations about peace and nonviolent communication, it was so easy for me to become verbally violent in a fraction of second when I felt threatened. The encounter invited me to think about why I acted the way I did and what would be necessary for me to handle a situation like that differently in the future.

As to the personhood of the boy, I wonder what he learned. He might have learned not to do such a dangerous thing again, but what did he learn about how he could expect to be treated by men when he does something dangerous? The modeling he received from me about how to confront dangerous behavior was undoubtedly toxic. If he was receiving good modeling from his own father, then my treatment of him would have been absorbed in a sea of parental love with no lasting negative effect. But if his relationship with male figures in his life was characterized by anger and violence, then I probably reinforced that image of masculinity. I never saw the boy again and regretted that I could not offer him an apology and explain to him that I was concerned that his actions were potentially endangering the small children who lived next door. We might have even got on to a conversation about his interest in motorbikes and established a neighborly connection.

My interaction with the boy was a missed opportunity for mutually *making* the personhood of each other in a positive way because the encounter was characterized by my power *over* the boy rather than power *with*. My emotional outburst was activated by a survival need (touchstone 2) that was not evil or illegitimate but was, in the moment, unaware (the opposite of contemplation) of its relational impact. As a result, I stripped the boy of his power to speak because of the brute force of me being a larger and stronger male.

Communication as a practice of peace is always a dance between the active advancement of a value that we hold to be important (assertion/intention) and doing this in a way that makes space for the perspectives and needs of others (kenosis/humility). In the above story, I had a clear value that was important to assert in the interests of community safety, but I did not do this in a way that kept open the possibility of relationship. Martin Luther King Jr. frames this balance as a dance between power and love, each of which has a shadow side, in the following way:

> Power without love is reckless and abusive, and love without power is sentimental and anemic. Power at its best is love implementing the demands of justice, and justice at its best is love correcting everything that stands against love.[1]

Adam Kahane elaborates beautifully on this dynamic,[2] as do Anderson and Adams,[3] using slightly different language (see appendix C). In an effective dialogue, a fluid movement occurs between the *assertion* of our own position and listening with *flexibility* to the position of others. The shadow side of assertion could be summarized as being a *control freak* where we stop listening and start to dominate others. The shadow side of flexibility could be summarized as being a *doormat* in which we lose our backbone, subsumed by the desires of the others.

---

1. King, "Martin Luther King."
2. Kahane, *Power and Love*. I love this book and highly recommend it to everyone.
3. Anderson and Adams, *Mastering Leadership*, 88, 274–94.

CONVERSATION SHAPES THE WORLD

It is through conversations that dance skillfully between power (assertion) and love (flexible, kenotic humility) that our everyday conversations can be embodied practices of peace. This dynamic lies at the heart of nonviolent leadership. As J. Parker Palmer regularly reminds us, we cannot *not* make a difference in the world. The only question is what kind of difference we are making and how aware we are about what it is.[4] Our leadership is not restricted to being in a formal role but is an inherent part of being human. Whether we know it or not, we are always leading through our conscious or unconscious actions.

As a coach and professional supervisor, I support church leaders as they reflect, in a structured way, on their identity, vocation, faith, spirituality, and relationships. When people get stuck in their efforts to accomplish a goal, they sometimes frame this as another person *getting in the way* or *not cooperating*. The presenting question is "How do I get that other person to change?" The true but flippant answer is "You can't." Having acknowledged this annoying reality and laughed about it, we can then explore what *is* possible. What is possible is our capacity to examine what is going on within ourselves and use this knowledge to frame the next conversation. We must do this preparatory *inner work*, so that our hearts are predisposed to undertake the subtle dance between power (intention) and flexibility (love) in the dialogue to come.

THE INNER WORK OF CONVERSATION: JESUS AND THE INNER VILLAGE

Have we ever given any thought to *who it is* that engages in conversation with others? As I reflected on my encounter with the boy on the motorbike, I noticed how an angry part of me had suddenly risen from the depths of my psyche and taken control in my deliberative consciousness. This does not absolve me of ethical responsibility. I can't say, "The devil made me do it!" The experience and others like it have highlighted that if I want to act consciously and nonviolently, then I need to develop a capability to notice and manage the forces of my psyche rather than them managing me, particularly in stressful situations.

---

4. Palmer, *Let Your Life Speak*, 73–94.

A colleague of mine describes the psyche as something resembling an "inner village," containing multiple aspects of self.[5] Perhaps you have had the experience of trying to decide between two good courses of action. One helpful way of framing this is to say, "Part of me wants to do *x*, but part of me wants to do *y*." Our psyche carries a range of different, sometimes competing, needs. We might imagine sitting in a circle and inviting each *person* (aspect of self) to speak in turn about how they are viewing the situation and what their respective needs are. To have an internal *conversation with self* is to have a conversation with characters in the inner village.

This is well and good when we have time and space for deliberation, we might be thinking! But what about when an aspect of our psyche erupts from the unconscious, as it did in my encounter with the boy on the bike, and takes possession of our decision-making? This is an example of what the psychologist Carl Jung described as the shadow. The shadow is comprised of all those aspects of ourselves that are inconsistent with the way we like to think of ourselves in the public gaze. For example, if a significant part of my sense of identity is to be a person of peace, then anything in me that smacks of violence will most likely get denied and held under lock and key in the unconscious, only to erupt in embarrassing outbursts that seem outside my conscious control. Part of the nature of the shadow is that it expresses itself in ways that take us by surprise. We think later, "That was not like me," and feel embarrassed.

An eruption of the shadow can not only be embarrassing but can sometimes be violent and dangerous to others. If we aspire to *practice peace*, then we are going to have to pay attention to hidden, disguised, and sometimes violent aspects of ourselves. The more heavily invested our ego consciousness is in an aspect of *light*, the more potentially dangerous we can be to others, if we deny our darkness. While this is true for every human being, perhaps we can see how any moral or ideological system, religious or otherwise, can be a seedbed for violence. Rather than say "I am a good upright moral person," it would be much more honest and much safer to say "God, be merciful to me, a sinner!" (Luke 18:13).

So, if the shadow is often invisible to our ego consciousness, how do we become aware of it and thence engage with it through inner dialogue, so that it is less likely to erupt in damaging ways? The following are several ways by which we can become more aware of our shadow.

---

5. I am grateful to George Trippe for this term. The animated movie *Inside Out* delightfully explores the same concept.

(i) Attend through prayer

I mentioned above that the goal and purpose of contemplative prayer is not *primarily* to examine ourselves but to say yes to union with God (touchstone 1). Having said that, anyone who has practiced contemplative prayer knows that it takes only a few seconds before aspects of our psyche stage a hijack attempt on our good desire for God, symbolized by our prayer-word. The hijacker could take any number of forms, particularly those outlined in touchstone 2, such as mimetic rivalries, survival and belonging needs, and manifestations of shame. If we catch the hijack attempt quickly, we can return to our prayer-word within moments. However, if the hijacker is equipped with sophisticated weapons of distraction, then it can sometimes be minutes before we realize that a takeover has occurred. We then return to saying our prayer-word.

(ii) Reflect on the embarrassing moments

Because aspects of the shadow break out in unexpected and embarrassing moments, it is useful to notice these moments rather than dismiss them. If I am having a conversation with someone and I realize afterwards that I said something or behaved in a way that was unhelpful—even offensive (touchstone 2)—then it's worth debriefing that conversation with a trusted and skilled listener, inviting the kind of *judgment as illuminating light* discussed in chapter 7. A pastor, spiritual director, professional supervisor, or therapist can help us to get insight into what aspect of our-self was trying to have their voice heard in that moment, what we can learn, and what steps of relationship repair may now be needed.[6] In a similar vein, it can be instructive to notice what parts of our lives persistently trip us up, block our relationships, or annoy us about ourselves or other people. These are all potential pointers to aspects of our shadow.

---

6. There is a crucial difference between a psychologically well person having this dialogue with the inner village and someone who is clinically psychotic. In the former case, the self-aware ego remains in control of the process and always retains ethical responsibility for action. Dialoguing with the inner village is a simple form of mindfulness. In psychosis, inner aspects of the psyche overwhelm the ego (pastoral carers should not be encouraging people suffering from acute psychological conditions to engage in this kind of inner dialogue without professional psychological or psychiatric support).

(iii) Reflect on our rivalries

As we discussed in touchstone 2, mimetic desire and mimetic rivalry are nearly always invisible (unconscious) to us in the first instance. René Girard points out that once rivalry starts to escalate, we forget the original object of our rivalry and find that we are now caught up in imitating each other's emotional state. For example, as the person with whom we are arguing gets more anxious, we get more anxious. As they blame us, we blame them. As they get angry, we get angry (and vice versa, in each case).

Whenever we find ourselves in conflict with another person, it is worth asking, "How has this person become my rival?" Rivalry does not always have to be about material possessions. Rivalry can also ignite over such things as being right, being powerful, or being in control. When we notice the nature of our rivalry, then we can begin to consciously disengage the emotional load (through contemplative prayer, for example) and refocus on the actual issues. We need to focus on *performance (shared goal) over personality*. In a similar vein, in reflecting on Jesus's warning about wasted words,[7] Rowan Williams says:

> The times when we can be absolutely sure that we are wasting words are when we are reinforcing our reputation or defending our position at someone else's expense—looking for a standard of comparison, a currency in the market of virtue.[8]

(iv) Give thanks for affirmations and humiliations

Other people often see us more clearly than we see ourselves. We are blessed if we have a relationship with a partner, friend, colleague, or boss who will give us feedback with genuine love and concern. Let us be grateful for their compliments, because they may be pointing to something good in ourselves that we have refused to see or respect. Say thank you! Such a dialogue is an expression of the loving judgment discussed in chapter 7, which bears fruit because the judgment occurs within the context of a loving covenantal relationship. Could we even be grateful for an occasional unwanted humiliation, which is painful precisely because

---

7. Matt 12:36.
8. Williams, *Silence and Honey Cakes*, 76.

it touches a raw nerve, shedding light on an emotional program for happiness (yeah, I know—it's hard to hear!)?

(v) Pay attention to dreams

Another way of attending to the shadow is to pay attention to who is showing up in our dreams. To give a personal example, in my early thirties, I had a series of dreams in which Nazis were attacking other people with extreme brutality. These dreams occurred with some regularity, and I started to explore them with my spiritual director. We discussed how Nazi violence is a manifestation of the dark side of power and control (touchstone 2). We started to explore my feelings about power and control and how it showed up in my relationships. It became clear that I had a complex relationship with power. I was afraid of having power because I had been the recipient of its misuse by others, and yet I also knew that I could misuse power myself by being overly controlling.

Because of this sequence of dreams and discernment with my spiritual director, I decided to accept a new role that required me to exercise structural power in my organization in a responsible way. As Martin Luther King Jr. observed, what is necessary in nonviolence is not to deny power but to exercise power with love. Once I started to put this into practice, the Nazi dreams stopped entirely. When such a dream very occasionally shows up, I now know that it is inviting me to reflect again on how I am using power in my relationship with others.

(vi) Invite Jesus into the village

Brother Roger of the Taizé Community used to say that the risen Christ is near to every person. How often do we invite Jesus into the conversations in our inner village? Or do we just talk *about* Jesus at church on Sunday or read *about* him in the Scriptures? I am writing these words while doing a house-sit for a friend. Just outside is a little hut not much bigger than a children's cubbyhouse in which is stored swimming pool equipment. I wonder if we sometimes relegate Jesus to the little storerooms of our psyches. We might ask him for help in a moment of crisis, but the rest of the time, we are happy for him to remain in his box.

In recent years, I have tried to invite Jesus more actively and consciously into dialogue in my village. I picture Jesus sitting in the circle and ask him what he would like to say. I speculate that one of the reasons we might *not* do this imaginative exercise is because part of us thinks that it is nuts. The skeptical part of our ego might say, "You're just having a conversation with yourself; you're in fantasy land." To that part of myself, I respond, "Thanks for your thought and for being a devil's advocate, but I'm still going to listen to what Jesus has to say."[9]

One such practice of dialoging with Jesus was taught by St. Ignatius of Loyola in the sixteenth century. It became the heart of prayer for the Jesuit order (Society of Jesus) that he established. Ignatius also advocated a regular examination of conscience in which we reflect on how the Spirit has been moving in our lives and where our attention has been in relation to God. Ignatius invited us to consider where we have been moving *towards* greater love for God, self, and others and where have we been moving *away*. This contemplation will invariably reveal aspects of our shadow (touchstone 2) with which it may be beneficial to have a conversation.

(vii) Be open to feedback

Organizational psychology has given us useful tools (questionnaires) to get feedback on aspects of ourselves that are relational blind spots. In my experience, most people find such tools, when responsibly facilitated by well-trained persons, to be a helpful entrée into greater awareness of how their behavior affects others.[10] While sometimes this is painful, I have seen numerous cases of how such awareness has transformed people's relationships in a positive way.[11]

(viii) Be open to the gold

So far, we have been talking about the negative or destructive aspects of the shadow. However, the shadow can also contain surprising gifts

---

9. It is true that evil can masquerade as an angel of light (Lucifer). One principle of discernment is that Jesus, sitting in our inner village, will never commend something that is inconsistent with the fruits of the Spirit (Gal 5:22–25). Having the wise counsel of a spiritual director/friend is advisable when doing this work.

10. The safe use of such instruments in the workplace relies on using the tool as a way of *describing* observable relational behaviors in the workplace rather than *diagnosing* people's psyche, character, or ability.

11. An example of such a tool used commonly in organizations is the Leadership Circle (Anderson and Adams, *Mastering Leadership*).

of which we had been previously unaware. We might discover, in our dreams, figures of wisdom, courage, sensitivity, and beauty. It can be transformational for men who have difficulty with vulnerability and relationships, and may even be outwardly violent, to begin to discover gentleness and kindness in their dreams. Frequently, these dreams images emerge in the form of wise and gentle women, representing aspects of the man's soul. When sufficient trust is established, men can be invited to talk about their dreams. This is another way of practicing peace.

In my thirties, I had a sequence of dreams that pointed to something new and creative opening within myself, but it took a long time to figure out what it was. For over a year, I had recurring dreams about trying to get to an airport, but something kept getting in a way: a taxi would not show up; or the taxi got stuck in traffic; or the taxi would break down. I would be anxiously looking at my watch and knowing that I would miss my flight. I talked about these dreams with my spiritual director, and, for months, we could not get a breakthrough about what the dreams might signify. At the time, I had started to wonder about cutting back my full-time work in the church in order to grow a part-time business in coaching and facilitation but was procrastinating out of fear of failure and loss of income.

One day, my spiritual director speculated about whether catching a flight might represent launching a business and that the frustrations in not getting to the airport could be related to not taking concrete action to do so. As a result of our joint ponderings, I decided to take a leap in faith by reducing my stipendiary work in the church by a day a week and trust that I would cover the financial shortfall by launching a small business. As I took the initial steps to start a business, my dreams started to change: I started to get closer and closer to the airport, eventually arriving at the luggage terminal and checking in to my flight. When I finally registered a legal business name and actively sought work, I had a dream in which I was taking off in a 747 jumbo jet. After that dream, the recurring dreams stopped entirely. They had done their job. It was clear that the unconscious was pressing me in a particular direction, calling for a sacrificial commitment that would be life-giving for others as well as myself.

RECAP: WHY ALL THE INTROSPECTION?

I worked once with a manager in human resources who said that part of orienting new people to an organization is introducing them to "who's who in the zoo." My reflections in this chapter are a bit like getting to know who's who in the zoo of our own psyche. The value of this for the practice of peace is that the more we get to know our own complexity and how it may show up in conversations with others, including possibly erupting in the stress of conflict, the better placed we are to navigate complexity in the outer world. The Franciscan priest and teacher Richard Rohr says, "If we do not transform our pain, we will most assuredly transmit it."[12] Practicing peace means avoiding dumping our unresolved inner *stuff* onto other people. Consciously inviting Jesus into our inner village as an active dialogue partner is a way of asking Jesus to shape our inner village into a reconciled community of love. This can happen at both the intra-psychic and outer-communal levels:

> Listen! I am standing at the door, knocking; if you hear my voice and open the door, I will come in to you and eat with you, and you with me. (Rev 3:20)

It seems evident to me that one of the primary ways that God can lovingly work around our ego's defensive security and belonging needs (touchstone 2), without violence, is through contemplation and dreams. Within ourselves, we may discover a pearl of great value, which needs to be shared with the world rather than buried (touchstone 4). Or we might discover dark aspects of ourselves, with which some conversation is required to prevent them being transmitted to other people—the kind of loving judgment to which I referred in chapter 7. The Roman poet Terence says, "Nothing human is alien to me."[13] If I know that violent Nazi-like characters occasionally inhabit my own psyche, then my compassion for violent people can be evoked—not in any way to justify a person's violence but in order to recognize their humanity and the ways in which ordinary people can do inhumane things—what Hannah Arendt calls "the banality of evil." It is useful to know that, given the right set of circumstances, I have it within me to commit atrocities. Getting to know the complexity of our psyche, including those parts of it we might be

---

12. Rohr, "Transforming Pain."
13. Terence, *Heauton Timorumenos*.

embarrassed to share with others, increases our compassion for the human condition, beginning with compassion for ourselves (touchstone 4).

Lest we think that this level of introspection is narcissistic, it is worth noting that the fifth, sixth, and seventh degrees of humility outlined in the Rule of St. Benedict all relate to rigorous inner examination in order to be more truthful with ourselves.[14] As we take the veil off the darker aspects of our inner self, we stop shoring up false public images of ourselves. To realize we are no better, or more moral, than anyone else can be humiliating to the ego but is also a liberation from any need for the public posturing that is just another emotional program for happiness. How can anyone diminish us or shame us, when we have already honestly faced our fragility, our inner demons, our vulnerabilities, and know that God loves us—and hence that we have value and dignity (touchstone 1)? Being honest about ourselves opens the possibility of loving our enemies —people who do violence to us (touchstone 4). And so, we turn now to the practical issue of forgiveness.

SUMMARY

1. Contemplative prayer develops a capacity to notice and detach from our inner agendas, survival and belonging needs, and mimetic rivalries. This is a particularly useful capability in nonviolent communication and therefore helps us to love our neighbors (including enemies).

2. We relate to the world and love our neighbor through conversation. Conversation shapes our personhood and the personhood of others. We inescapably cocreate each other. This involves a dance between power and love (asserting ourselves and being responsive to the needs of others).

3. We can develop more flexibility in our dance between power and love by developing a conscious awareness of the complexity of our inner village, so that parts of that village are less likely to get transferred onto others in situations of stress or high conflict. Learning to love *all* of ourselves correlates with loving others as ourselves.

---

14. Benedict, *Rule*, ch. 7.

REFLECT

1. What do I notice when I meditate? Are there particular concerns, memories, or anxieties that frequently show up? What names/faces would I give to these aspects of my inner village? Is there something I would like to say to some aspect of my inner village, or is there something they would like to say to me (later, once my meditation is finished)?

2. Make a list of people or characters in my inner village. Draw a picture of them sitting around a campfire. Invite Jesus to be there around the campfire, too.

3. If I am in conflict with someone, is it possible that the person has become my rival in some way? What change of thinking would I need to disengage from the rivalry and refocus on the actual issues?

4. Do I have a soul-friend, spiritual director, priest, coach, or therapist whom I would trust to talk about what I am noticing in my inner village?

12

The Inner Work of Forgiveness

IN TOUCHSTONE 3, I TALKED about the forgiveness of God as a manifestation of God's liberating and healing activity. As such, to have the mind of Christ is to practice forgiveness. This is treacherous territory, because forgiveness can be difficult. Forgiveness does not come naturally or easily to humans. To guilt-trip ourselves or others to forgive before we are ready can be a form of violence.[1] On the other hand, to fail to respond to the life-giving possibilities of forgiveness is also to do violence to ourselves (because our resentments poison us) and to others (because it perpetuates active or passive hostility).

I recently heard a well-known journalist and public intellectual in Australia say, "Some acts are beyond forgiveness." There are times when we can know, at a cognitive faith-level, that nothing is beyond God's forgiveness and still find forgiveness incredibly difficult. One of the gifts of the psalms is that they cover the full range of human emotions, including desperate cries for vengeance by people who have experienced appalling injustice and violence.

> Remember, O LORD, against the Edomites
> the day of Jerusalem's fall,

---

1. Neither should we confuse forgiveness with trust. As an example, it is conceivable that a person may choose to forgive someone, but it doesn't mean that they should put themselves in a position where continued abuse is enabled. This is why restorative justice principles refer to "resetting" relationships rather than assuming relationships will be "renewed."

how they said, "Tear it down! Tear it down!
  Down to its foundations!"
O daughter Babylon, you devastator!
  Happy shall they be who pay you back
  what you have done to us!
Happy shall they be who take your little ones
  and dash them against the rock! (Ps 137:7–9)

To forgive means to let go of my hostility towards another person. Forgiveness is a decision we make in response to being hurt. When we experience hurt, loss, and pain, there are two paths we can choose. One path is to return harm with harm—to retaliate—to pay back. The other path is to choose to heal, starting within ourselves. Why does Jesus talk so much about forgiveness? Partly because it is God's nature to forgive and partly because unforgiveness is a disease rooted in mimetic rivalry that perpetuates the continued pattern of tit for tat violence. It makes us sick—which is why forgiveness is part of God's work of healing and deliverance.

- Then Peter came and said to Jesus, "Lord, if another member of the church sins against me, how often should I forgive? As many as seven times?" Jesus said to him, "Not seven times, but I tell you, seventy-seven [or seventy times seven] times" (Matt 18:20–22; here, Jesus counters the vengeance of Lamech in Gen 4:2).
- But I say to you, love your enemies and pray for those who persecute you (Matt 5:44).
- Do not judge, so that you may not be judged. For with the judgment you make you will be judged, and the measure you give will be the measure you get. Why do you see the speck in your neighbor's eye, but do not notice the log in your own eye? Or how can you say to your neighbor, "Let me take the speck out of your eye," while the log is in your own eye? You hypocrite, first take the log out of your own eye, and then you will see clearly to take the speck out of your neighbor's eye (Matt 7:1–5).
- Go and learn what this means, "I desire mercy, not sacrifice." For I have come to call not the righteous but sinners (Matt 9:13).
- Forgive us our sins, for we ourselves forgive everyone indebted to us (Luke 11:4).

- [Jesus on the cross] Then Jesus said, "Father, forgive them; for they do not know what they are doing" (Luke 23:34).

Before continuing to talk about the inner work of forgiveness, I want to clearly state what forgiveness is *not*. We need to be clear on this, lest we do violence in the name of forgiveness. Forgiveness does not mean:

- That what happened to us was right or excusable
- Accepting pressure to forgive, to make someone else feel better
- That we must forget—try to forget where you left your car keys!
- Denying our feelings of anger, sadness, and loss
- Having to hurry and get on with it—healing takes time
- That we must have an ongoing relationship with the person we forgive—we may choose to renew the relationship under new terms, or we might release the relationship and never see the person again
- Saying "I forgive you," when I really don't!

Forgiveness is firstly an inner-work journey that we intentionally undertake, because we know that, at some level, we do not want to carry around the load of resentment anymore. We may sense that forgiveness will not only liberate ourselves but also liberate the other person from the load of our unforgiveness. A good synonym for forgiveness is *letting go*. In *The Book of Forgiving*, Desmond and Mpho Tutu propose a fourfold path that can lead to forgiveness. The four steps they suggest are: telling our story, naming how we have been hurt, deciding to forgive, and renewing or releasing the relationship.

Appendix B contains a list of questions that may be helpful to ask ourselves as we embark on a journey of forgiveness. If we have an introverted personality, we may find that writing responses to the questions will help, or, if we are more extroverted, it might help to talk the questions through with a trusted listener.

In this short chapter, I have put a particular focus on forgiveness, because it is one of the most demanding forms of inner work. It is now time to shift the focus from inner work to outer work. Having located ourselves in God through the practice of contemplative prayer and being mindful of aspects of our inner village (including what we can know of our shadow), we have laid the groundwork for engaging in the *outer work* of conversation.[2] We know what we want to say and how we want to say it, and we have resolved to treat the other with respect—as a sacred thou rather than as an object to get our own needs met. We are therefore approaching the other with curiosity and openness to what may emerge in conversation.

In part 3, we will explore how to structure conversations in ways that optimize love for neighbor and love for self by creating conditions for the delicate dance between power and love.

SUMMARY

1. Accepting and giving forgiveness is a manifestation of the deliverance of God. It is liberating for others as well as ourselves.
2. Forgiveness is a process that starts within. If a hurt is significant, it can take time and work to accomplish.
3. We can do violence to ourselves (or others) if we try to force ourselves (or others) to forgive out of a sense of obligation or guilt and before we are ready to declare genuine forgiveness.

REFLECT

1. Is there anything in my life for which I need to be forgiven? What is the next step?
2. Is there anyone in my life I feel an urge to forgive? What is the inner work I need to do?

---

2. The path is not linear. Inner and outer conversations are constantly interacting. Parker Palmer uses the metaphor of a mobius strip. Our inner contemplation may catalyze an outer conversation—and an outer conversation will provoke new awareness of our inner life.

Part 3
ACTION

The glory of God always shows itself in an empty space.
  —Timothy Radcliffe, OP

13

Natural Living Systems

THE LAST CHAPTER FOCUSED ON contemplative practice through which we love God and do necessary inner work to prepare for conversations with other people. It is through conversations that we love our neighbor as ourselves, shape the world in which we live, and are shaped by it. The chapters that now follow explore a range of frameworks and tools that help to *structure* a backwards and forwards movement between power (*intention*) and love (*flexibility*) through the inherent design of the processes themselves. Organizations spend a lot of time and money on forming the character traits and capabilities of individual leaders and less attention to the group processes by which people engage with each other.[1]

We could think of dialogic conversations between individuals and groups as being like a choreographed dance routine. This analogy occurred to me while watching people coming together every Sunday afternoon at Scarborough Beach, Western Australia, to learn to salsa dance. There are a handful of body movements and rhythms that constitute the basic choreography. The basic choreography of practicing peace I have called Collaborative Emergent Design. Once people learn these steps, people of different capabilities can happily dance in close quarters to each other. As people become more capable with the basics, they add

---

1. As an example, capability frameworks upon which organizations' professional development courses are based typically focus on individual skills and traits. Most performance reviews in organizations focus on individual performance. Team coaching, which is concerned with team relationships and team performance is a new but growing initiative.

more advanced moves and then become teachers of others. The teachers often wander around the dance floor, dancing with different people as they go—a highly effective form of action-learning.

The conventions (dance routines) of interaction in organizations vary greatly. In some contexts, the conventions are highly ordered and controlled, with one person or group telling others what to do and when to do it. However, the social complexity and speed of change in our world at the present time is requiring more flexible, organic, and collaborative approaches in many situations.

Because I am concerned for how Christian communities become catalysts and prototypes of peace, most of my focus in this chapter will be on how conversations in groups and teams are choreographed.[2] I will be paying particular attention to how we develop collaborative cultures in which groups of people work together to get things done with and through each other. As mentioned in the preface to this book, being a heroic and controlling leader was one of my greatest stress points as a young priest. As a professional supervisor I have now found it is often the Achilles heel of many people in formal leadership, lay and ordained. Those of us who have imported hierarchical leadership practices from the business or government environments have often discovered that they do not work as well in churches. Much of this failure is because leadership practices in business assume contractual relationships between persons rather than covenantal. Contractual employment relationships include legal obligations to follow orders, which do not exist to the same extent in church communities.

In church communities, we get things done only when people want things to happen, rather than because people are being forced to do so. Collaborative practice is not only desirable but necessary. But it turns out that collaborative practice has a range of other advantages in terms of working together, even outside churches. To understand why this is so, it is worth reflecting a little on how human systems function as natural living systems.

---

2. A 'group' is comprised of people doing different activities who meet for information sharing and coordination. A 'team' is a group who have shared goals and must work effectively together to achieve those goals.

NATURAL LIVING SYSTEMS: THE BODY THAT DANCES

One of the products of the modern scientific age and the Industrial Revolution was that we began, unconsciously, to think of the world in mechanistic terms. This was underpinned by a philosophy of science that sought to understand the world by breaking things down into component parts to analyze how they worked and related to each other. The sixteenth-century philosopher Francis Bacon said, "Nature is only mastered by obedience to her laws,"[3] implying that it was, in fact, a good aspiration to have mastery over the natural world. As an example, Newton's laws of physics reliably describe how forces between objects work, and this enables us to do useful and interesting things, like driving cars or putting satellites into orbit.

When we think of the world in mechanistic terms, we may automatically also think of organizations as machines and humans as component parts in the machines. This is precisely what Frederick Taylor did when he brought his mechanical engineering thinking to developing scientific management and efficiency in production lines in the early twentieth century. Such language frames people as things to be *managed*, along with infrastructure, money, and information. One of the textbooks given to me in the 1980s when I studied management described the main components of management as "planning, organizing, directing, and controlling."

Significant movements occurred during the twentieth century, which has led to a rethinking of paradigms (taken-for-granted models) of the physical universe and our relationship to it.[4] Advances in mathematics and quantum physics have demonstrated that the universe is far more complex than we previously thought. What we considered to be fixed *laws* turn out to be useful descriptors of the way in which the macro-environment works, but everything becomes less certain and predictable at the subatomic level. The science that I learned at school in the 1970s, about the universe being made of protons, neutrons, and electrons, has changed. Mathematicians and scientists now talk about probability fields rather than physical objects. It turns out, we are all made of fields of

---

3. "Non nisi parendo vincitur" appears on the crest of the University of Western Australia.

4. I am speaking here primarily of the industrialized Western world. For Aboriginal cultures and any other spiritual tradition that has a deep connection to land, this knowledge of relational interconnectedness has always been deeply embedded.

energy and that we cannot *know* something as it exists, in and of itself, because the very process of observing something changes it (for example, if you fire an electron beam at something under a microscope, the beam changes the object being viewed). Biologists are also learning that the natural world is not just a collection of species fighting tooth and claw for dominance (Darwin's notion of survival of the fittest) but that the world is more like a network of intricate, mutually supportive, collaborative relationships.

This confluence of factors has also led to significant rethinking over the last forty years about the nature of organizations. Rather than thinking of organizations as machines, we find that organizations behave much more like natural living systems—sometimes called complex adaptive systems or self-organizing systems.[5] The new insight was that if nonhuman species are constantly adapting themselves in cooperative ways for the best adaptive fit to their environment, for the sake of the advancement of life, then could it be that human systems operate in similar ways? In turns out that they can and do.

Consider, for example, the extraordinary phenomenon of a city of ten million people that self-organizes to feed itself every day. There is no Chief Executive Officer (CEO) of Metropolitan Feeding. No one developed a master plan. No one person or group is in control. How does it happen? In short, it happens through millions of conversations—simple *linguistic acts* of declarations, requests, offers, and promises, all held together and made functional by the glue of stories, relationships, and trust. Formal organizations like churches and companies, and informal organizations like cities, are enormous networks of conversation and mutual commitments. All the action is happening in the conversational spaces between us.

On the face of it, has my assertion about the capacity of systems to self-organize naturally and collaboratively just contradicted my earlier observations about humans being mimetically rivalrous? Well, it seems that both realities exist together—like two pieces of music playing simultaneously. The creative miracle of self-organization, through which God brings about the marvelous diversity of life that has evolved on earth, seems to *incorporate and utilize* the rivalries and violence that humans do to each other. In God's ecosystem, nothing is wasted, even our sin!

---

5. The Santa Fe Institute has been a significant contributor to this emerging way of thinking.

God opens a creative space, extends an invitation of love, and constantly draws life into greater and more interesting complexity, as the system responds in freedom. To say a system *self-organizes* does not evacuate God from the equation. David Bentley Hart says that "a species in whom love dwells has a genetic heritage because it loves. There is no 'gene' for love. We have been shaped by transcendental ecstasies."[6] Later, I will contend that processes like Open Space Technology and Talking Circles optimize the natural conditions of self-organization while simultaneously minimizing the dynamics of mimetic rivalry. As a result, these processes *create* nonviolent conditions.

If systems have a natural capacity to self-organize for optimal fit to the environment and the creation of life, then at least two other implications emerge in relation to leadership. Firstly, our attitude to disruption and change will not be to panic and say "How do we *fix* this problem?" Change and disruption are not problems to be fixed. When change is occurring, useful questions to ask are "What does this disruption signify, and what new life might be *emerging* here?"

The phenomenon of emergence is a key aspect of a self-organizing system. Peggy Holman defines emergence as "higher order complexity arising out of chaos in which novel, coherent structures coalesce through interactions among the diverse entities of a system."[7] What Holman describes as disruption, differentiation, and novelty bears a significant resemblance to the paschal journey of dying and rising.[8] The role of formal leadership in the process of disruption is to walk with the community through the kenotic journey of death and resurrection, listening carefully for the new life that may be emerging.

The second implication of a system's capacity to self-organize is that we, as formal leaders, need to restrain our instinct to control. Yes, formal leaders have a role to play as part of the system, but it is not to the crush the system's self-organizing creativity. The good news is that in our current world of mind-bending complexity and exponential change, the only thing adequate to the challenges facing us is the power of collaborative self-organization, rather than individuals or small groups trying to be in control. The latter does not work for several reasons. It assumes stable environmental conditions where we can plan for the future (we

---

6. Hart, *Experience of God*, 271.
7. Holman, *Engaging Emergence*, 18.
8. As does Otto Scharmer's *Theory U*.

can't, because things are changing too quickly); it assumes we alone have all the necessary knowledge, information, and expertise (which is hubris); and it assumes we have the capacity to control the execution of the plan (which is impossible, because multiple independent parties all need to be involved).

Saint Paul's metaphor of the *body* to describe the church[9] has striking similarities to envisaging an organization as a natural living system. The body has many members, all related to one another in an organic unity. Each part of the body has a unique and important contribution to make, and no part of the body is disposable. How then are we to envisage formal leadership within such a body?

SUMMARY

1. Human beings are not separate from the ecosystems that we inhabit. We are part of an interdependent natural living system.
2. All natural living systems are in a constant process of self-organizing themselves for optimal relationship with the environment. If the system cannot or will not adapt (either through its own choice or because the environment is changing too quickly to allow time for adaption), a life-form will go extinct.
3. Believing that we are in control of a complex system is an illusion.

REFLECT

In what ways do I notice human systems/organizations to which I belong demonstrating self-organization? Is this self-organization in alignment with formal management structures and/or working in a different direction(s)?

---

9. 1 Cor 12.

14

Collaboration

HOSTING THE DANCE

WE CAN THINK OF A human natural living system (group, organization, city, or country) as a *network of conversations* through which the various components adapt to each other for the best fit to the emergence of life in a particular context. Such a system in inherently *collaborative* rather than competitive. Collaboration means to "co-labor" or to "work together." This requires a mindset shift, particularly for those of us in the church where we still use terms like rector (ruler) or priest-in-charge on clergy licenses. The way that the church self-organized for centuries was through a hierarchy, with clergy holding educational, teaching (preaching), and decision-making power. The church describes an ordained person as being in holy orders. There is nothing wrong with this per se. The good ordering of a community can be in the interests of the peace of a community. As we saw in our discussion of mimetic rivalry, having certain categories of persons who are set apart can serve to reduce the chance of unconstrained mimetic rivalry in a community.[1] Hierarchical ordering also has significant benefits in preserving core stories of a community through time, particularly through liturgy, which is a highly ordered way of transmitting corporate memory.

But there is also a major weakness in this kind of highly structured ordering of churches. It can distort the original vision of the church as a

1. The Anglican Ordinal has the phrase "set apart by the laying on of our hands" (*A Prayer Book for Australia*, 796).

community of baptized persons called to ministries based on spiritual gifts,[2] because it tends to reframe the ordained person as *the* minister. This framing of ministry is common in churches. It frequently creates overworked, stressed clergy and/or lay persons who tend to unconsciously set themselves up (or be set up by others) as heroic leaders.[3] Under such conditions, the self-organizing capacity of a system to adapt itself rapidly and flexibly to the environment is constrained. This is problematic in this period of unprecedented disruption and change, where we need to develop collaborations across traditional organizational boundaries. Organizational psychologist Dr. Neil Preston points out that the more complex challenges become, the more collaboration is needed. And here is the clincher: Preston boldly states, "If you are in control, then you are not collaborating!"[4] Setting up a systemic expectation that formal leaders have the answers or being overly controlling in one's leadership will degrade both collaboration and collective intelligence.

Collaboration aims to release the collective intelligence of a group through fostering the *emergence* of something that did not exist before the individual egos got together. Collective intelligence is an emergent property of safe (nonviolent) dialogic conditions within a group, rather than adding up the IQs of all the individuals in a room. To create collaborative conditions, we need to make a paradigm shift from heroic to hosting-style leadership. A person who is adopting a hosting style of leadership will:

- Be creating conditions of participation safety so members of the group can speak their truth, explore options, and cocreate new realities together. Participation safety is essential to catalyzing collective intelligence, because people will speak their truth and take risks only if they feel it is safe to do so and that they will not be scapegoated, named, blamed, or shamed (sometimes shaming is masked by the term *called out*) by the group.

- Understand the complexity of the system in which they are operating and not try to heroically figure out a single answer and then try to impose this on a group.

---

2. 1 Cor 12, Eph 5, Rom 12. See also Pickard, *Theological Foundations.*

3. Wheatley with Frieze, "Leadership."

4. Personal conversation with Neil Preston. For more information, see http://www.psyopus.com.au/about/.

- Not confuse collaboration with consultation. Consultation is sometimes appropriate where we need technical expertise. For example, a surgeon in an operating theater or a pilot in an airplane may consult with other members of the team before making an executive decision. A priest in an Anglican church might ask for advice from others, but they retain the authority to make final decisions in relation to liturgy. In contrast, the host of a *collaboration* has no more structural power than anyone else in the circle beyond their hosting role. The architecture of collaboration is a circle, and the host sits in the circle as an equal member of the conversation, along with everyone else. It is then up to the group to decide how it will make decisions and distribute power. Genuine collaboration is inherently nonviolent, because it is about doing things *with* people rather than *to* them or *for* them.

To return to our metaphor of the dance between power and love, the *heroic* leader decides on what the dance is going to be and, if they are a male in a ballroom dance, will largely control the choreography. A *hosting* leader takes a different approach. Having noticed that something is changing in the environment, the hosting leader creates conditions where a group can figure out the way forward together, drawing on the collective intelligence of the group.

Hosting a collaborative dance is not dissimilar to community theater, where a small team will collaborate with a community to conceive, design, script, and enact a piece of theater in which members of the community may also become the actors. Let us now look at the main aspects of this collaborative emergent design process.

SUMMARY

Collaboration is about fostering creative and safe conditions where shared understanding can lead to shared commitment to address complex challenges.

REFLECT

1. Read Margaret Wheatley's reflection "Leadership in the Age of Complexity: From Hero to Host" (see bibliography for its availability

on the web). Does my current style of leadership tend in one direction more than another? Does this depend on the circumstances? What are the costs and benefits of my leadership style for me and my community?

2. To what extent is my church or organization tapping into the collective intelligence of the church and broader community, in relation to complex challenges we are facing? What is my evidence for this?

15

Collaborative Emergent Design

STRUCTURING THE DANCE

LET US IMAGINE SOME COMMON scenarios in the life of any organization. Something or someone has disrupted the peaceful functioning of the system. Perhaps an angry young person has burned down a church;[1] or a virus has struck, and, virtually overnight, people cannot meet as they used to; or changing demographics in an area has resulted in decreased membership and financial giving, resulting in finances no longer being able to sustain existing infrastructure costs such as buildings and salaries. These are examples of external factors that disrupt our system.

There could also be internal disrupters. Formal leaders sometimes need to compassionately disrupt a system that has ossified. A compassionate disruption might be catalyzing a compelling vision and/or redrawing previous boundary conditions. For example, the church in Australia has gone through significant external disruption over the last fifty years as society shifts to a post-Christian society. An internal compassionate disruption could be a bishop deciding to enable creative new structures that are better adapted to contemporary missional needs. Disruptions can vary in scale and complexity. For example, the disruption might be:[2]

- Simple—there is a leak in the roof, which needs to be fixed

1. I mention this dramatic example, because I personally know of two situations where this happened.

2. This four-factor diagnostic framework is called Cynefin. David Snowdon created it.

- Complicated—we have discovered asbestos in the roof
- Complex—a church is faced with closure or major restructuring
- Chaotic—a pandemic has occurred

The nature of the disruption will shape the response needed. We do not need to engage in a hosting style of leadership for every decision. Collaborative group process is not needed for simple or complicated disruptions. For a *simple* disruption, an authorized person will decide and act (we do not need a committee meeting to change a light globe). For a *complicated* disruption, we may need to engage specialized consultancy advice and apply a best-practice engineering solution (a car engine that stops working is a complicated challenge, but it will yield to the appropriately skilled investigation). If a disruption is *chaotic*, the immediate crisis needs to be stabilized (lockdowns during the COVID pandemic were an example of restraining an exponential growth in sickness, which would have chaotically overwhelmed health systems).

The place for Collaborative Emergent Design process comes into play to address *complex challenges* (sometimes called *wicked problems*). Complex challenges have some or all the following features:

- Multiple stakeholders—individuals or groups
- Different strongly held beliefs, needs, or aspirations
- Urgency
- Unclear cause/effect linkages—we discover the nature of the problem only as we start to solve it
- High stakes—you get only one go to construct a new building, bridge, or freeway
- Social complexity—how people act is less predictable than how a machine operates

Complex challenges are surprisingly common, and yet leaders commonly make the mistake of applying mechanistic (simple problem) or best-practice (complicated problem) responses to what are extraordinarily complex questions, which, amongst other things, includes the unpredictability of human relationships. This can result in anger, frustration, and conflict, because people instinctively sense when a simple response to a complex challenge is being thrust upon them. One reason for this error could be related to an overestimation of the importance of individual experts and an underestimation of the complexity of the system and the capacity of a self-organizing system to deliver high performance outcomes. The latter is possible only if we allow the system to self-organize rather than tightly controlling it.

I once facilitated a meeting in which the sponsor of the meeting, an engineer, understood the problem of applying simple solutions to complex challenges. The sponsor therefore took a different approach. In addressing a problem that had previously proved intractable over a lengthy period, when viewed through engineering lenses alone, she decided to expand the group of people involved to include government policy makers, politicians, investors, environmental specialists, indigenous community leaders, and interested community members. This diversity gave rise to rich new insights and the development of promising collaborative relationships.

Even at the level of everyday decision-making, formal leaders may fail to recognize the underlying complexity of any system where people are involved. Even constructing an inanimate object like a bridge happens within the context of a local community and ecosystem. If we do not bring the complex interests of affected people into dialogic engagement with each other, divergent voices will inevitably go u*nderground* in the form of subversive hallway, elevator, and water-cooler conversations. Such conversations are frequently characterized by nitpicking, passive-aggressive behaviors, and scapegoating.

Having discerned that a disruption, question, or issue is complex, the next step is for the leader to initiate a Collaborative Emergent Design process. Emergent design creates the *conditions*, both human and technological, to develop *shared understanding*, leading to *shared commitment*. I have outlined the main principles below. This framework for Collaborative Emergent Design is significantly influenced by Harrison Owen's work on Open Space Technology and self-organizing systems.[3] I have been experimenting with Owen's work for many years, and what follows both validates and fleshes out his work, with additional material and anecdotes from my own experience. The idea is not to replicate these principles as mechanistic steps but to think about how the principles might apply to a particular complex question with which we are dealing.[4]

3. Owen, *Wave Rider*.
4. Much of what follows represents the personal experience of myself and colleagues road testing across hundreds of facilitated meetings. The process draws on Owen, *Wave Rider*; Holman, *Engaging Emergence*; and Scharmer, *Theory U*. All these

(i) Invite an initial coalition of the willing

The seed of an idea, which later becomes a collaboration, often begins in the mind of just one or two people. Have you ever had the experience of sharing an idea which you are excited about with someone else, and the other person's eyes glaze over? You know within seconds that the other person is simply not interested. But you talk about it with someone else, and their eyes light up and they become excited. Do not expend time and energy trying to sell something, especially if people's eyes are glazing over.[5]

Developing collaborations comes from inspiring interest through *invitation* rather than hard *sell*. If we have enough of these exploratory invitational conversations, we will find a small group of willing participants. If we do not, then we might need, with all humility, to reassess if the idea is viable. Jesus once told a parable about a person who sowed seeds. Jesus sowed seeds of a vision called the kingdom of God. Some listeners were not interested; some were interested but quickly got distracted by other things; and some got excited and received the vision, and it grew.[6]

When Jesus says "Where two or three are gathered in my name, I am there among them" (Matt 18:20), I think Jesus is saying something about the Spirit working through the relational process of being human. Perhaps he is even speaking to the pitfalls of individualism and heroic leadership. Just as God is a communion/relationship (Trinity), so all our work done in Jesus's name will be relationally constituted. To express this in more colloquial terms, "better together," or "two minds are better than one—three even better."

So, if we have an idea we are enthusiastic about, the first step is to find others who may be similarly interested and create a small coalition of the willing.[7] An ideal initial size for a coalition of the willing is around four to seven people, but it might take some time to even get to that number. Initially, it might just be two people yarning over a coffee. Working together

---

writer-practitioners take a natural living systems approach and, most importantly, have extensive on-the-ground experience of doing the work and not just talking about it.

5. Jesus counsels his disciples at one point, "If anyone will not welcome you or listen to your words, shake off the dust from your feet as you leave that house or town" (Matt 10:14).

6. Matt 13:1–23; Mark 4:1–20; Luke 8:4–15.

7. I am keen to reclaim this excellent phrase, in the service of nonviolence, from George W. Bush who infamously used it in relation to the Iraq war (2002).

provides many practical benefits, including mutual encouragement and support, as well as developing important shared understandings around identity, intention, and the principles of collaborative engagement.

(ii) Clarify identity (who) and intention (what)

A primary role for leaders is to help groups to develop a shared understanding and articulation of the group's identity and purpose. *Identity* can sometimes feel a bit nebulous; it's hard to pin down. I have found that a sense of shared identity often comes from storytelling about shared experiences. As well as personal storytelling, a key role for formal leaders is to hold the feet of the community to the fire of the shared story (gospel, in the case of churches). Just as we can talk about our own personhood only by sharing stories about our relationships with others, the same is true of the identity of a group. What brought us together? What trials or adventures have we been through? What do we care about? Who or what do we belong to? The Scriptures, preaching, and teaching are, at their best, constant reconnections with founding stories. Saint Paul makes a significant statement of identity when he says to the church, "You are the body of Christ and individually members of it" (1 Cor 12:27).

In the context of a faith community, *intention/purpose* typically has a sense of vocation. It often feels like something that we *must do*. Abraham is called to a new land, Moses is called by the divine voice out of a burning bush to lead a group of slaves out into the desert, Jonah is called to Nineveh, Samuel is called by a quiet voice in the night, the prophets are called to speak a word of judgment and hope to Israel, Jesus is driven by the Spirit into the desert and then calls others to follow him to Jerusalem. The first apostles are called by the risen Christ to announce his resurrection and invite others into his life. Saint Paul is called to be an apostle to the gentiles. The church is called to repent, believe the good news, heal, forgive, make disciples, baptize, teach, forgive, receive the gifts and fruits of the Spirit, be ministers of peace and reconciliation.

We might protest that these purposes are doable only by extraordinary people. But the Scriptures go to great length to point out that God's call is frequently to very fallible people. King David, purported to be the greatest king of Judah, was an adulterer who sent his rival to his death. Peter, the first bishop of Rome was, at one point, called 'Satan' by Jesus. St. Paul oversaw the persecution and murder of early followers of Jesus. The

character of spiritual vision is that it is always a new possibility emerging from God's resurrection future and unfolds through love. It has the character of an in-breaking and out-flowing life. The way a *coalition of the willing* discerns and expresses its intention will be based on the discernment of emergent life rather than getting fixated on problem-solving for personal survival. As Peggy Holman says, we are being invited to take responsibility for what we love as an act of service to the world.

One of the ways of framing this approach in secular language is "appreciative inquiry." This phrase was coined by David Cooperrider. Cooperrider had been an organizational consultant who at one point was hired to diagnose why the performance of a company was dropping. Rather than asking what is not working here, he decided instead to structure his interviews with staff around what was happening when they were performing at their best—to track the flow of life in the system. To his surprise, the performance of the company started to improve even before Cooperrider had presented his report. This led him to the thesis that *organizations move in the direction of the questions we ask*. If we frame questions in the negative (e.g., how we fix a problem), we may well make the problem worse. But if we ask questions about what is working and build on this, the system will move in the direction of its best self.[8]

In framing a clear intention, we are stalking the flow of God's resurrection life and fanning the emergent flames of possibility. Or as Jesus puts it: "Do not worry about what you will eat and drink, but strive first for the kingdom of God and his righteousness, and all these [other] things will be given to you as well" (Matt 6:33). This is particularly important for those in churches to recognize, since it is so easy for our agendas to get driven by problem-solving such as stressed budgets and leaking roofs. Such questions may be important, but we need to locate them in relation to bigger aspirational intentions.

Harrison Owen says that a key job of leaders is to use story to cast vision. When faced with crisis, organizations sometimes ramp up demands on their beleaguered members by more stridently telling them what they *should* be doing. That does not work very well, because nobody likes to be "should-ed" on. Storytelling is a more effective approach for inspiring people.

Revisiting, reclarifying, and recommitting to *identity* and *purpose* on a regular basis contributes to strong and enduring communities. One

---

8. There are strong thematic correlations with assets-based community development and positive psychology.

of the by-products of liturgy is precisely this kind of remembering. Liturgy is an anamnesis (an antidote to amnesia). Remember whose you are and the good end to which you are called![9] People get reignited when they (re)connect to a powerful story, which gives shape and coherence to their lives and a visionary possibility of what might be, which is an outworking of that story. Collaborative Emergent Design does not start with answers, plans, or strategies that we try to impose on others. It is not a more sophisticated way of trying to get *other* people to change. Collaborative design starts with a shared story and a compelling vision of what could be possible. We then invite people to work together on the realization of that vision (the how-to).

As an example, I once worked with others on an initiative to bring a guest from another country for a series of speaking and facilitation engagements. We began our work by sitting in a circle and sharing responses to the following questions:

- What is my interest in this project? What do I like about the idea? How does this idea resonate with my values?[10]
- Is this idea consistent with the core vocation of our existing community, or is it sufficiently different that we would need to auspice it under another name/structure?
- What are we trying to achieve?—purpose/intention
- What gifts/talents/interests do I bring?
- How much time (or other resources) can I contribute?
- What do I know about myself which could get in the way of our shared work together, that I need to declare? What do I want others in the group to do if they notice me doing this?
- Who else do I know might be interested in this idea?

When visiting the Taizé Community in France, I heard a story (which I have not been able to verify) about the founder, Brother Roger.

---

9. The essential and often neglected question in churches about purpose inevitably invites us into deeper epistemological reflection about how we discern truth (the leading of the Spirit). This may also lead us to reflect on which of our beliefs or commitments are primary/central and which are secondary/peripheral.

10. For the Christian, this question could include "How does this resonate with our purpose as a church?" The second and third degrees of humility in Benedict, *Rule*, ch. 7, invite us to consider if we are being obedient (hearing) to the loving will of God.

When Brother Roger arrived in the small French Village of Taizé before the Second World War, he initially prayed on his own in the little old village chapel for five years before he was joined by another brother. The pair grew to a handful of brothers. The initial circle of prayer kept growing, and now, a hundred years later, there are close to a hundred brothers, and the community is visited by five thousand young people a week, in summer, from all over Europe. This is an inspiring example of the fruit of clear identity and purpose, and the work of the Spirit.

(iii) Clarify the boundaries

After getting sufficient clarity of purpose, the initial coalition of the willing will want to expand the circle of interest and engage the energy and contribution of a broader group of people. Before doing this, it is advisable to articulate any relevant constraints (boundary conditions). In short, what is up for grabs, and what isn't? Boundaries help provide focus and direction. As discussed above, the first and primary boundary condition is the shared intention. *What do we care to do together and invite others to join us in doing?*

Typical boundary conditions (constraints) for collaborative meetings in churches might include:

- The convening theme/question—which then shapes which subsequent conversations are central and which are peripheral
- Clarity about whom we are inviting—restricted invitation or open invitation? (For reasons that we will explore below, open invitations have many advantages in dealing with complex questions.)
- How we will raise money/resources? (For example, one church set a boundary condition that all operating costs for the church needed to be raised from the giving of parishioners rather than external fundraising.)
- Clarity about how we will assign local decision-making authority (what decisions can be made, and within what financial constraints, without coming back to the parish council)
- Credal statements or articles of faith
- Statutes and policies (government or ecclesial)

This work of clarifying boundaries can be quite delicate. If we draw the boundary too tightly, it can quash the new life of the Spirit. Saint Paul says, "Do not quench the Spirit. Do not despise the words of prophets" (1 Thess 5:19–20). The more we unconstrain a system, the more potential creativity is unleashed. If an existing boundary (say, within an institutional system) will not allow the emergence of new life, there is nothing to be accomplished by getting angry and frustrated it. Rather, it might be possible to create a new enabling structure. Such a structure might be short-term, just for the life of a project, or long-term. I have a friend who started a contemplative prayer community. It eventually become quite large. Because the style of prayer could not be accommodated within the boundaries of the existing church structures, the community decided to create a new legal entity for governance purposes while retraining a harmonious relationship with the original church.

On the other hand, if a boundary is too loose, then the system can lose energy, direction, and focus as it becomes detached from its founding story. Some people may feel nervous about whether primary identity/purpose is being compromised. Saint Benedict's third degree of humility,[11] in which monks are to submit to authority, is an example of a boundary condition that not only nurtures humility in the exuberant but also maintains unity and cohesion in a community.

There is one more important piece of boundary-setting that the convening group needs to do. This is to decide how to decide. Collaborative process is always navigating a delicate balance between top-down and bottom-up decision-making and authority. If there is too much top-down power, then *responsibility* becomes split from *passion*, and we are no longer collaborating. But if we insist on absolute consensus for all decisions, the system can lose its momentum and turn into endless talk with no action, which can be an evasion of responsibility to act. There is no right way of making decisions, but the question of *how* decisions will be made is also a collaborative decision in the first instance. Then we need to communicate this clearly to anyone who is being invited. Options for decision-making include:

- Complete empowerment and authority are given for people with passion to make their own decisions and implement what they are passionate about

---

11. Benedict, *Rule*, ch. 7.

- Empowerment and authority to act is given but with a mechanism for sub-sections to meet regularly for coordination and resourcing purposes
- Consensus decision-making—everyone must agree on all substantive points
- Majority vote
- Delegation of decision-making to a group-endorsed person or small group
- Sociocratic decision-making—collaboratively naming and dealing with any compelling objections before moving to a good-enough decision

(iv) Check cultural blind spots

The collaborative frameworks and tools that I describe in chapter 16 are highly transferrable across cultures, because the geometry of the circle is so universal and the principles are adaptable enough to allow for cultural distinctiveness. However, it is always worth being attentive to our potential cultural blind spots. Some cultural aspects that may need careful consideration in collaborative work include:

- How an invitation to participate is extended—if groups are coming that have traditionally been in conflict with each other, one-to-one conversations may need to be held with groups to ensure they understand the nature of circle process and are comfortable (enough) with what will happen, rather than just relying on a written invitation.
- Starting time—with some communities, particularly Aboriginal groups, the meeting may not start before certain elders have arrived.
- Sponsor's welcome—who has authority to welcome and speak first?
- Warm-up—in some cultural settings, it will be necessary to dedicate a fair bit of time at the beginning of the meeting to allow people to introduce themselves in terms of place and family.
- Symbols—it is quite common to have a symbol in the middle of a circle to represent the focus and intention of the meeting. Because

symbols can evoke historical narratives, containing emotional load, the symbol needs careful selection.

- Authority vested in the facilitator—it is important that the facilitator and the sponsor (host) have shared understanding on the facilitator's role and who will make what decisions in the unlikely event that a meeting needs to be suspended.

(v) Expand the circle: invitation to collaboration

Once the coalition of the willing feels it has a coherent sense of its shared story, intention, and any relevant boundaries and cultural factors, the next step in the Collaborative Emergent Design process is to expand the circle to a broader group of people who will contribute to the expansion of the vision/intention and bring it to life. We start to move from the *who* (identity) and *what* (intention) to the *how* of implementation. As mentioned earlier, collaborative process is commensurate with complexity—where we have a challenge or opportunity that is too big for any one person or group to accomplish alone. We collaborate when we *need* or *want* others to partner with us, not just because we think it is a *nice* thing to do. If we can do something alone, like changing a lightbulb, we do not need to collaborate.

Regrettably, with human control needs being what they are, we often *underestimate* the complexity of systems and therefore how much collaboration is desirable and necessary. At this point, we may fall into a trap for the unwary, which is to mistake *consultation* for collaboration. A consultative mindset keeps us firmly in control of what happens while convincing ourselves that we are being collaborative. Sometimes, we hear these two words being used as synonyms in organizations. This might fool the formal leader but leaves others feeling annoyed and frustrated. You may have heard yourself or others in an organization say, "They (management) ask us our opinion, but they have already made up their minds."

A useful indicator of whether we are collaborating or consulting is where decision-making power resides. The definition of leadership in a collaborative system is *passion (without which no one is interested) combined with responsibility (without which nothing happens).*[12] In a consulta-

---

12. Paraphrase of Owen, *Open Space Technology*.

tive process, passion and responsibility are split from each other. Person *a* (management) asks person *b* (staff) what they are passionate about. Person *a* then takes this away and makes executive decisions about what is important (responsibility), which then gets unilaterally declared and pushed back down to person *b* to enact, regardless of what person *b* may think about the wisdom of the delegated action. Sometimes, consultation is appropriate. But if so, be honest about it, and do not pretend we are collaborating.

With complex challenges and collaborative partnerships, the power relationships are more horizontal than vertical. For example, a colleague of mine has worked on a major infrastructure project involving an alliance of ten private companies. The power relationships between the alliance partners are mainly horizontal, even though the alliance as whole is accountable, vertically, to the government. In this situation, the vertical interface between the alliance partners and the government occurs through a management group that has representatives from the different alliance partners. In churches and community groups, participants in the collaborative process are typically not employees, and there is no legal power to give orders to people. In this situation, power relationships are also horizontal, and things happen only because people voluntarily agree to collaborate. Results happen when those with the *passion* for doing something also exercise *responsibility* for making it happen.

Therefore, when we are doing Collaborative Emergent Design, we are asking ourselves, "Who has leadership (*passion* and *responsibility*) to contribute?" In deciding how to expand the collaborative circle, I found Marvin Weisbord's acronym AREIN[13] to be helpful in brainstorming potential invitees. We sit in front of a white board and ask who has:

- Authority to make decisions—having decision-makers present can save time later
- Resources to contribute—money, infrastructure, energy, ideas, time
- Expertise in the areas to be considered
- Information that no one else has
- Need to be there—because they will be affected by decisions made (e.g., clients, suppliers, etc.)

13. Weisbord and Janoff, *Don't Just Do Something*, 17.

The aim of this is to diversify the group beyond the regular participants. If we keep putting the same people in a room together, we can expect to get similar results (which might be fine, if you are happy with the results you are currently getting). Based on the principle of a natural living system, the more diversity in the human ecosystem that we can get together, the more interesting and creative will be the outcomes. As an analogy, a permaculture garden gives rise to more species and plants than a monoculture garden.

However, we need to go one step further. In wondering about who has *passion and responsibility* to contribute, part of the answer to this question is that we don't entirely know. This is where we can usefully apply the principle of the open invitation, making it possible for anyone to attend who wants to be there. We might not know why a particular person has shown up, but they do and often offer surprising new insights.[14]

I once saw a lovely example of emergent leadership in an Open Space in a large independent school, attended by ninety people. The topic was related to how to foster positive and supportive relationships between students and cut down on bullying. A third of the group were parents, a third staff, and a third students. When it came time to post the agenda, a twelve-year-old student walked confidently into the circle to convene a conversation about why this single-gender school (for over one hundred years) should become coeducational. While she did not prevail in changing school policy, on that occasion, it was a striking example of providing a space for smaller voices to be heard.

In another Open Space, the convening question was about how to stop the fracturing of families and the removal of children from their parents during the first two years of life. The meeting was jointly sponsored by three large non-governmental organizations (NGOs) that provided care to families and children. About one hundred people attended, including parents who had experienced removal of their own children into state care, government agencies, service providers, and other interested persons. It would be difficult to imagine a more complex and emotionally charged issue.

Parents and government agency representatives sat in circles sharing highly personal stories (note the difference here from a consultation

---

14. This is particularly true in church and community-based meetings where we wish to optimize the potential for community partnerships. In other organizations, it may be less feasible to have completely open invitation, for reasons of space, cost, confidentiality, or other reasons.

process, in which service providers would have more likely been separated from clients by a third-party consultant). Much grief was expressed. By the end of the day, there were about thirty people left in the closing circle, undoubtedly related to the emotional intensity of the conversations. Professional counselors had been on hand during the day to support people if needed but, to the best of my knowledge, were not called upon by participants. When empowered with the Law of Two Feet, people demonstrate an impressive capacity to self-regulate their emotional engagement rather than be protected from strong emotions by well-meaning facilitators.

Day 2 of the meeting opened with ninety people. Conversations continued, and action plans were developed. In the closing cycle, participants spoke about how the process had enabled them to engage with and withdraw from difficult conversations as they needed to, how mutual understandings had grown, and how useful it all was for the development of better policies and practices between clients, government, and service providers. The participants launched a dozen new initiatives, including new collaborative processes between NGOs and hospitals.

The invitation to this expanded circle of collaboration will contain the main components of what has been discussed above:

- The name of the sponsoring person or person—the core *coalition*
- The convening theme—the expression of *intent/purpose* of the collaboration
- Background/context—how the intention fits within our *core story/identity*
- What the group is asking of participants and what will happen next—decision-making, authority, and action planning
- Logistical details—when, where, RSVP

(vi) Sit in a circle and cocreate an agenda

The circle is the architecture of collaboration. It signifies in a physical way that we are all in this together, and everyone's contribution is valuable. The circle is also the heart of dialogic practice. The word *dialogue* comes from two words, *dia* (across) and *logos* (meaning). The power of a good dialogue is to *create meaning in the space between us*. This is a different dynamic than debate, which aims to prove that we are right or have the best answer to a problem. Debate can be useful to rigorously test the logic of ideas and plays a part in evidence-based science as well as in the law, when trying to discern a communal agreement on what constitutes fact or objective truth. However, as we have noted, one of the features of complexity is that there may be different epistemological and hermeneutic assumptions to navigate. There are also multitudes of potential ways of getting to an outcome, and each of those ways is affected by the diverse needs of stakeholder groups. To use the earlier example of building a freeway, the engineering science may be quite clear; but how does a community put a value on a threatened species of bandicoot whose habitat lies in the path of the freeway, or the meaning to an Aboriginal community of a songline[15] or sacred site? Rather than a debate between two proposals, a complex scenario may give rise to hundreds of concerns in a group. The only process that is adequate to this kind of complexity is the self-organizing capability of the natural living system itself.[16]

Fortunately, we have some well-tested circle processes available to us, which can create effective conditions for dialogue (shared meaning-making) through the power of self-organization. These processes are *inherently nonviolent because of the way in which they structure out rivalry and structure in* the possibility of cooperation (see appendix D for a longer explanation of how the design of dialogic circles structures in peace by mitigating mimetic rivalry).[17]

---

15. In Australian Aboriginal cultures, a *songline* is a highly sophisticated oral technology that can serve multiple purposes, including mapping local identity, meaning, history, geography, identifying cultural sites, and navigation.

16. A strength of synodical processes in the Anglican Church, which are conducted using parliamentary conventions of debate, is that it is possible to bring large numbers of people (often 500+) to a decision point. This is useful for simple or complicated issues. However, when debate is used to try to engage highly complex questions, it frequently fails to cope with the complexity. We inevitably end up making decisions at the cost of creating winners and losers who may remain in unresolved conflict with each other.

17. I am choosing to focus on just two processes because of their robustness and flexibility for use in a wide range of situations, including churches. To locate these processes within many group methodologies, see Holman, *Change Handbook*; the free app by Holisticon AG, *Liberating Structures*; and Scharmer, *Theory U*.

Talking Circles

One simple and yet powerful process for circle dialogue is the *Talking Circle* (sometimes called a Listening Circle). People have been sitting around campfires in a circle for centuries talking about what they care about. In the university in which I work, I notice at lunchtimes that students sit on the lawns with their friends, naturally self-organizing into small circles. The Talking Circle simply formalizes this fundamental human conversational configuration around a key question or theme. Commonly, a Talking Piece is used. This is an object that participants pass around the circle, enabling each person to speak without being interrupted by anyone else. Before the Talking Circle commences, the facilitator explains the principles of engagement and requests the group's consent (see appendix E).

The architecture of the circle and the shared commitment to the use of the Talking Piece create conditions of respectful speaking and listening and equalize power in the group by preventing persons with more structural power from shutting down people by talking over them. Talking Circles are generally structured in a way that parallels the epistemological lenses being used in this book:

- Heart—gathering, recalling attention to the intent of the circle, introductions, background stories, where we have come from, what has drawn us to this circle, commitment to the use of the Talking Piece
- Head—exploration of issues and opportunities in relation to the specific focus question(s)
- Hands—decision-making about next steps, who is doing what and by when

In a Talking Circle, it is not always necessary to create an agenda before the meeting, because the agenda emerges as the Talking Piece is passed around. However, if the group wishes to structure its thinking, there is a simple self-organizing way of doing this. When it comes to the exploration of issues and opportunities phase of the circle, participants may be invited to write questions on separate pieces of A4 paper (using brightly colored markers). Participants put these in the middle of the circle, where they are clearly visible to everyone. The group members then all contribute to moving the pieces of paper around on the floor so that related questions are clumped together thematically. The Talking

Circle then proceeds as normal using the Talking Piece, with the added benefit that the group now has developed a shared sense of the territory which the group will be covering.

The careful preparation and structuring of a Talking Circle create conditions of participation safety in which honest and respectful speaking and listening occur. Otto Scharmer summarizes three aspects of this deep listening, all of which are commonly observable in a Talking Circle, given sufficient time:[18]

- Open mind—speaking the truth as I see it, rather than what I think others want to hear, and seeking to understand the views of others. This is listening from the perspective of *my* story, while recognizing the potential truth of other stories. The opposite of the open mind is *preemptive judgment* (I am right, so I don't need to listen to you).

- Open heart—hearing the deeper truth of others, at a heart level, including underlying concerns and values. This also involves listening from the perspective of *our* story—being alert to patterns and themes that are emerging. We try to feel concerns that we share. The opposite of the open heart is *cynicism* (listening like this is a waste of time, and I don't really trust these people anyway).

- Open will—coming to a place of stillness, where we know we need to let go of the past to receive something new that is bigger than our constituent parts and individual ideas. This convergence cannot be forced by anyone, and, when insight emerges, it typically evokes both surprise and delight. The opposite of open will is *paralyzing fear, domination, and control* (theologically, "*my* will be done" rather than "*thy* will be done")

The Talking Circle process is being used increasingly in schools, restorative justice, peacemaking, community development, mediation, conflict management, and church leadership.[19] Just a few examples of Talking Circles that have been held in church and chaplaincy contexts are:

---

18. Scharmer, *Theory U*, 40.

19. For a detailed elaboration on the principles and mechanics of hosting a Talking Circle, see Baldwin and Linnea, *Circle Way*. The Art of Hosting network is also doing excellent work with dialogic circles, including offering training. See http://artofhosting.org/.

- Debriefing a responder team following the death of a student in a university residential college
- Helping workplace teams to review what is working well, areas of friction that the groups want to address, and refocusing goals
- Supporting a group to name their grief, tiredness, and what was sustaining them after months of COVID lockdown
- Bringing people together in a parish to talk about human sexuality at the time of debates in Australia about same-gender marriage
- Developing relationships and shared understandings among members of a newly elected parish council
- Bible and book studies where the Benedictine Lectio Divina process was combined with a Talking Circle process
- Grief support for a group of work colleagues who had experienced a series of deaths of family and friends
- As a regular way of structuring a community of practice of professional colleagues

One of the lessons of the COVID lockdowns is that Talking Circle conditions can also be created in an online (Zoom) environment. The mechanism for doing this is to create a simple PowerPoint slide with the names of all the participants illustrated in the shape of a circle. The facilitator screen-shares the PowerPoint slide with the Zoom participants, and an imaginary Talking Piece is passed around the virtual circle. Extra fun can be created by inviting participants to select their own personal Talking Piece and hold it up when they start speaking. Participants are asked to say "finish" when they have finished speaking.

The Talking Circle is very functional with small numbers (less than twenty) but can become quite time-consuming as numbers grow. One way of managing this is to divide large groups into smaller groups of six to ten. I was once involved in such a meeting with ninety clergy. We arranged the group into circles of ten, each with a trained circle facilitator. When numbers are large, and/or when we are trying to create even greater degrees of self-organization, I recommend using Open Space Technology.

Open Space Technology

Open Space Technology (OST) is a process devised by an Episcopal priest, Harrison Owen. Open Space has been used in hundreds of thousands of meetings in all continents and across all cultures. Harrison Owen conceived Open Space after noticing that the most energetic conversations in conferences occurred outside the preplanned sessions—in other words, during coffee times and meal breaks. Anyone who has ever been to a conference can relate to this. It is in these informal spaces that people have conversations about things they care about, with whomever shows up. Relationships are established, business cards get exchanged, and future actions get decided, all without any formal control or facilitation. The question that occurred to Owen was how to design a conference that was 100 percent coffee break (oral tradition says that he did this in twenty minutes over a couple of martinis). The self-organizing principles that we observe in a typical coffee break include:

- Conversations are convened by people with passion and responsibility
- Whoever comes are the right people—trust that whoever shows up has something to offer
- Whatever happens is the only thing that could have happened—trust what emerges
- Whenever it starts is the right time
- When it's over, its over
- The Law of Two Feet—leave the conversation if you're not contributing or learning

In the same way as a Talking Circle, Open Space begins with everyone sitting in a circle (or, in the last of large meetings, in concentric circles). However, the agenda of the meeting is created in a different way. Instead of everyone staying together in the same circle, which is impractical with large numbers, participants write conversation topics on pieces of paper and post these on an agenda wall. The wall is structured as a grid with multiple time slots and breakout spaces. When this is completed, participants self-organize into the conversations that they want to be part of and use The Law of Two Feet to move freely between spaces. This creates a buzz of high engagement and creativity. Towards the end of the allocated time (typically anywhere between a half-day and three days), the same self-organizing process is used to create action-planning groups. The advantage of the Open Space process is that it is scalable to large groups (meetings of two thousand to three thousand people are possible) and is a process that enables an organization to deal with remarkably high levels of complexity and conflict.

As a newly ordained priest, I spent the first five years of my ministry producing what I thought were good ideas (i.e., answers) for all the wonderful things that our little struggling communities could do to revitalize. I had great ideas in worship, Bible studies, prayer groups, and connecting to the local community—one idea after another. All of these were consistent with the core kingdom-vision of the Christian community. The congregations in which I worked were endlessly patient and supportive with what I was putting before them. Nothing seemed to shift. I started to feel depressed and a failure in my leadership. My bishop was encouraging and assured me to press on faithfully. The problem was, in hindsight, that the ideas were mine. I was unknowingly stuck in a heroic mode of leadership.

Then, one day, I noticed some patterns starting to occur in my conversations with different people in different settings. In an experience similar to what Carl Jung calls synchronicity, I found in conversations I was having with people that the theme of community gardens kept popping up. Several people, completely unknown to each other, were saying things like "Wouldn't it be great to have a community garden in our suburb." Someone suggested that we could start a prototype garden on the church block and one day even extend across to the piece of disused land, owned by the local shire. It would have been so easy for me, as the parish priest, to go into heroic leadership mode and try to thrust this excellent idea on our patient parishioners. However, I had recently been introduced to Open Space Technology and its principles of collaboration. Rather than treat a community garden as an answer, plan, or objective, we decided to treat it as a lightly held *intention*. Ten people got together and formed an initial coalition to explore the idea. We subsequently convened an OST meeting and cast the invitation as widely as possible in the broader suburb. In short, people responded. Community passion combined with responsibility.

Twenty years later, the community garden that emerged out of that Open Space meeting is still a thriving part of that local community. Many people got involved, including the shire, local schools, residents, refugees, ex-prisoners, and art-funding bodies. It has waxed and waned and gone through different iterations of self-organizing leadership. This is an example of emergence in a self-organizing system. The mood is characterized by a vibrancy of spirit and a detachment of anxious ego.

More recently, in the diocese in which I work, an Anglican parish convened its annual two-day parish camp in Open Space format. Seventy people attended, with thirty conversations and nine action plans convened. At the end of the meeting, the parish priest outlined a mechanism for getting formal endorsement from the parish council. The role of the parish council was to encourage, enable, and support the action initiatives and help with how the new initiatives could be coordinated with existing programs through ministry team leaders.

In another case, in 2019, the Anglican Diocese of South Queensland convened the first full day of its annual synod in Open Space around the question "What is God calling us to be and do?" Imagine four hundred and fifty people sitting in concentric circles, with no preplanned agenda (a very courageous act on the part of the bishop and his diocesan council). Within an hour of starting, participants had convened sixty-five conversations and had got to work. At the end of the day, nineteen action plans were convened and next steps decided. Many participants observed that the opportunity to engage in wide-ranging conversations, including a number on issues of conflict, created a more settled atmosphere in the second day of synod, which was conducted in traditional parliamentary style.[20]

Open Space Technology offers the following advantages in the context of dealing with high complexity:

- Keeps passion and responsibility connected—rather than having responsibility taken out of the hands of people who care the most
- Mitigates blind spots (things that experts don't know that they don't know)—through the principle of open invitation
- Creates conditions of peace by structurally mitigating mimetic rivalry and scapegoating (see appendix D)
- Optimizes networked communication by bringing as much of the system as possible into one place at the one time
- Diminishes the tyranny of controlling individuals and empowers quieter voices

20. Interviews with participants can be viewed at https://anglicanfocus.org.au/2019/09/23/synod-2019-open-space-insights/.

- Dissolves organizational silos
- Provides a safe container for high conflict
- Enables collective (sometimes called *hive*) wisdom to emerge

(vii) Wait for coherence to emerge and pivot to convergence

Diverge to dialogue; converge to commit
As we have seen, dialogue is a process of *making meaning between persons through* speaking and listening—the delicate dance between power and love. We have also seen how we sometimes get thrust into the need for effective dialogic process because the system has become disrupted by an external event (or because we choose to initiate a compassionate disruption from within) and the challenges are sufficiently complex that we *need* to collaborate.

For whatever reasons, we have opened the circle, conversations have been convened, and people are at work. This is the *divergent* phase, where multiple parallel conversations are occurring, and it might seem, initially, that there is no pattern or similarity between the conversations. As an Open Space facilitator, I have occasionally had a nervous sponsor come up to me partway through a meeting and say, "People don't seem to be talking about what they are *supposed* to be talking about." This is partly a pointer to the sponsor's own control needs (the group is talking about exactly what it *needs* to be talking about), but it's also a legitimate desire by the sponsor to get to action and outcome. So, as a meeting sponsor or facilitator, how do we know when a group has talked enough and we need to invite the group to commit to action?

To some extent, we make an assessment in the design phase about how much time needs to be allocated to the divergence phase. The general principle is that the more people, complexity, or conflict are present, the more time is needed. To create genuine space for dialogue, rather than just an *appearance* of space, an Open Space meeting requires anywhere from a half-day to a full day for most meetings. However, the existence of high complexity or conflict nearly always demands two or even three days. If a Talking Circle process is being used, it may be necessary to schedule several meetings over a period (sometimes referred to as a sustained dialogue). If the host does not allocate sufficient time, the group will not be able to process the complexity of the topic and/or their depth of emotional load and will most likely leave frustrated and annoyed.

The divergence phase provides time and space for the expression of strong emotion and for exploring issues that are personally important. Until this work is done, people are not psychologically ready to commit to actions for the future. However, at the right time, the group will be ready to pivot to action. The signals that a pivot point is approaching can include:

- Strong emotions witnessed early in the meeting are starting to settle
- No new topics are being posted
- Themes in conversations are starting to repeat

At this point, it is usually time to invite the group to convene action-planning conversations. This is called the convergence or commitment phase. It is typically associated with lots of positive energy, because the group is psychologically ready to move to action.

I once observed this process unfold over a period of about three months in a sustained dialogue process in a university setting. A staff working group was coordinating the development of a significant strategy to address the underrepresentation of women in the science, technology, engineering, math, and medicine (STEMM) disciplines. A traditional consultative approach would have involved putting together a small task force of specialists who would then survey/consult a range of stakeholders before developing a plan and submitting it for approval. However, the sponsor wanted to take a more collaborative approach, in which the women who would be most affected by such a plan would be actively involved at every stage of its development, from conception to approval to implementation.

The sponsor established a small steering group (coalition of the willing) to clarify intention. The steering group then hosted an Open Space meeting for a full day. Anyone who was interested could attend, from the vice chancellor to students. About ninety people attended. Instead of pivoting to action on the day of the Open Space, the steering group collected the group-report notes and worked with a facilitator who was experienced in a process called issue mapping.[21] This process identified about eight key emergent themes from the Open Space, along with preliminary issues and opportunities. The third step involved another

---

21. Issue mapping is outlined in Culmsee and Awati, *Heretic's Guide*.

half-day meeting to which anyone from the original Open Space was invited. The eight themes were posted on walls in various parts of the room, and participants could freely move between the themes (Law of Two Feet) to flesh out the implications and practicalities of each theme. Participants could also add a new theme, if they felt something important had been missed. This collaboratively designed material formed the main content of a project submission that was approved by senior management (some of whom had been present at the Open Space) and implemented by those who had been involved in the design.

(viii) Prototype: fail forward

With action plans constellated, another key role for formal leadership comes into play. For collaborations to be effective, we need to continue to keep passion and responsibility linked as closely as possible. Yes, there usually needs to be coordination of activity, but sponsors need to give action-plan leaders sufficient resources and decision-making authority to move ideas forward, without being tightly controlled from above. This is called *unconstraining* the system, and it can be a challenge for organizations that are used to a command-and-control approach.

Because this relaxing of constraints can activate deep organizational immunity to change, it is best to not try to change organization-wide policies before acting; otherwise, nothing will happen. Rather, it often works to frame new initiatives as *prototypes*—small pilot projects, which can be given special conditions (such as temporary exemptions from standard policies) as well as permission to fail without threatening the entire organization.

I witnessed a fun and effective example of prototyping while facilitating for a very innovative training and development company that had about twenty staff. The whole team went to a house in the mountains for a residential Open Space meeting. The theme of the weekend was to develop new market niches/opportunities. The executive team had flagged that they would make two seed-funding grants available after the Open Space for developing prototypes. This sent a strong message that the company was serious about creativity and innovation.

After a full day of exploration of ideas (divergence), the convergence phase on day 2 involved the group deciding on three new project possibilities. The criteria were that projects needed to have "energy (passion)," "impact," and "do-ability." The commercial and practical potential of the projects was fleshed out, by the participants, over a couple of weeks before being presented to the board that selected one of them for prototyping. Within six months, this initiative had resulted in the acquisition of a major client, a doubling in the size of the company, and the opening of international operations. The sponsors commented that a weekend of Open Space had provided a good return on investment!

(ix) Establish minimum necessary structure to sustain spirit

No one puts new wine into old wineskins; otherwise, the wine will burst the skins, and the wine is lost, and so are the skins; but one puts new wine into fresh wineskins (Mark 2:22).

When we are developing a new initiative, the initiative is going to need an enabling structure to support momentum. Structure includes such things as people with the requisite skills, motivation, and time; equipment; communications infrastructure; bookkeeping, banking, and cashflow; action-reflection coaching support; and legal compliance. None of these needs to be elaborate, but we need to consider them all, so that initiatives are sustainable.

When an organization has been operating for a long time, its structures may be maladapted to current circumstances. For example, over time, organizations tend to develop rafts of policies and procedures that were originally devised as useful quality assurance or risk-management devices but that are not well suited to being lean and adaptive. If we try to squeeze spirit into old structures, we can kill (human) spirit. Because structures and policies are frequently so hard to change, it is sometimes useful to experiment with parallel pathways that will enable spirit rather than working against it.

I know of one church community that has replaced traditional planning processes with an annual Open Space Technology meeting to which everyone is invited. The sponsor summarized it by saying, "What happens at the Open Space is our plan for the next year." After the Open Space meeting, a member of the parish council meets with people who convened action-conversations to discuss what enabling structures will be needed, issues of coordination and communication, and what simple financial support and reporting is required. This places members of the parish council in more of a coaching role than a command-and-control role.

In another case, a previously large congregation became smaller over time. The parish treasurer, who had been doing the job for twenty years, became increasingly tired, because she wanted to give up the job but did not want to resign unless someone else stepped up to the job first (this did not happen). When an intentional interim minister arrived, she was able to help the congregation to see that they had an "enabling structure" challenge that needed to be resolved. In the absence of any volunteers, the parish council decided to hire a part-time administrator to take over bookkeeping as well as most administrative compliance requirements being generated by the denominational office. This was liberating for everyone.

(x) Support people who are grieving

Death is a natural feature of all natural living systems. Christians proclaim the "resurrection of the dead and the life of the age to come."[22] Hence, we do not need to be afraid of death. We don't need to keep organizations on endless life support. Life support systems for churches can include shoring up unsustainable systems with grant funding or refusing to draw the necessary boundaries that would catalyze transformational change. I once heard the abbott of a Benedictine monastery being interviewed. He was asked whether he was worried about how his previously large monastery, with two schools attached, now had only six brothers and no schools.[23] The abbott observed that, over the centuries, monasteries go through life cycles. They close in some places and open in new places. We could apply the Open Space principle "When it's over, it's over."

One of the painful responsibilities of people in formal leadership roles is to declare end of life and bury something that is no longer viable. Leaders may *avoid* doing this for several reasons. Sometimes, it's because we, as leaders, don't want people to dislike us. Sometimes, it's because the organizational end-of-life conversations are painful and likely to evoke strong reactions. Sometimes, a reluctance to act is theologically justified, in terms of hope that things will get better. However, quite often,

---

22. Nicene Creed.

23. In this case, the decline was not due to poor leadership but changing demographic conditions over a fifty-year period.

everyone knows that a life needs to end, and they are just waiting for someone to take responsibility to lead them through the grief process.

Organizational grief work has similarities to individual grief work when a person physically dies. For example, it could involve inviting people to come together to:

- Tell the story of the origins of a ministry
- Celebrate what has been achieved
- Reflect theologically on death, resurrection, and hope
- Ritually place symbols of thanksgiving
- Celebrate the Eucharist
- Have a wake/party

One church with which I worked in a rural area had four properties. Two were standing empty, one had a semi-regular Sunday congregation of five persons, and the main center had twenty regular attendees. The congregations realized that the economic demography of the areas was changing. As small family farms were taken over and aggregated by corporate agribusinesses, the population of rural towns was decreasing. Congregational members started to ask questions of legacy, such as "What is the best way we can leave something for our grandchildren?" Rather than unilaterally closing churches and selling property, the central church body hosted a series of Talking Circles and Open Space meetings, where members of the community could come together to explore options. They realized that their old building, built for a congregation of three hundred people and sitting on land now worth many millions of dollars, and could be redeveloped through a partnership with a Christian mission agency to provide a smaller chapel, social services, and cash-creating rental property. This led to a sense of excitement about new possibilities rather than their previous despondency about declining numbers.

(xi) Review and reiterate

Someone (I forget who) has said that organizations start as *movements* of the Spirit, progressively morph into *machines* (complete with ossified structures, systems, policies, and procedures), and finally become *monuments*. When an organization becomes detached from its identity, purpose, and environment, it will face a crisis. The crisis will either precipitate a reconnection to passion and purpose, with associated adaptive restructuring, or result in death. This is a feature of all natural living systems.

Organizations need regular processes of collaborative review to intentionally reflect on connection to identity and purpose and to reassess whether the enabling structures are fit for purpose. We can have a whole bunch of highly inspired or highly dispirited people and still not be *aligned* in shared understandings and shared commitments. We tend to make ungrounded assumptions that everyone is happy or is happy about the same things. Creating review-and-reflect spaces is designed to bring *hallway and elevator conversations* into the open. Examples of review-and-reiterate meetings are:

- Conducting Talking Circles with newly elected parish councils to grow relationships and to develop shared understandings on purpose, roles, and responsibilities (a church I know does this as a weekend residential retreat each year)
- Conducting an annual Open Space Technology meeting for the whole congregation to review and refocus ministries
- Conducting structured Talking Circle review meetings annually (and whenever else is required) in existing home groups to check on what is working well and where people may have buried things they need to talk about
- Regular structured coaching and/or professional supervision conversations with ministry team leaders

Collaborative Emergent Design principles do not always unfold in the linear order described above and will typically go through repeated cycles of reiteration. One example of this has been the development of a Peace and Nonviolence Education network.[24] The network was inspired by a papal statement on peace (*connection to identity*). A small group (*coalition of the willing*) began to explore an *intention/purpose* to develop and make available peace and nonviolence education resources to teachers in Christian-based schools in Australia and New Zealand. This group collaborated with an Anglican school system to *develop and prototype* a ten-lesson religious education (RE) unit. This was aided by some grant funding (*enabling structure*). The *review* principle included

---

24. See www.peaceandnveducation.org

getting feedback from staff and students who did the prototype unit. The *reiteration* involved hosting a national *Open Space Technology* meeting and inviting RE teachers and representatives of school systems interested in peace education, to which about fifteen persons came.

A *second reiteration* occurred with another national Open Space gathering one year later, to which forty people came. In each reiteration, the steering group applied the same basic principles of Collaborative Emergent Design to *expand the circle of interest and engagement*, with local variations and new initiatives emerging. After three years, four school systems, across five Australian states and New Zealand, were involved. All this was achieved by enthusiastic staff contributing time and energy from within their existing workloads, along with a small amount of grant funding. At the time of writing this book, an *enabling structures* question is emerging about what will be necessary to support long-term development. This example shows the iterative nature of collaborative design, which frequently moves more like a circle than a straight line.

SUMMARY

If a question, challenge, or opportunity is complex, then it invites (if not requires) a Collaborative Emergent Design approach.

REFLECT

1. Do the steps in the Collaborative Emergent Design process make sense to me? What questions emerge for me?

2. What is a complex challenge or opportunity that is calling my attention? With whom could I share my thoughts? From there, whom else might we invite to a conversation? Extend an invitation, and use the Talking Circle process to develop clarity around identity, intention, and next steps. Once these things are clear, expand the circle of interest by:

    - reading Christina Baldwin and Ann Linnea's book *The Circle Way: A Leader in Every Chair*. What opportunities can we see to experiment with hosting a Talking Circle on something we care about?

- reading Harrison Owen's book *Open Space Technology: A User's Guide*. What opportunities can we see to experiment with hosting an OST meeting about something we care about?

16

Conversational Frameworks and Tools

LEARNING THE DANCE STEPS

THE PREVIOUS SECTION OUTLINED THE broad principles of Collaborative Emergent Design, which enable a community dance to be collaboratively choreographed. To this foundational choreography, we can add a range of specific dance steps (skills of dialogue) that enable us to move fluidly between power and love. These will make the dance even more enjoyable and with less risk of injury to each other on the dance floor. This chapter describes a range of these tools and frameworks that groups can use in the interests of enabling conditions of peace.

FIVE-STEP NONVIOLENT CONVERSATION STRUCTURE

This five-step conversation structure[1] is a versatile framework for planning a conversation when there is conflict (emotional load) or dispute (a difference of fact or opinion over what has happened or what should happen). With sufficient practice, we can apply this process in the heat of the moment, if we need to respond immediately to a demanding situation.

---

1. From the Pace e Bene Nonviolence Service (https://paceebene.org); also adapted by Brendan McKeague. This framework has parallels to Gervase Bushe's structuring of communications in *Clear Leadership*: the Aware Self (parallel to steps 1 and 2), Curious Self (parallel to step 3), and Descriptive Self (parallel to step 4).

(i) Observe what is going on inside myself in response to what I am observing in my surroundings.

This step requires me to pay attention, in the first instance, to what is happening in my body in response to an external stimulus—particularly one that I may interpret as a threat. As we discussed in part 2 (contemplation) our perception is a complex interaction of affect (body), emotion, and story. Generally, my body will *tell me* when it is sensing a threat. The threat may not necessarily be a *real* danger to me; it might just be that one of my internal survival or belonging needs has been activated.

Noticing what is happening in my body, especially when I am afraid or angry, is the first step to acting nonviolently rather than automatically *reacting*. Even before I utter a word, it might be that I have broken into a sweat, stopped breathing, or slumped in my chair. Everyone's reactive patterns are unique. Automated reactions might include getting angry (fight), getting tongue-tied (freeze), or avoiding certain people or situations (flight). None of these strategies will serve loving relationships well.

> *Reflect*: When I am in a conflict with someone, what is going on in my body? Be as specific as possible about where and how in my body my reactions show up.

(ii) Center myself

Once I have noticed the reaction in my body, the next step is to find my strong internal equilibrium point. If my emotional energy is high, then I need to put myself in touch with a place of support, strength, or peace within myself that will help me in this moment of reaction or confusion. I need to find a *circuit breaker* to my body's physical reaction. I need to connect with my own nonviolent values and act from there, rather than getting mimetically trapped in the emotional state of others who, within themselves, might be feeling angry or afraid. If I have the luxury of preparation time prior to a conversation, then doing careful inner work can also contribute to my centering (appendix A).

> *Reflect*: What helps me to relax and recenter my body when I am stressed? As I do this, does it change the way I am thinking about the situation?

(iii) Listen to the truth of the other

Listening to the other person can be quite difficult, if a person seems determined to insult, abuse, or hurt me. Nevertheless, it is what I need to learn to do, if I am to understand why another person is behaving the way they are and/or to care for myself. I can develop my skills in this regard by practicing regularly in situations of low threat. Demonstrating to myself and the other person that I am listening may include:

- Not interrupting the other person
- Asking questions of clarification
- Recognizing that what I am feeling may be an intuitive mirroring of the other person's feelings—e.g., if I am feeling angry, then it might be that I am picking up the other person's anger
- Summarizing (paraphrasing) what the other person has said or may be feeling before trying to assert my own position.

> *Reflect*: Listening to the truth of another requires me to make an intentional mental shift into a mood of genuine curiosity about what is going on in the other person's universe. If I am currently not happy with an aspect of a relationship with someone and want/need to improve it, is there anything I can get curious about? What genuine questions might I ask the person about what life is like for them? (Note that steps 3 and 4, "Listen to the truth of others" and "Speak my own truth," are interchangeable, depending on the situation.)

(iv) Speak my own truth

Speaking my own truth requires at least two things. Firstly, I need to know what my own truth is. Any sense of my truth might be buried under years of family/social conditioning, such as what is *polite/appropriate* to say. Have I prepared myself to speak my truth without demeaning or accusing the other person? Speaking my truth might include:

- Naming how I am feeling about something that has happened rather than criticizing, accusing, or attacking the other person. In conflict situations, we may be dealing with a lack of conversational competency rather than maliciousness. When a person hears about the impact of their behavior on me, they may be surprised and even grateful that I have pointed this out.[2]

- Making transparent my underlying assumptions about my truth sources and claims. A key communications challenge that has been emerging in recent years is the loss of shared agreements about what constitutes fact. As trust in fact-verifying institutions erodes, and avenues for the rapid promulgation of alternative truth claims increase (social media), I might find myself talking at cross-purposes with someone, simply because we do not share an agreed reference point for establishing facts. If I spot this happening in a conversation, I may need to drop down to a deeper level of curiosity about how the other person is forming their view of reality. In some cases, I might need to declare, "I believe this (fact) to be true based on . . ."[3]

- Making clear requests about what I need from others to care for my needs or making clear offers to others about how I might care for their needs.[4]

- Making declarations about what I am going to do next within my own authorized sphere of influence. This could be personal decisions related to my own life or decisions affecting others, if I am in a position of authorized decision-making, such as a parent, manager, teacher, umpire, judge, arbitrator.

---

2. Saint Benedict provides guidance in his tenth and eleventh degrees of humility (*Rule*, ch. 7), where we must be particularly careful not to humiliate others but be gentle in our communications.

3. Daniel Kahneman (*Thinking Fast and Slow*) has demonstrated through extensive research how what initially seems most obvious is not necessarily true—hence the need for rigorous research and published peer review in science. Some of Kahneman's and other writers' work is summarized in a readable abbreviated form in McRaney, *You Are Not So Smart*. A variation on "truth sourcing" in church contexts includes differences in hermeneutical assumptions about how to interpret the Bible. Someone sayin, "The Bible says . . ." can be a dialogue stopper unless the dialogue partners are willing to exchange their deeper suppositions about *how* they discern truth in Scripture.

4. Alan Sieler's work on linguistic acts offers an extremely useful toolbox for using language effectively. Sieler proposes that all spoken language falls into six categories: assertions (facts that can be grounded in philosophically sound rules of evidence and communally accepted authoritative sources); assessments (opinions, feelings); declarations (a statement of authority, such as an umpire saying "the ball is out of bounds"); promises; offers; and requests (Sieler, *Coaching to the Human Soul*).

> *Reflect*: Think about a conversation I need to have. Would the questions in appendix A be useful as a guide to get clearer on what I want to say in the conversation?

(v) Discern a larger truth

A larger truth is something that transcends the initial starting points of the persons involved in a dialogue. A larger truth is an emergent property of the dance between power (speaking my truth) and love (being open to the truth of the other[s]). We should not reduce this *emergent* truth to just a negotiated settlement where each person reluctantly agrees to trade off parts of their own interests. Rather, an emergent truth typically has the character of genuine surprise, novelty, and gift.

This bigger truth does not necessarily mean that we need to walk away as best friends or that we have even agreed on our points of difference. We might end up agreeing to disagree, or suspending, or even ending a relationship that continues to be abusive or manipulative. Or, we may agree that we need some outside assistance to help us move forward, such as engaging a facilitator, mediator, or arbitrator. I may need to withdraw my cooperation, my collusion, or my tacit approval in situations that remain unjust. Even though there may not appear to be an immediate, successful outcome to the listening and the speaking, there is always the possibility that something will emerge, as seeds sown during a dialogue take root and sprout in their own time. That is the gift of hope that participants in a genuine dialogue[5] can offer each other.

A structural variation on the five-step structured conversation is called "A Coaching Approach to a Conversation." This applies the same principles of moving between power (speaking) and love (listening), within the context of a coaching model. See appendix F for an example of how to structure a conversation in this way.[6]

---

5. A genuine dialogue is where parties enter in good faith to speak their own truth and listen to the truth of others. This is different from bargaining where participants may intentionally hide truth and/or engage in strategic gaming. If I find myself in such a situation, I may still choose to engage nonviolently (I am in control only of my own actions and responses.)

6. In "pure" coaching, the agenda of the conversation is set entirely by the client, with the coach helping the client to clarify the client's situation, explore options, commit to action, and then reflect on that action later. However, this structure can also be

> *Reflect*: If I am entering a conversation with someone, and I notice I am attached to getting a particular result, could I trust that the dialogue might give rise to something surprising emerging—something that could serve both me and the other persons involved? Could I give myself permission to relax my strong grip on winning?

THE TWO HANDS OF NONVIOLENCE

In this book, I have maintained that we can think about nonviolence in terms of *loving power in action*. Nonviolence is not pacifism before violence but a loving response to violence, as we assert a nonviolent, creative alternative to dominant powers. As such, nonviolence includes a strong no to abusive or intimidating power directed towards us, like Jerusalem closing her gates against an invading force.

> Praise the LORD, O Jerusalem!
>   Praise your God, O Zion!
> For *he strengthens the bars of your gates*;
>   he blesses your children within you.
> He grants peace within your borders;
>   he fills you with the finest of wheat. (Ps 147:12–14)

Nonviolently maintaining our personal or communal boundaries against aggression is one way of loving ourselves *and* our neighbor. Martin Luther King Jr. constantly asserted that a community based on principles of respect and dignity, regardless of race (the kingdom of God on earth), was not only beneficial for victims of injustice but would also be a humanizing gift to oppressors, through which such oppressors would regain their dignity.

One way of symbolizing this dynamic of loving, nonviolent assertion is through the symbol of two hands.[7] Imagine myself standing in front of someone who is hostile towards me. Imagine holding up one hand with my palm facing towards the other person like a stop sign. This

---

usefully adapted to everyday supervisory conversations where a supervisor/manager/leader needs to introduce their agenda into the conversation while also creating an effective space for listening and learning.

7. This exercise originates from Pace e Bene Nonviolence Service.

signifies a firmly and calmly held boundary against abuse, whether emotional, spiritual, or physical. While continuing to hold that hand up, I put my other hand in front of me with my palm facing upwards and oriented slightly towards the other person. This signifies "Even though I will not accept your violent behavior towards me, I commit to treating you with fairness and dignity and not imitating your aggressive behavior towards me" (theologically, this could include the intention "I want for you what Christ wants for you").

A colleague, who facilitates Open Space Technology meetings in a country where there has been a history of significant violence between disputing parties, told me a stark story about necessary boundary-setting. When these parties come together to meet in Open Space, the meeting convenor makes a clear stipulation that no guns can be brought into the room! Creating a level of participation safety is a necessary precondition for dialogue.

> *Reflect*: Is there a person who is pressing into my boundaries of safety and dignity and with whom I want or need to have an ongoing relationship? I could practice the two-hands exercise in a quiet space on my own. What did it feel like? Did the exercise result in any new thoughts on how I might engage with this person in my next conversation with them?

CREATION OF THIRD-WAY ALTERNATIVES

One of the dynamics of violence is that it is frequently framed in terms of a binary win-lose outcome—sometimes expressed as a zero-sum game (I win only if you lose; I can only be right because you are wrong). When situations are set up as a binary, there is an increased risk of escalating mimetic rivalry as we mirror each other's desire to win. We have seen how dialogic processes such as *circle work* (groups) and the *five steps* (one-to-one conversation) open the possibility of emergent outcomes that transcend the initial positions of participants. This can include the creation of third-way collaborations involving all parties or creating entirely new parallel pathways.

A powerful example of the creation of a third-way alternative comes from sixth-century Europe—a time that had similarities to our own. Benedict of Nursia, the son of a nobleman, was concerned about the deeply troubled times in which he lived following the breakdown of the Roman Empire. His initiative was to create an alternative way of living in the form of monastic communities, driven by a law of simplicity, work, and prayer. Benedict established twelve monasteries within his lifetime, and the number expanded rapidly in subsequent years. These monasteries became hubs of community, learning, agriculture, and health care and have significantly influenced the development of European culture and civilization for over a thousand years.

> *Reflect*: Are there any situations in my life right now where I am stuck in a binary win/lose situation? What third-way alternatives might be possible? With whom could I start a conversation to explore such possibilities?

REFLECTIVE PRACTICE

An essential contributor to the practice of peace is reflective practice, particularly for persons in formal leadership roles. A good reason for engaging in reflective practice is that doing any work in situations involving interpersonal conflict will certainly activate some of the unconscious or semi-conscious dynamics that we touched on in part 1 (touchstone 2) namely, interpersonal mimetic rivalry and shadow aspects of the psyche, including survival and belonging needs. Learning to spot how these dynamics show up in our relationships and how we deal with them is a type of mindfulness practice that can save us from acting, unconsciously, in ways that cause harm.

Professional supervision uses reflective practice, and it can also be used in professional coaching and in communities of practice. Reflective practice has a long history in the military, in the form of the after-action review (AAR) following military exercises or actual combat. In civil aviation, pilots and copilots commonly do after-flight debriefs to pick up even the smallest aspects of what could have been done better. At its simplest level, reflective practice involves asking questions like "What happened? What did we learn? What would we do differently next time? What changes do we need to make to systems to structure in improvements?" Christian groups will wish to add questions that provoke theological reflections. See appendix G for an example of a template for a reflective practice conversation.

> *Reflect*: What might be the value to me and others, for me to engage in reflective practice in a more intentional and disciplined way? With whom might I partner to do this work?

RESTORATIVE GROUP CONFERENCING

In part 1, we reflected on how God's justice is restorative rather than punitive. God repairs harm by liberating humanity from the rivalrous violence and destructive internal mindsets of scarcity and fear that are so destructive of human relationships. God, through love, heals deep grief and shame associated with fractured relationships with God and other people. Regrettably, our justice systems are oriented almost entirely towards punishment, particularly for adults. I was speaking to a criminal justice lawyer recently about the situation of a teenager who had been involved in the perpetration of a serious assault while under the influence of drugs and alcohol. The offender had also been subject to violence as a child, which had led to mental illness. The community's needs in a situation like this are best protected by combining high accountability with high support. The juvenile justice lawyer in this case said that youth justice in his state of Australia places high emphasis on, and mechanisms for, healing and repair for both victims and offenders. Research has shown that this leads to reduced recidivism and higher satisfaction rates for victims of crime.[8] However, the lawyer said as soon as a person is legally an adult (the day they turn eighteen), the system immediately shifts to punishment/deterrence. Due to a single determinative date on a calendar, both victim and offender are denied the possibilities for accountability and healing that come with a restorative justice approach.

Restorative justice invites us to a paradigm shift in which we reconceive harm as a *crime against the state, which needs to be punished*, to a

---

8. Restorative justice practice (RJ) came to Australia through youth justice family conferencing in the early 1990s, following New Zealand's work in 1988–1989. The New Zealand justice system has embedded restorative approaches in the form of pre-charge conferencing, and this has been expanded to adult criminal justice in many situations. In Australia, restorative justice varies from state to state but tends to be available only for juveniles. At a theological level, the early pioneers of restorative justice, such as Howard Zehr at Eastern Mennonite University, shaped their thinking about restorative justice based on the Christian understanding of justice as setting relations right, reconciliation, and forgiveness. See Dubler and Lloyd, "End of Punishment."

tear in the fabric of community relationships, which needs to be repaired.[9] Restorative justice focuses on the *harm* that is caused by crime and the *needs* in both victim and offender that flow from harm. It is based on three foundational principles:[10]

- Do no further harm.
- Work with people (rather than to or for them).
- Set relations right.

In a restorative group conference, everyone who has been affected by an act of harm comes together voluntarily in a facilitated meeting to explore three questions:

- What happened?
- Who has been affected and how?
- What is needed to repair harm, prevent recurrence, and reset (renew or release) relationships?

Because of the success of restorative justice in criminal law, the principles have now expanded into other areas, including family conflict, schools, and universities. In a school, for example, when a student is being disruptive in a classroom, a restorative approach would include the teacher talking privately with the child about the impact of their behavior on others, whether there are any background contributing factors, and what the child could do to set things right. Rather than assuming that the child is being intentionally naughty and needs to be punished, a deeper exploration may uncover hidden trauma, grief, loss, or something happening at home, which is leading to the student acting out their pain.[11]

The restorative justice movement has evolved over the years to move beyond only responding to harm. Practitioners have developed a range of group conference processes (founded on the basic architecture

---

9. The distinction is not always as clear cut. Courts can sometimes divert cases to RJ, recommend pre-sentencing conferences, or refer parties to optional post-sentencing conferences. The latter may take place months or even years after a conviction, when the persons involved are ready.

10. See Australian Association for Restorative Justice, www.aarj.org.au

11. This is called trauma-informed restorative practice. Regrettably, schools sometimes use restorative practices in a mechanistic way as just another form of behavioral control and punishment. Restorative practices in schools should ideally be located as part of a whole-school approach to relationship management, including for staff.

of the circle), which also serve the proactive purposes of *developing* and *maintaining* relationships.

Restorative practices are demonstrably effective *practices of peace*, grounded in the theological principles outlined in part 1. These include:

- God's justice understood as setting relations right
- Peace understood as a communal state of harmonious relationships (shalom)
- Personal accountability through truth-speaking
- Creating conditions for personal accountability (repentance)
- Creating conditions for repair of relational harm (healing)
- Creating conditions where forgiveness may emerge
- Loving our neighbor—including our enemies (not necessary to like them but to create space for them as fellow humans)
- The making of persons through conversation, especially difficult conversations
- Creating a community movement that offers a tangible alternative to demonizing and scapegoating[12]

This book was written not long after a major criminal trial in the USA following the murder of an African American man, George Floyd, at the hands of a white policeman. The murder was one of many where police and justice systems were accused of systemic racism, including disproportionate violence towards persons of African American origin. This fueled the international Black Lives Matter movement. Even though the police officer was found guilty of murder, it was recognized by many community leaders that finding one person guilty of murder, and having that person being punished, did not in itself constitute justice. In a short speech following the guilty verdict, Minnesota Attorney General Keith Ellison distinguished between the concepts of accountability and justice:

12. To find someone guilty of a crime and for them to experience consequences is not scapegoating as Girard defined it. However, a person who has perpetrated a harm/crime against someone can find themselves swept up in a broader scapegoating impulse in society if they happen to come from a particularly identifiable cultural group. This was a key point raised to greater consciousness by the Black Lives Matter movement. An indicator of a scapegoating mindset developing is the language used to describe persons. If language like "animals," "sub-human," or "nonhuman" is being deployed, it is easier for people to justify their violence.

I would not call today's verdict "justice," however, because justice implies true restoration. But it is accountability, which is the first step towards justice. And now the cause of justice is in your hands. And when I say your hands, I mean the hands of the people of the United States.[13]

This points to the need to listen more deeply to what people are wanting when they cry for justice.

The Anglican Diocese of Perth, in 2021, became the first diocese in Australia to embed Restorative Engagement and Alternative Dispute Resolution processes as the first step, wherever possible, for dealing with conflict and (non-child-related) harm in the diocese.[14] Previously, the default option was for people to make a formal complaint to a Professional Standards Unit,[15] which would need to investigate, make findings, and issue sanctions. The latter approach, by replicating similar conditions to a court, can create conditions of increased conflict, personal stress in all parties, minimal or no reconciliation and forgiveness, and virtually no relational learning.

> *Reflect*: Have I ever been involved in a situation that may have benefited from a well-facilitated restorative group conference, with voluntary participation, to explore the nature of a conflict or harm and collaboratively seek ways to put relationships right?

STRUCTURED APOLOGY

A frequent feature of a restorative conference is a formal apology for a harm caused. Most often, the apology will be delivered face to face as part of the conference. Occasionally, where there has been a major injury

---

13. Ellison, "Today's Verdict Isn't 'Justice.'"

14. A key principle of restorative practice is voluntary engagement by all parties and a willingness by parties to acknowledge the harmful impact of their behavior on others. Participants are not required by the process to admit any contravention of a law or policy. This reflects a key distinction in restorative practice between intention and impact. We may not have intended to do harm, but we did, in fact, hurt someone. A restorative conference creates conditions in which the nature of harm can be explored in a non-legalistic way.

15. Making a formal complaint is still available to those who do not wish to engage in a restorative process. The latter is always voluntary.

or crime, a harmed party may not want contact with an offender but will have signaled a willingness to receive a written apology.

A well-structured apology delivered soon after realizing the impact of one's actions can be healing and prevent escalation of conflict. On the other hand, a disingenuous apology can do more damage than good. An example of a disingenuous apology is to say, "I'm sorry you feel that way, but . . ." Such a statement expresses an avoidance of responsibility by the person making the apology.

Genuine apology starts with honest self-reflection. It requires me to acknowledge that my actions have had a negative impact on another person regardless of what I may have intended. A genuine apology does not demand that the other person respond in any way, including forgiving me. It will include some or all of the following components:

- Naming what I did
- Acknowledging the (probable) impact of my actions on the other (empathy)
- A simply worded, unqualified apology—not hedged with self-justification, not saying "I didn't intend to hurt you," not overdoing it with groveling, not requesting anything from the other person
- Indicating, where possible, that I have learned something about myself that could help prevent recurrence to the harmed person or anyone else
- If appropriate, offering a conversation about how I can make things right—but not expecting this will be taken up by the other person, just to make me feel better

> *Reflect*: Do I feel a need to make an apology to someone? Write out an apology using the above points as a guide. Practice saying it. How does it feel? Does it feel authentic? Keep tweaking it until it does. If in doubt, consult an independent third party. Remember: an apology does not have to produce any particular result. The exercise has its own value.

MANAGING INDIVIDUAL AND COLLECTIVE SHADOW

In part 2, I wrote about psychological *shadow* as those parts of ourselves that are inconsistent with our egoic self-identity, which may pop out and surprise us in relationally unhelpful and embarrassing ways. If someone acts in a very surprising and uncharacteristic way, it *may* be that an aspect of their shadow is showing up. How might we deal with this, if we are in a formal leadership or management role?

Firstly, we need to treat very carefully and very compassionately. We need to tread carefully, because eruptions of the shadow can precipitate a huge amount of emotional energy in a relationship. For example, if another person has an outburst of anger, it is very easy for us to mimetically reciprocate their anger. We also need to tread compassionately, because the other person might be feeling very vulnerable and possibly ashamed about their behavior (the same will be true of ourselves, if our own shadow has been activated). It is safest to approach a *possible* manifestation of the shadow at the level of observed behavior. Drawing on the five-step communications model described above, we are safe to start with *curiosity* (listen to the truth of the other).

For example, let's say a friend or colleague had a sudden outburst of anger in a meeting. We could catch up with the person, in a safe environment, soon after the meeting (so as not to publicly shame or embarrass the person further). We might say something like "I noticed you seemed very angry in that meeting. You're normally very calm, so I was surprised when you yelled at Jane. I am wondering if you are OK?" This could allow space for the person to talk through what was happening (internally) for them at the time. We might also have a conversation about what relationship repair with Jane may be needed.

As well as individual shadows, organizations can manifest a *collective* shadow.[16] An *organizational shadow* is an aspect of the collective story that people in an organization have placed off limits for discussion, either explicitly or implicitly. For example, if a group identifies itself through its *success*, then the group may not wish to entertain any discussion about its *failures*. Rather than address their collective failure, the group may instead choose to *blame/shame* an individual within the group. If an organization defines itself by being *loving*, then it may not wish to consider how it is *afraid* or *hateful*. The latter is a particularly perilous trap for

---

16. Refer to Hollis, *Why Good People*.

churches, because those of us in churches tend to develop strong internal narratives about being *nice*.

The practice of personal and corporate repentance is one mechanism that churches have used to address negative expressions of shadow, although churches have not necessarily used this psychological language. The challenges come when certain aspects of our shared life are so buried in the shadow that we cannot even name them sufficiently to be able to repent.

There are simple practices that we can build into our shared life to identify and mitigate negative manifestations of personal and collective shadow:

- Do a *check-in* at the beginning of all meetings. Begin with one minute of silence, during which we invite participants to pay attention to their breathing and/or listen to the sounds around them. Then go around the circle and invite each person to briefly say how their energy level is (on a scale of one to ten) and whether there is anything that is distracting them, which they would like to acknowledge (and it is OK to say nothing). Do not go into problem-solving; just listen! This check-in process can help people to identify and acknowledge feelings and concerns lying just below conscious awareness, which, unless named, might reduce group effectiveness or, worse, break out in relationally unhelpful ways.

- Build in meeting protocols that make it clear to participants that dissent from the dominant group perspective is welcome. This can be done through intentionally asking questions like "Does anyone have a different perspective on this? What might we be overlooking? Would anyone like to propose an alternative? Does anyone have any reservations about the course of action being proposed?"

- Include a period of process-reflection at the end of team meetings. This means stepping out of the content of the meeting (issues and decision-making) and asking "How well did we work together in this meeting? Did we say what we wanted to say? How well did we listen when someone said something with which we disagreed?"

- Include a brief check-out round. Each person briefly says something that they are grateful for, a take-home insight from the meeting, and/or a personal commitment to action.

> *Reflect*: Can I recall a situation where my shadow was activated in an unhelpful or embarrassing way? Where might I have observed this happen in someone else? If the latter, how did I manage the situation?

> *Reflect*: Do I use any of the strategies described above in regular meetings (check-in or check-out processes, group learning questions)? If not, is this something with which I could experiment at a future meeting?

COMMUNITIES OF PRACTICE

A community of practice is a group of people who meet voluntarily to do action-reflection learning on an initiative or project of shared interest. Establishing a community of practice is also a wonderful way of mutually encouraging and resourcing people who are prototyping something new.

The underlying principles of a community of practice are entirely consistent with Collaborative Emergent Design principles. As with Open Space Technology, we form communities of practices out of a constellation of passion (what we care about) and responsibility (what work and learning we would like to do together).[17]

The university in which I work made grant funding available for groups of staff who wanted to develop new initiatives that would contribute to teaching and learning. One of these projects brought together a group from across the university, both academics and professional support staff, who wanted to explore the development of restorative practices to grow relationships and address conflict and harm in a more relational, less punitive manner. We used the Collaborative Emergent Design process described in the previous chapter to develop our work and expand the circle of interest. From an initial small group conversation, we grew a community of practice of eighteen persons. Over a period of a year, this expanded to a broader circle of interest of about seventy people, with many participants each taking small steps towards implementing restorative practices within their own spheres of influence.

---

17. On the nexus of caring, see Wenger et al., *Cultivating Communities of Practice*, 27.

> *Reflect*: Is there an area of my life/work that would benefit from support and shared learning with other people who are working on a similar area of interest? Could I invite some people together, sit in a circle, and explore what a community of practice might look like?

> *Reflect*: If you would like to learn more about how communities of practice work, a web search will provide sources of useful information.

DIALOGUING WITH THE PLANET

In this chapter, I have talked about how human systems are natural living systems. This raises the question about how human systems interact with other natural living systems of the planet and what it would mean to *give voice* to the planet in the process of human dialogue. Within the paradigm of a natural living system, humans are not separate from the ecosystem but are an integral *part* of it. Indigenous communities have a much deeper appreciation of these relational dynamics than the industrialized West, which has become increasingly disconnected from the natural environment.

Are there ways in which churches might reconnect with our own biblical traditions of being steward-gardeners of the natural world?[18] There is a fascinating story in the Gospel of John, where Mary meets the risen Jesus near the tomb. The text says, "Supposing him to be the gardener, Mary said . . ." Could it be that Mary was intuiting something about Jesus being the true human being, whom God commissioned to be a gardener/steward?[19]

Peter Hawkins, a leader in the field of team coaching, says that the inescapable context of all coaching conversations is the natural living system that sustains us. There is never a conversation in which a dialogue participant is *not* the planet itself. Hawkins has said that he will sometimes place an empty chair in a team meeting and ask people to

---

18. Gen 2:15.
19. John 20:15; Gen 2:15.

reflect on what the planet might be saying in relation to the topic of the conversation.[20]

> *Reflect*: In my family, community, or church, what place does the planet have in my thinking and conversations? How do I listen to the planet's concerns in my decision-making? Could one aspect of kenosis involve emptying ourselves of some of our acquisitive desires, in order to reduce our personal and communal environmental footprint?

DECOUPLING FROM SYSTEMIC MIMETIC DESIRE

In my reflection on mimetic desire (pt. 1, touchstone 2), I suggested how easy it is for us to get swept up into the desires of people around us. In the movie *School of Rock*, the main character, Dewey Finn (played by Jack Black), is a music teacher in an elite private school. Finn teaches the students that the basic ethos of rock 'n' roll is to resist "The Man," by which he means the dirty rotten commercial system that would have the students conform to the dominant values of their parents and the school system.[21]

Putting aside the irony of the students using the resources of their expensive school and becoming thoroughly enmeshed in the mimetic rivalry of a rock and roll competition, the movie is a lighthearted invitation to think about the nature of how the *system*, of which we are inescapably a part, shapes our desires. Saint Paul says in his Letter to the Galatians, "For freedom Christ has set us free. Stand firm, therefore, and do not submit again to a yoke of slavery" (Gal 5:1).

Part of a personal practice of peace may involve reflecting on how I may have become trapped in habits of acquisition and mimetically formed assumptions about what success means. Have such desires led to violence towards ourselves (anxiety or burnout) or violence towards others (using other people in an instrumental way for our own purposes)? The spiritual disciplines of *sabbath* and *asceticism* help heal the mimetic and addictive forces in us that underly violence.

---

20. I cannot find this in writing. Hawkins made the point in an online team coaching workshop run by the International Coach Federation in 2021.
21. Linklater, *School of Rock*.

> *Reflect*: Am I currently doing things that I find hard to give up? (Can I disconnect from social media for one day a week? Can I turn off my phone for a day? How financially indebted am I? What might it mean to materially simplify my life? What conversations would I like to start with my family or friends about this? What percentage of my net income am I giving away?)

NONVIOLENT DIRECT ACTION

Sometimes, dialogue and the creation of third-way alternatives can be difficult, particularly if there is a huge structural imbalance of power or a general lack of motivation by a large system to change the status quo (the current system seems to be *working* for the majority). In such situations, some people will feel called to engage in nonviolent direct action to raise consciousness of issues, educate people, begin a groundswell of changed behavior, or bring people with structural power into dialogue.

Direct action always has the potential to become violent, because there is a temptation to demonize and scapegoat the opposition. A distinctive positioning for the Christian activist will be how to engage in direct action while being obedient to Jesus's command to love your neighbor as yourself. Nonviolent direct action can be a form of what Walter Brueggemann calls the prophetic imagination, in which we reflect on the way we are shaping the world through the mind of Christ and the practice of peace.

Nonviolent direct action will always be focusing on the *issues* rather than demeaning *persons*. Nonviolent action creates conditions of moral dilemma for the system by revealing the unjust nature of a situation and forcing people to choose how they respond. Martin Luther King Jr.'s approach to direct action during the civil rights movement was to expand the orbit of love to try to win over (persuade) the opposition, rather than shut them down. Direct action sometimes has an aspect of strategic noncompliance, which enables people without structural power to embody the collective power of moral force.[22]

---

22. Babette Smith shares some entertaining stories about the way in which convict women transported to Australia utilized song, dance, and voice to maintain their spirits and resist some of the worst aspects of incarceration (Smith, *Convict Women*). See also the website of the Albert Einstein Institution, which lists 198 methods of nonviolent

The Love Makes a Way movement in Australia has been an example of a Christian nonviolent direct action, in which small groups of Christians have done strategic sit-ins at the offices of members of parliament to protest and raise consciousness about the treatment of asylum seekers. The group typically includes young and elderly persons (early twenties to eighties). When asked to leave by the police, the group refuses just long enough to require the police to charge them with trespass. They then politely make their way into waiting police cars while invited journalists record video for the evening news. The goal in this direct action has been to raise awareness of the issues without demonizing politicians or police.

> *Reflect*: What do I think of the ethics of nonviolent direct action? Can I imagine any situations in which I would be prepared to protest nonviolently and be arrested?

---

action, summarized from Gene Sharp's book *The Politics of Nonviolent Action*.

17

Conclusion
Joining the Dots

THE PEACE OF CHRIST OFFERS humanity something distinctively different and hopeful in comparison to the way the world commonly thinks about and practices peace.

Human cultures tend to think of peace as the absence of conflict, achieved by shoring up our tribal identities through expelling troublesome and disruptive persons. Humans have become adept at rationalizing violent peacemaking by creating narratives about the *other* as fundamentally disordered and lacking humanity. How do we know this? Because Jesus, the entirely innocent one, was a victim of this kind of collective victim-making, with its associated communal self-justifications. Both religion and state argued that it was expedient that one person die for the sake of the nation.[1] Jesus died for (on account of) our sins (violence). In light of the life, death, and resurrection of Jesus, we can perceive how violence is fundamentally a human problem—not unique to any group or religion. The myth of redemptive violence is still the dominant narrative in human cultures after two thousand years.

The peace of Christ offers a peace that the world cannot give, because it does not rely on the making of victims. Neither is the peace of Christ a kind of therapy that we use to cope better with and thereby normalize our individual or collective violence. Rather, the peace of Christ is God's cruciform love in action, drawing us into communion with God as

1. John 11:50.

an act of divine grace. God is simultaneously liberating us from violence and inviting us to participate in an existence governed by a nonviolent logic—the Logos (Word) of Christ.

This is not something we achieve by our own efforts. The Holy Spirit grafts us onto the pattern of God's inner life by way of kenotic (self-emptying) dying and rising. The path of peace therefore has a cruciform shape. The contemplative life and the practices of peace are our yes to God.[2] We not only think our way into a new way of being; we pray and act our way into knowing the God of peace ever more deeply.

Contemplative prayer is a kind of dying and rising with Christ. It is kenotic. In contemplative prayer, we notice and let go of our mimetic rivalries and deep-seated insecurities, which cause us to perceive other people as objects for our own wish fulfillments.

Collaborative Emergent Design and the skills of dialogue are also a kind of dying and rising with Christ. Through the design of the processes themselves, we structure out, as far as possible, mimetic rivalry and structure in deep and respectful communal listening (love) and clear, intentional, humble, loving service of the world (power).

All three aspects of our perception—the way we think about God, the way we pray, and the way we engage in communion with each other—work together in a cycle of positive reinforcement (see appendix H).

The amazing thing is that it is precisely through God's complete physical immersion in the vortex of our disoriented desires, and becoming a victim of them, that God nonviolently reconciles it all—all the mess and the goodness of the human condition.

The death and resurrection of Christ are not an afterthought by God to clean up an unforeseen catastrophe but reveal, within our space-time, the loving, kenotic pattern of the inner life of God's very being. God was, is, and always will be Christlike. God is drawing all creation to God's self. Like the love of a parent for a child, this love is covenantal—irrevocable.

So where does this lead those of us who constitute the church? I carry a quiet hope that Christian communities might be places where every member is on a lifelong journey of practicing peace, not just because it seems like a good idea, but because peace is the very nature of God, and because, in practicing peace, we become more fully human. Imagine a church that:

- Loves in a cruciform way

---

2. 2 Cor 1:20.

CONCLUSION

- Is shaped by the desire of Jesus
- Is a place where everyone can be at home
- Is a sign/pointer to the kingdom of God and an anticipation of the new creation
- Envisages justice as setting relations right
- Is experiencing deliverance, forgiveness, and joy
- Practices Christlike peace
- Is living non-anxiously, because we know that, in the end, it is all in the hands of the Christlike God

This is a vision gifted to us by Christ. It might sound like a big vision, given the human frailties of the church. I do not think I am being an ideologue. God will work in and through our frail dust. We will always fail, and, hopefully, we will extend forgiveness to each other for doing so, just as God forgives us. If we want to practice peace more intentionally as the central vocation of the church and are open to this journey, we can be confident that the Prince of Peace will lead us along our various roads to Emmaus.

Imagine the church throughout the world as constituting an *international academy of peace*, focused on the Christlike God, shaped by contemplative prayer, and practicing the art of dialogue. This could be a small contribution that Christians could make to the world. I hope and pray that this book might be useful as a resource for the journey. If you are not sure how to start, start small. Take the next small step. Invite a few people together. Sit in a circle, and get to work.

Appendix A

The Inner Work of Planning for a Conversation

IS THIS MY CONVERSATION TO HAVE?

1. Is this my conversation to have, or have I been drawn into a triangle between two other people who need to sort it out between themselves?
2. Is this a battle worth fighting? Would I feel resentful or guilty if I let it go?

DOING MY INNER WORK

1. How am I feeling? (angry, anxious, happy, sad, afraid)
2. What do these feelings tell me about what I value, need, or want?
3. Is this person "pressing buttons" (touching my shadow) related to my life scripts?
4. Has this person become my rival in some way? (possessions, position, power, influence, control, to be right)
5. How attached am I feeling to getting my own way?
6. How am I sometimes like those things that I dislike in the other person?
7. What is at stake?
8. What is not negotiable, and on what would I be prepared to be flexible?

9. What has been my contribution to any conflict that has occurred?
10. What might the Christlike God want in this situation? For me? For the other?
11. After meditating for twenty minutes, have my feelings or thoughts changed?
12. Has this person harmed me in some way that I would like to be acknowledged?
13. Do I need to declare a 'no' to a particular behavior?
14. What do I want from this conversation? Is my primary intent to nurture the relationship, to get shared understanding/commitment, or to coordinate action (or some combination of these)?
15. Have I given this person sufficient benefit of the doubt?
16. How might this person be suffering or in pain?

SPEAKING MY OWN TRUTH

1. What do I want to declare?
    - about what I've been thinking and feeling
    - about my underlying concerns, values, needs, or desired outcomes
    - about the impact of not having the conversation (the impact on me, on my relationship with the other person, on the organization)
2. What do I want to offer to support the other person?
3. What do I want to request from the other person to get my legitimate needs met?

LISTENING TO THE TRUTH OF THE OTHER

1. What am I curious about in relation to the other person's situation or view of the world?
2. What do I want to ask to understand the other person's view of things?

Appendix B

The Inner Work of Forgiveness

1. Describe the pain, grief, anxiety, bitterness, vengeance, anger. Let a loving inner gaze (either our own or Jesus's) fall on the range of emotions without needing to change or fix these emotions. Ask myself, "What did I want from this relationship that has been lost and might never happen?"
2. Work through any "bargaining" fantasies I have been carrying (e.g., I will forgive you *if* you do *x*). While it may, in some situations, be appropriate to request restitution, do an honest assessment on the limits of my capacity to compel restitution or the other person's willingness or capability to deliver it.
3. Do an honest assessment on my own contribution to the injury, including whether I have been withholding forgiveness in order to "punish" the other person.
4. Ask myself, "Am I genuinely ready to forgive?"
5. Ask for God's grace to help me to forgive. Wait for the gift of compassion to begin to rise within me—compassion for myself and compassion for the other person.
6. As compassion arises, can I consider the possibility that the other person was limited in their capacity for love through their life circumstances (while remembering this is not an excuse for their actions)?
7. Do I want to declare parameters or limits to my future relationship with this person? For example, I may decide that I want no future contact, or contact might be limited to certain durations, locations,

or in certain company. What supports from others will I need to hold these boundaries?

8. Do I want to declare forgiveness in person? In writing? Or by a personal ritual such as writing a letter to the other person and then burning it? (This might be needed where physical contact is dangerous, not logistically possible, or if the other person has died.)

9. If there are several people affected, do I want to explore the possibility of a restorative group conference for collective repair of harm?

10. Could there be value in sharing these reflections and my planned next steps with a trusted listener?

Appendix C
The Dialogic Dance between Power and Love

Power without love is reckless and abusive, and love without power is sentimental and anemic. Power at its best is love implementing the demands of justice, and justice at its best is love correcting everything that stands against love.

—MARTIN LUTHER KING JR.

POWER WITH LOVE	LOVE WITH POWER
Power *with* others Unattached advocacy Clear intention/direction Intention aligned with shared story/values Clear declarations and requests "God who is at work in you, enabling you both to will and to work for his good pleasure" (Phil 2:13)	Openhandedness Humility (kenosis) Curious listening Making space for others Clear, unattached offers "You must understand this, my beloved: let everyone be quick to listen, slow to speak, slow to anger" (Jas 1:19)
SHADOW (POWER WITHOUT LOVE)	**SHADOW (LOVE WITHOUT POWER)**
Control freak Power *over* others Intimidation Diminishment of others Objectification of others Overactivated need for security Demanding Strategic (nontransparent) game playing	Doormat Sentimental and anemic Endless talk and no action (avoidance) Diminishment of self Overactivated need for belonging Failure to speak one's truth Submissive Naïve

Appendix D
How Circle Processes Help to Structure Out Rivalry and Structure In Collaboration

THE CIRCLE PROCESSES DESCRIBED IN this book create conditions of effective collaboration by creating participation safety and the power of self-organization. We observed in touchstone 2 that violence originates in interpersonal mimetic rivalry and personal survival and belonging needs. Because these mechanisms are largely unconscious, they will inevitably show up in sabotaging ways in any group that is under pressure, even with the help of a skilled facilitator. As the number of people grows in a complex systems collaboration, so does the potential for destructive conflict.

Circle processes of the kind described in part 3 do not attempt to control or manage conflict or even to assume that conflict is a problem. In most complex challenges, conflict is inevitable, because people care deeply; and, because people care, conflict is signaling creative potential. Circle processes such as Open Space Technology and Talking Circles allow the passionate *caring* (which underlies conflict) to find positive expression rather than becoming destructive. Circle processes minimize the potential for destructive conflict by dealing with common forms of mimetic rivalry, emotional contagion, and the dynamics of structural power, which frequently occur in meetings. For example:

RIVALRY FOR CONTROL OF THE AGENDA (QUESTION, CONCERN, ISSUE)

If there are a hundred people in a meeting, there could be a hundred different agendas. Normal meetings limit the agenda to what the meeting convenor (controller) considers manageable. This can raise anxiety. As a participant, I will either need to suppress my own concerns (do violence to myself) or try to dominate others, so that my concern is discussed (do violence to others). Either way, other people in the meeting become my competitors. In a circle meeting, everyone at the meeting can put items on the agenda and give the item the time needed. I am invited to accept that I cannot control how other people will respond to my agenda, but at least I have the capacity to name it.

RIVALRY FOR HOW MUCH TIME AND PRIORITY IS GIVEN TO DIFFERENT AGENDA ITEMS

In controlling how an agenda is managed, chairpersons or facilitators typically find themselves being a lightning rod for participant discontent, as the facilitator becomes a rival for consideration about what is most important. Eventually, the facilitator may even be cast as a scapegoat by the group. Anyone who has been in a traditional town hall meeting or church annual general meeting (with everyone sitting in rows in front of a high table) to discuss a major community concern may have experienced the very tense atmosphere that can emerge, sometimes even to the point of emotional violence to others. Alternatively, people bury their feelings within and leave the meeting with a deep sense of suppressed anger and mood of resignation that the system cannot be changed (violence to self).

However, in an Open Space meeting, after introducing principles of self-organization, the facilitator walks out of the room (or at least some distance from the group). This achieves two things. It sends a powerful signal to participants that they have complete freedom to post agenda items (the agenda is not predetermined by someone else). Secondly, it makes it virtually impossible for the facilitator to become the recipient of collective transferences and scapegoating. The resulting dynamics of voluntary association (Law of Two Feet), collaboration, and co-creation are all forms of positive mimeses. That is, participants imitate (join/co-operate with) emergent ideas and questions with which they resonate.

RIVALRY TO WIN OTHERS TO MY AGENDA

The background to any rivalrous dynamic is a paradigm of *scarcity* or what we might call a zero sum game. If I get my way, then you, my rival, loses. However, the architecture of the circle, the clearly specified convening theme, an open invitation, the cocreation of the agenda, and the circle's power to give voice by using a Talking Piece (Talking Circle) or by using the self-organizing agenda (Open Space Technology) all contribute to creating an environment of *abundance*—abundant ways of getting one's voice heard and an abundant space for listening. The circle of participants at the beginning of the meeting all looking at each other, along with the apparently empty space in the middle of the circle, both symbolically communicate that this question is bigger than all of us: we are in this together, and, together, we are hopeful we can find ways forward. There is an implicit assumption of the possibilities of synergy, with the collective intelligence of the group being greater than the sum of individual intelligences.[1] Sitting on the edge of this empty space, with no agenda in sight, can initially be unsettling for participants. The facilitator calmly walking the circle models (positive mimesis) a trust that the empty circle is a safe space. For Christians, theologically, the space is not empty but already filled with resurrection hope and the presence of the Spirit.

EMOTIONAL REGULATION IN A GROUP

Sponsors are sometimes worried about the outbreak of strong emotions in meetings where there is potential conflict—that is, where people care deeply about different things. In normal facilitated meetings, the meeting chair/facilitator tries to monitor and regulate the emotional state of the group. This is a virtually impossible task, especially in large groups. It can be done only by forms of command/control, including appealing to people to behave nicely to each other, controlling who meets with whom, developing strategies to deal with "disruptive" participants, closing down conversations that become uncomfortably noisy or angry, or terminating a meeting. All these strategies can increase tension, as people experience their legitimate concerns and strong emotions being shut down. The risk of violence to the facilitator is that a person who steps between fighting dogs is very likely going to get bitten.

---

1. Some people have said to me that a bunch of stupid people cannot result in collective brilliance. Acknowledging that there is some element of truth to this, good preparation for the circle will have ensured, so far as possible, that people with the right mixes of skills and expertise will be present. But regardless of who attends, the dialogic process regularly produces surprising collective outcomes that would be beyond the capacity of individuals engaged in combative rivalrous conversations.

Circle meetings deal with strong emotions a different way—through the principles and structures of the circle design. The principle of the Law of Two Feet provides a powerful and effective tool that participants can use to emotionally self-regulate. It enables participants to individually discern the value (or not) of heated conversation and decide whether to stay engaged, walk away, or walk away for a period and then reengage when ready. All the experienced OST facilitators whom I have met have said that in hundreds or even thousands of Open Space meetings, they have never witnessed a single act of physical violence—albeit they have occasionally seen some yelling and foul language. I have personally witnessed on multiple occasions participants alternating between *engagement* and *withdrawal* from heated conversations in circles. Circle work trusts that groups can self-regulate in ways that would be completely impossible for any individual facilitator to *manage*.

The role of the circle facilitator is to calmly hold collective projections of anxiety by neither fighting (trying to control people into calming down) or flighting (closing a meeting down). By holding, I mean providing a physically and emotionally calm, non-anxious presence in a room, which has positive mimetic effect on others. The most verbal intervention that a circle facilitator may ever need to do is to simply recall the group to the convening question that brought the group together, the four principles, and the one law. The fourth principle, "when it's over, it's over," gives permission to the group to stay together as long as it takes to work through a tricky or emotive issue—rather than having the conversation shut down prematurely by a nervous or controlling facilitator.

THE ROLE OF PEOPLE IN THE ROOM WITH STRUCTURAL POWER

A common question I have been asked by sponsors prior to a circle meeting is whether the chief executive officer (CEO) or other senior staff should attend. They worry that people may not speak freely if the CEO is in their group. My answer is nearly always the same: the CEO is part of the natural living system, and to not have them present would be to risk reverting to a consultation dynamic rather than collaboration. The presence of persons with structural power in a group simply needs to be acknowledged as part of the reality of organizational life. A good question for the CEO to reflect on is their own mindset and behaviors that they carry into the meeting. How aware are they of their own dance between power (acknowledging the reality of their structural power) and love (genuinely curious listening)?

MITIGATING THE SOCIAL CONSTRUCTION OF DESIRE

One of Girard's key points is that people desire according to the desire of others. An implication of this is that in any group or any meeting process, people risk getting swept up by the desire of others and stop thinking for themselves. This is a particular risk in the presence of charismatic personalities. Most meeting processes provide no explicit permission for a person to extract themselves from the group mind if they are feeling uncomfortable.

Circles provide no inherent protection against the social construction of desire, since it is ubiquitously present as part of the human condition. However, there are some useful mitigators of the potential trap of group-think:

- The *self-organized agenda* gives permission for the individual to post their own agenda/topic rather than having to work only with the agenda created by others.
- *The Law of Two Feet* provides explicit provision for people to absent themselves from the group when they need to. This also provides an important form of self-care (nonviolence to self), psychological safety, and efficient self-regulation of energy (hence, by extension, productivity).

Appendix E
Talking Circles Principles (Generic)

1. The convening theme/question(s) on which we are focusing in this Talking Circle is/are . . .
2. The sponsor for this conversation is . . . (name/group)
3. The facilitator for the meeting is . . .
4. The latest finishing time for this meeting will be . . .
5. When holding the Talking Piece, you can

    - speak respectfully; or
    - hold the Talking Piece in silence (create space for yourself to think); or
    - say nothing and pass the Talking Piece to the next person.

6. When not holding the Talking Piece, listen without interrupting.
7. Record of meeting (if applicable, agree with the group what kinds of things, if any, will be written down, who will take notes, and what access the group will have to those notes afterwards).
8. Leave quietly if you need to, and return when you wish (no need to say anything).
9. If you have a question for an individual or the group during the circle, the process is to state your question when you have the Talking Piece. The relevant person(s) can choose to respond, if they wish, when they are holding the Talking Piece (hence you may or

may not get an answer to your question while the Talking Circle is in progress).

10. Each person accepts responsibility for how long they speak, taking account of the time and giving everyone an opportunity to speak.
11. The facilitator will not interrupt anyone, unless there is a need to recall the group to these principles.
12. Talking Circle guidelines apply once the Talking Piece is picked up from the middle by the first speaker and end when the Talking Piece is returned to the middle by the last person after one complete round.
13. Agreement with the group about not making audio or visual recording by any member (unless agreed on by whole group).

Any other requests that anyone wants to add to this list or anything that needs clarification? Then obtain group consent to these principles by show of hands (unanimous consent is required before proceeding).

Appendix F
Coaching Approach to a Conversation

Adapted by Michael Wood, drawing on John Whitmore's GROW model and Gervase Bushe on clear leadership

1. CONVERSATION TO CLARIFY INTENT/AGENDA FOR THE MEETING

Descriptive self (speaking)	Curious self (listening)
I'd like to talk about . . . In this conversation I'd like to cover . . . I have this much time for this conversation . . . I suggest we structure our conversation by . . . Given our objectives/targets, I need to focus on x in this conversation . . . Let's clarify how we decide (e.g., consensus; or we discuss, then I decide; or we discuss, then you decide; or majority vote)—most relevant for group decision-making I will be bringing a mix of directive and eliciting approaches here. That means . . .	Is that okay with you? Is there anything you want to cover? How much time can you give this conversation today? Out of the things you've mentioned, what is most important for you to resolve? How directive would you like me to be here (i.e., advising/directing or more of a coaching approach)?—relevant where there is a direct reporting relationship, rather than for collegial conversations

2. CONVERSATION TO SHARE ASSESSMENTS OF CURRENT REALITY—PERCEPTIONS/STORIES

Descriptive self (speaking)	Curious self (listening)
What I have observed is (name facts) . . . Some of the things I value are . . . My interpretation of what's going on here is . . . (and I admit I may be wrong or not seeing everything) What I am curious about is . . . What I'm worried about is . . . With my manager hat on, my concern is . . . I understand that the way you see things here is . . . Have I understood correctly? Would you mind repeating back to me what you believe my concern is, so that I know I have communicated my concern clearly?	Do you see it differently? How do you see it? What do you think has been working well, and what hasn't been working so well? How do you respond to what I'm saying? How do you see it? What's happening at the moment? How do you know that's accurate? What's the impact of that? What else is relevant? What have you tried so far? What results has that produced? How do you feel about the situation? Is there anything I can do to help you in your role (I may or may not be willing to do it, but I'd like to hear your view)? What I heard you say is . . .

3. CONVERSATION TO EXPLORE FUTURE POSSIBILITIES/OPTIONS

Descriptive self (speaking)	Curious self (listening)
I would like to talk about some options . . . I think some possibilities are . . . In the past I have/others have found that (option *x*) has worked well . . . Keeping in mind the goals/development areas we've discussed in the past, I want you/us to consider . . . Let's look at the benefits and drawbacks of that option to help you/us decide . . .	What do you think could happen from here? What options/possibilities can you see? What else could you/we do? If you did know . . . , what would you say? Do you know anyone who has solved something like this? What has worked in the past? That's fine to not know; take some time and get back to me tomorrow with your thoughts . . . If you could wave your magic wand and solve this, how would it look?

4. CONVERSATION FOR COMMITMENTS (AGREEING ON NEXT STEPS)

Descriptive self (speaking)	Curious self (listening)
I need you to . . . (if a supervisor/manager giving a legal instruction)	Given what we've discussed, what are your suggestions for next steps?
My request is . . . Can you do that?	Out of the options we explored, what would be a good first step?
Would you be willing to . . . ?	What will you do? By when?
I can offer you . . . Would that help?	Can you feed back to me what you understand we (and I) have agreed to?
I can't/won't offer you . . .	What support do you need from me or from others?
As I understand it, this is what we have agreed to . . . Is that your understanding?	What could get in the way of you/us achieving this?
There seem to be some points on which we still have different views. I'd like to arrive at a solution that is workable for both of us. I suggest we continue the conversation on . . . (get commitment and set date)	How are you feeling about the next steps that we've agreed on? Any lingering or unspoken concerns?
If we've become stuck, do we need to involve someone else in this conversation?	How committed are you to this action (scale of one to ten)?
I would like to review this with you on . . .	

Appendix G
Sample Questions for Reflective Practice

1. What happened? Who said/did what? (sometimes verbatim)
2. On what specific moment in time would I like to focus my reflection?
3. What was I noticing in my body at the time?
4. What emotions was I feeling at the time?
5. What was I thinking at the time?
6. Do I have any theories about what might have been going on for me at a deeper level? For example, what were my underlying concerns/needs during the encounter?
7. What about at a deeper level? Were my survival or belonging needs being activated? Did any aspect of my shadow show up in an unhelpful way? Was I caught up in mimetic rivalry?
8. Where was God (Christ) in this encounter? Does the situation remind me of a particular biblical story or metaphor?
9. Are there any transferable learnings/principles (take-home insights) that I would like to apply in future situations like this?
10. Do I need to take any specific restorative or constructive action in relation to the people involved? What is the nature of my next conversation with this person(s)?
11. Are there any other next steps for me to take?

Appendix H

Joining the Dots: Integrating Theology, Contemplation, and Action in the Practice of Peace

Theological Touchstones	Contemplation	Action
Touchstone 1 Christlike God Promise of union Revelation Grace Irrevocable covenant Personhood as mutually cocreating Relational	Contemplative prayer (love God with all your heart) Prayer word as symbol of trust Perceiving other as sacred thou "Our Father in heaven, hallowed be your name"	Loving action (doing right things vs. doing things right) Giving and receiving within the Trinity = theological basis for dialogue Do no harm Nonviolence/collaboration Starting with core identity and purpose (gospel of Christ = gospel of peace) Appreciating inquiry (start with what is working) Open invitation to dialogue (the dignity of difference) Natural Living (Self-Organizing) Systems Lens "Your kingdom come on earth as in heaven"

Touchstone 2 Disoriented desire Mimetic rivalry Survival and belonging Shame, grief, and loss Scapegoating Law Ritual Myth	Contemplative Practice Recognizing and releasing internal mimetic desires and rivalries Reconciling in the inner village Recognizing and withdrawing shadow projections	Circle design structurally mitigates mimetic rivalry (creating conditions of peace) Managing shadow in organizations Decoupling from systemic mimetic desire
Touchstone 3 Kenosis (humble self-emptying) Dying and rising Participation Deliverance Healing Forgiveness Reconciliation Justice = setting relations right Solidarity—not retaliation Sacrificial love Judgment of mercy	Prayer word as a symbol of reorienting desire (thy will be done) = participation Inner work of forgiveness Inner work of healing "Forgive us our sins"	Listening with an open mind and open heart "as we forgive those who sin against us" Motivation and grounding for nonviolent, collaborative practices of peace Conceiving dialogue as a dance between power and love

Touchstone 4	Inner silence as foundation for listening to others	Listening with open will
Becoming human	Cultivating attention	Collaborating as the practice of peace
Mind of Christ	Inner work of conversation (dancing between power and love)	Hosting-style leadership
Fruits of the Spirit		Passion + responsibility
Courage		Architecture of the circle
Peace and joy		Inviting/engaging enemies (whoever comes)
Kenotic space making		Detaching from egoic definitions of success (whatever happens)
Positive mimesis		Trusting timings (whenever it starts)
Restorative justice		Accepting endings (when it's over, it's over)
		Five steps
		Two hands of NV
		Third ways
		Reflective practice
		Restorative conferencing
		Structured apology
		Managing shadow
		Communities of practice
		Dialoging with planet
		Decoupling from systemic mimetic desire
		NV direction action

Bibliography

Abramson, L., and D. B. Moore. "Promoting Positive Peace—Block by Block: Community Conferencing in Baltimore." In *Moving toward a Just Peace: The Mediation Continuum*, edited by Jan Marie Fritz, 189–212. Clinical Sociology: Research and Practice. New York: Springer, 2014.

Alison, James. *Jesus the Forgiving Victim*. 4 vols. Glenview, IL: Doers, 2013.

———. *Knowing Jesus*. London: SPCK, 1998.

———. *On Being Liked*. London: Darton, Longman, and Todd, 2003.

———. *Raising Abel: The Recovery of the Eschatological Imagination*. New York: Crossroad, 1996.

Anderson, Robert J., and William A. Adams. *Mastering Leadership: An Integrated Framework for Breakthrough Performance and Extraordinary Business Results*. New Jersey: Wiley, 2016.

Athanasius. "On the Incarnation of the Word." Translated by Archibald Robertson. In *Nicene and Post-Nicene Fathers*, edited by Philip Schaff and Henry Wace, 2nd ser., 4. Buffalo, NY: Christian Literature, 1892. Revised and edited for New Advent by Kevin Knight. https://www.newadvent.org/fathers/2802.htm.

"Australian of the Year Awards: Australia Day 2021." YouTube, from *ABC Australia*, Jan. 25, 2021. https://www.youtube.com/watch?v=FQbok_RtSrM&t=2412s.

Axel, Gabriel, dir. *Babette's Feast [Babettes Gæstebud]*. Copenhagen: Nordisk, 1987.

Bachelard, Sarah. *Experiencing God in a Time of Crisis*. Oldham Lancashire, UK: Meditatio, 2017.

———. *Resurrection and Moral Imagination*. London: Routledge, 2016.

Bailie, Gil. *Violence Unveiled: Humanity at the Crossroads*. New York: Crossroad, 1995.

Baird, Julia. *Phosphorescence: On Awe, Wonder and Things That Sustain You When the World Goes Dark*. Sydney: Fourth Estate, 2020.

Baldwin, Christina, and Ann Linnea. *The Circle Way: A Leader in Every Chair*. San Francisco: Berrett-Koehler, 2010.

Ball, Jennifer. *Doing Democracy in Circles: Engaging Communities in Public Planning*. St. Paul: Living Justice Press, 2009.

Bargen, Catherine, et al. *Serving Crime Victims Through Restorative Justice: A Resource Guide for Leaders and Practitioners*. Edmonton: Alberta Restorative Justice Association, 2018.

Barry, William A. *Paying Attention to God: Discernment in Prayer*. Notre Dame, IN: Ave Maria, 1990.

Barth, Karl. *Theological Declaration of Barmen.* In *The Church's Confession Under Hitler*, by Arthur C. Cochrane, 237–42. Philadelphia: Westminster, 1962. https://sacred-texts.com/chr/barmen.htm.

Behr, John. *Becoming Human: Meditations on Christian Anthropology in Word and Image.* New York: St. Vladimir's Seminary, 2013.

———. *The Mystery of Christ: Life in Death.* New York: St. Vladimir's Seminary, 2006.

Borg, Marcus J., and Wright, N. T. *The Meaning of Jesus: Two Visions.* San Franciso: Harper, 1999.

Broughton, Geoff. *Restorative Christ: Jesus, Justice, and Discipleship.* Eugene, OR: Pickwick, 2015.

Brueggemann, Walter. *The Prophetic Imagination.* Minneapolis: Augsburg Fortress, 2001.

Buber, Martin. *I and Thou.* Translated by Walter Kaufman. New York: Charles Scribner's Sons, 1970.

Hamerton-Kelly, Robert G., ed. *Violent Origins: Walter Burkert, René Girard, and Jonathan Z. Smith on Ritual Killing and Cultural Formation.* Stanford, CA: Stanford University Press, 1987.

Bushe, Gervase R. *Clear Leadership: How Outstanding Leaders Make Themselves Understood, Cut Through the Mush, and Help Everyone Get Real Work Done.* Palo Alto, CA: Davies-Black, 2001.

Campbell, Douglas A. *Paul: An Apostle's Journey.* Grand Rapids: Eerdmans, 2018.

———. *Pauline Dogmatics: The Triumph of God's Love.* Grand Rapids: Eerdmans, 2020.

Carnley, Peter. *Yellow Wallpaper and Other Sermons.* Melbourne: Harper Collins, 2001.

Cassian, John. *Conferences.* Translated by Colm Luibheid. New York: Paulist, 1985.

Chesterton, G. K. *The Everlasting Man.* New York: Dover, 2007.

Clément, Olivier. *Taizé: A Meaning to Life.* Chicago: GIA Publications, 1977.

Coakley, Sarah. *The New Asceticism: Sexuality, Gender and the Quest for God.* London: Bloomsbury, 2015.

Consedine, Jim. *Restorative Justice: Healing the Effects of Crime.* Lyttleton, NZ: Ploughshares, 1995.

Cooperrider, David, and Suresh Srivastva. "Appreciative Inquiry in Organisational Life." In *Research in Organisational Change and Development*, edited by W. A. Pasmore et al., 1:129–69. Oxford, UK: JAI, 1987.

Cowdell, Scott. *René Girard and the Nonviolent God.* Notre Dame, IN: University of Notre Dame, 2018.

———. *René Girard and Secular Modernity: Christ, Culture, and Crisis.* Notre Dame, IN: University of Notre Dame Press, 2015.

Crenna-Jennings, Whitney. "Young People's Mental and Emotional Health: Trajectories and Drivers in Childhood and Adolescence." Education Policy Institute, Jan. 2021. https://epi.org.uk/wp-content/uploads/2021/01/EPI-PT_Young-people%E2%80%99s-wellbeing_Jan2021.pdf.

Culmsee, Paul, and Kailash Awati. *The Heretic's Guide to Best Practices: The Reality of Managing Complex Problems in Organisations.* Bloomington, IN: iUniverse, 2011.

De Mello, Anthony. *Awareness: The Perils and Opportunities of Reality.* New York: Image, 1992.

———. *Sadhana: A Way to God.* Melbourne: Harper Collins Religious, 1998.

Dennis, Marie, ed. *Choosing Peace: The Catholic Church Returns to Gospel Nonviolence.* New York: Orbis, 2018.

Dillard, Annie. *Pilgrim at Tinker Creek*. London: Pan, 1976.
Dubler, Joshua, and Vincent Lloyd. "The End of Punishment: Restorative Justice, Prison Abolition and the Christian Refusal of State Violence." *ABC*, Dec. 23, 2018; updated Jan. 23, 2019. https://www.abc.net.au/religion/restorative-justice,-prison-abolition-and-the-refusal-of-state/10630778.
Ellison, Keith. "Today's Verdict Isn't 'Justice.' But Accountability Is a First Step toward Justice." *Guardian*, Apr. 20, 2021. https://www.theguardian.com/commentisfree/2021/apr/20/keith-ellison-george-floyd-speech-minnesota-attorney-general.
Frädrich, Björn. *Taizé Readings*. iPhone ed., v. 3.0. Taizé, 2018. iOS 8.0 or later.
Francis, Pope. "Nonviolence: A Style of Politics for Peace." Vatican, Jan. 1, 2017. https://www.vatican.va/content/francesco/en/messages/peace/documents/papa-francesco_20161208_messaggio-l-giornata-mondiale-pace-2017.html.
Freire, Paulo. *Pedagogy of the Oppressed*. London: Penguin 2017.
Gibson, Mel, dir. *Hacksaw Ridge*. Santa Monica, CA: Lionsgate, 2016.
Girard, René. *Things Hidden Since the Foundation of the World*. Translated by Stephen Bann and Michael Metteer. Palo Alto, CA: Stanford University, 1987.
Green, Chris. *Sanctifying Interpretation: Vocation, Holiness, and Scripture*. Cleveland: CPT, 2020.
Griffiths, Bede. *The New Creation in Christ: Meditation and Community*. London: Darton, Longman and Todd, 1992.
Haidt, Jonathan, and Greg Lukianoff. *The Coddling of the American Mind: How Good Intentions and Bad Ideas Are Setting Up a Generation for Failure*. London: Penguin, 2019.
Hardin, Michael. *The Jesus Driven Life: Reconnecting Humanity with Jesus*. Lancaster, PA: JDL, 2010.
———. *Mimetic Theory and Biblical Interpretation: Reclaiming the Good News of the Gospel*. Eugene, OR: Cascade, 2017.
———. *Reading the Bible with René Girard: Conversations with Steven E. Berry*. Lancaster, PA: JDL, 2015.
Hart, David Bentley. *Atheist Delusions: The Christian Revolution and Its Fashionable Enemies*. New Haven, CT: Yale University Press, 2009.
———. *The Experience of God: Being, Consciousness, and Bliss*. New Haven, CT: Yale University Press, 2013.
———. *The New Testament: A Translation*. New Haven, CT: Yale University Press, 2019.
———. *That All Shall be Saved: Heaven, Hell, and Universal Salvation*. New Haven, CT: Yale University Press, 2019.
Hauerwas, Stanley. *The Peaceable Kingdom: A Primer in Christian Ethics*. London: SCM, 2009.
Haven, Cynthia L. *Evolution of Desire: A Life of René Girard*. East Lansing: Michigan State University Press, 2018.
Hawkins, Peter. *Leadership Team Coaching: Developing Collective Transformational Leadership*. London: Kogan Page, 2011.
Heim, S. Mark. *Saved from Sacrifice: A Theology of the Cross*. Grand Rapids: Eerdmans, 2006.
Hill, Jess. *See What You Made Me Do: Power, Control and Domestic Abuse*. Carlton, Aus.: Black, 2019.
Holisticon AG. *Liberating Structures*. Version 3.4.0. 2021. Android 5.1 or later.

Hollis, James. *Finding Meaning in the Second Half of Life.* New York: Gotham, 2006.

———. *Living an Examined Life: Wisdom for the Second Half of the Journey.* Boulder, CO: Sounds True, 2018.

———. *Why Good People Do Bad Things: Understanding our Darker Selves.* New York: Gotham, 2007.

Holman, Peggy. *The Change Handbook: The Definitive Resource to Today's Best Methods for Engaging Whole Systems.* 2nd ed. San Francisco: Berrett-Koehler, 2007.

———. *Engaging Emergence: Turning Upheaval into Opportunity.* San Francisco: Berrett-Koehler, 2011.

Ignatius of Antioch. "Letter to the Romans." Translated by Cyril Richardson. Order of St. Ignatius, n.d. https://www.orderofstignatius.org/files/Letters/Ignatius_to_Romans.pdf.

Ignatius of Loyola. *St. Ignatius of Loyola: Personal Writings.* Edited and translated by Joseph A. Munitiz and Philip Endean. London: Penguin Classics, 1997.

Isaacs, William. *Dialogue: The Art of Thinking Together.* New York: Currency, 1999.

Jersak, Bradley. *Her Gates Will Never Be Shut: Hell, Hope, and the New Jerusalem.* Eugene, OR: Wipf and Stock, 2009.

———. *A More Christlike God: A More Beautiful Gospel.* Pasadena, CA: Plain Truth Ministries, 2015.

———. *A More Christlike Word: Reading Scripture the Emmaus Way.* New Kensington, PA: Whitaker House, 2021.

———, and Michael Hardin, eds. *Stricken by God? Nonviolent Identification and the Victory of Christ.* Grand rapids: Eerdmans, 2007.

Johnson, Robert A. *Inner Work: Using Dreams and Active Imagination for Personal Growth.* San Francisco: Harper, 1986.

Kahane, Adam. *Solving Tough Problems: An Open Way of Talking, Listening, and Creating New Realities.* San Francisco: Berrett-Kohler, 2004.

———. *Collaborating With the Enemy: How to Work with People You Don't Agree with or Like or Trust.* San Francisco: Berrett-Kohler, 2017.

———. *Power and Love: A Theory and Practice of Social Change.* San Francisco: Berrett-Kohler, 2010.

———. *Transformative Scenario Planning: Working Together to Change the Future.* San Francisco: Berrett-Kohler, 2012.

Kahneman, Daniel. *Thinking Fast and Slow.* New York: Farrar, Straus and Giroux, 2011.

Kantor, David. *Reading the Room: Group Dynamics for Coaches and Leaders.* San Francisco: Jossey-Bass, 2012.

Karp, David R. *The Little Book of Restorative Justice for Colleges and Universities: Repairing Harm and Rebuilding Trust in Response to Student Misconduct.* New York: Good, 2015.

Keating, Thomas. *Open Heart, Open Mind.* New York: Amity House, 1986.

King, Martin Luther, Jr. "Martin Luther King on Love and Power." YouTube, 2011. https://www.youtube.com/watch?v=U0uEVTh0ios.

———. *Strength to Love.* London: Fount, 1963.

Lederach, John Paul. *The Moral Imagination: The Art and Soul of Building Peace.* Oxford, UK: Oxford University Press, 2005.

Lewis, C. S. *The Great Divorce.* London: Collins, 1946.

Linklater, Richard, dir. *School of Rock.* Los Angeles: Paramount, 2003.

Linn, Dennis, et al. *Don't Forgive Too Soon: Extending the Two Hands That Heal*. New York: Paulist, 1997.
———. *Good Goats: Healing Our Image of God*. New York: Paulist, 1994.
———. *Healing Religious Addiction: Reclaiming Healthy Spirituality*. London: Darton, Longman and Todd, 1994.
———. *Sleeping with Bread: Holding What Gives You Life*. New York: Paulist, 1995.
———. *Understanding Difficult Scriptures in a Healing Way*. New York: Paulist, 2001.
Llewellyn, Peter. *Lamb Power: The Victory of Jesus in the Book of Revelation*. Whadjuk Noongar Boodja: Mountain Top, 2021.
Lloyd, Vincent, interview guest. "Should Prisons Be Abolished?" *ABC*, Jan. 23, 2019. https://www.abc.net.au/radionational/programs/theminefield/should-prisons-be-abolished/10739838.
MacDonald, George. *Unspoken Sermons*. Radford, VA: Wilder, 2008.
Macy, Joanna, and Chris Johnstone. *Active Hope: How to Face the Mess We're in without Going Crazy*. Novato, CA: New World, 2012.
Marr, Andrew. *Tools for Peace: The Spiritual Craft of St. Benedict and René Girard*. New York: iUniverse, 2007.
Marshall, Christopher D. *All Things Reconciled: Essays on Restorative Justice, Religious Violence, and the Interpretation of Scripture*. Eugene, OR: Cascade, 2018.
———. *Beyond Retribution: A New Testament Vision for Justice, Crime, and Punishment*. Grand Rapids: Eerdmans, 2001.
———. *The Little Book of Biblical Justice: A Fresh Approach to the Bible's Teachings on Justice*. New York: Good, 1989.
May, Gerald. *Addiction and Grace: Love and Spirituality in the Healing of Addictions*. New York: Harper Collins, 2007.
McFague, Sally. *A New Climate for Theology: God, the World, and Global Warming*. Minneapolis: Augsburg Fortress, 2008.
McRaney, David. *You Are Not So Smart: Why Your Memory Is Mostly Fiction, Why You Have Too Many Friends on Facebook and 46 Other Ways You're Deluding Yourself*. London: One World, 2012.
McClaren, Brian. *Everything Must Change: When the World's Biggest Problems and Jesus' Good News Collide*. Nashville: Thomas Nelson, 2007.
Myers, Ben. *The Apostles' Creed: A Guide to the Ancient Catechism*. Bellingham, WA: Lexham, 2018.
———. *Christ the Stranger: The Theology of Rowan Williams*. London: T&T Clark, 2012.
Nathanson, Donald L. *Shame and Pride: Affect, Sex, and the Birth of the Self*. New York: Norton and Co., 1992.
Nouwen, Henri. *In the Name of Jesus: Reflections on Christian Leadership*. New York: Crossroads, 1993.
———. *Spiritual Direction: Wisdom for the Long Walk of Faith*. San Francisco: Harper, 2006.
Osborne, Carly. *The Theory of René Girard: A Very Simple Introduction*. Adelaide: Australian Girard Seminar, 2016.
Owen, Harrison. *Open Space Technology: A User's Guide*. San Francisco: Berrett-Koehler, 1997.
———. *The Power of Spirit: How Organizations Transform*. San Francisco: Berrett-Koehler, 2000.

———. *The Practice of Peace*. Circle Pines, MN: Human Systems Dynamics Institute, 2004.
———. *The Spirit of Leadership: Liberating the Leader in Each of Us*. San Francisco: Berrett-Koehler, 1999.
———. *Spirit: Transformation and Development in Organization*. Potomac, MD: Abbott, 1987.
———. *Wave Rider: Leadership for High Performance in a Self-Organizing World*. San Francisco: Berrett Koehler, 2008.
Palmer, Parker J. *A Hidden Wholeness: The Journey towards an Undivided Life*. San Francisco: Jossey-Bass, 2004.
———. *Let Your Life Speak: Listening for the Voice of Vocation*. San Francisco: Jossey-Bass, 2000.
———. *To Know as We Are Known: Education as a Spiritual Journey*. San Francisco: Harper One, 1993.
Pickard, Stephen. *Seeking the Church: An Introduction to Ecclesiology*. London: SCM, 2012.
———. *Theological Foundations for Collaborative Ministry*. London: Routledge, 2009.
Pranis, Kay. *The Little Book of Circle Processes: A New/Old Approach to Peacemaking*. Intercourse, PA: Good, 2005.
Preston, Neil. "Becoming a Collaborative Leader, Papers 1 and 2." Unpublished manuscript, in possession of author.
Radcliffe, Timothy, O. P. "The Throne of God: What Role Does Monasticism Play in the Church?" Monks and Mermaids, 2000; posted Feb. 21, 2017. https://fatherdavidbirdosb.blogspot.com/2017/02/monserrat.html.
Reynolds, Henry. *Truth-Telling: History, Sovereignty and the Uluru Statement*. Sydney: New South, 2021.
Roger of Taizé, Brother. *A Life We Never Dared Hope For*. London: Mowbray, 1980.
Rohr, Richard. *Everything Belongs: The Gift of Contemplative Prayer*. New York: Crossroad, 2003.
———. *Falling Upward: A Spirituality for the Two Halves of Life*. San Francisco: Jossey-Bass, 2011.
———. *Immortal Diamond: The Search for Our True Self*. London: SPCK, 2013.
———. *The Naked Now: Learning to See as the Mystics See*. New York: Crossroad, 2009.
———. *Simplicity: The Art of Living*. New York: Crossroad, 1997.
———. "Transforming Pain." Center for Action and Contemplation, Oct. 17, 2018. https://cac.org/transforming-pain-2018-10-17/.
———, with John Bookser Feister. *Jesus' Plan for a New World: The Sermon on the Mount*. Cincinnati: St. Anthony Messenger, 1985.
Rosenberg, Marshall B. *Nonviolent Communication: A Language of Life*. Encinitas, CA: Puddledancer, 2003.
Ruka, Jay. *Huia Come Home*. Raglan: Huia Ministries, 2017.
Russo, Anthony, and Joe Russo, dirs. *Captain America: Civil War*. Burbank, CA: Marvel, 2016.
Rynne, Terrence J. *Jesus Christ Peacemaker: A New Theology of Peace*. New York: Orbis, 2014.
Sacks, Jonathan. *The Dignity of Difference: How to Avoid the Clash of Civilizations*. London: Continuum, 2002.
Sandford, John A. *Dreams: God's Forgotten Language*. San Francisco: Harper, 1989.

Scharmer, Otto. *Leading from the Emerging Future: From Egosystem to Ecosystem.* San Francisco: Berrett-Koehler, 2013.

———. *Theory U: Leading from the Future as It Emerges.* New York: Berrett-Koehler, 2009.

Schwarger, Raymond. *Jesus in the Drama of Salvation: Toward a Biblical Doctrine of Redemption.* New York: Crossroad, 1999.

Shier, Michael. "President Biden Condemns Terrorist Attack and Vows to Hunt Down Those Responsible." *New York Times,* Aug. 26, 2021. https://www.nytimes.com/2021/08/26/world/biden-afghanistan-kabul-airport-attack.html.

Sieler, Alan. *Coaching to the Human Soul.* Vol. 1 *Ontological Coaching and Deep Change.* Blackburn, Aus.: Newfield Australia, 2003.

Sinclair, Amanda. *Leadership for the Disillusioned: Moving beyond Myths and Heroes to Leading That Liberates.* NSW: Allen& Unwin, 2007.

Slatery, Butigan, et al. *Engage: Exploring Nonviolent Living.* Oakland: Pace e Bene, 2005.

Smith, Babette, interview guest. "The Convict Women Who Defied Authority." ABC, Apr. 27, 2021. https://www.abc.net.au/radionational/programs/latenightlive/convict-women_-babette-smith/13319830.

Solzhenitsyn, Alexander. *The Gulag Archipelago 2: 1918–1956, Parts III–IV.* Translated by Thomas Whitney. [Glasgow?]: Collins/Harvill, 1975.

Taylor, John V. *The Christlike God.* London: SCM, 1992.

———. *The Go-Between God: The Holy Spirit and the Christian Mission.* London: SCM, 1972.

———. *Kingdom Come.* London: SCM, 1989.

———. *Meditations on the Cross and Resurrection.* Geneva: World Council of Churches, 1985.

Thibodeaux, Mark E. *God's Voice within: The Ignatian Way to Discover God's Will.* Chicago: Loyola, 2010.

Thorsborne, Margaret. *A Guide to Workplace Conferencing: A Restorative Approach to Transforming Workplace Conflict.* Brisbane: Margaret Thorsborne and Associates, 2014.

Tilling, Chris, ed. *Beyond Old and New Perspectives on Paul: Reflections on the work of Douglas Campbell.* Eugene, OR: Cascade, 2014.

Tuto, Desmond, and Mpho Tutu. *The Book of Forgiving.* London: William Collins, 2014.

Uluru Dialogue. "The Uluru Statement." Uluru Statement, 2017. https://ulurustatement.org/the-statement.

Wachowski, Lana, and Lilly Wachowski. *The Matrix.* Burbank, CA: Warner Brothers, 1999.

———. *The Matrix Revolutions.* Burbank, CA: Warner Brothers, 2003.

Ward, Benedicta. *The Sayings of the Desert Fathers.* Trappist, KY: Cistercian, 1975.

Weaver, J. Denny. *The Nonviolent Atonement.* Grand Rapids: Eerdmans, 2001.

Weisbord, Marvin, and Sandra Janoff. *Don't Just Do Something, Stand There! Ten Principles for Leading Meetings that Matter.* San Francisco: Berrett-Koehler, 2007.

Wenger, Etienne, et al. *Cultivating Communities of Practice: A Guide to Managing Knowledge.* Boston: Harvard Business Review Press, 2002.

Wheatley, Margaret J., with Debbie Frieze. "Leadership in the Age of Complexity: From Hero to Host." Margaret J. Wheatley, Winter 2011. http://www.margaretwheatley.com/articles/Leadership-in-Age-of-Complexity.pdf.

Wheatley, Margaret J., and Myron Kellner-Rogers. "The Irresistible Future of Organizing." Margaret J. Wheatley, July/Aug. 1986. http://www.margaretwheatley.com/articles/irresistiblefuture.html.
Whitehead, James D., and Evelyn Eaton Whitehead. *Shadows of the Heart: A Spirituality of the Negative Emotions*. New York: Crossroad, 1994.
Whitmore, John. *Coaching for Performance: The Principles and Practices of Coaching and Leadership*. London: John Murray, 2009.
Whyte, David. *The Heart Aroused: Poetry and the Preservation of the Soul in Corporate America*. New York: Crown Business, 2002.
Williams, Rowan. *Meeting God in Paul*. London: SPCK, 2015.
———. *Silence and Honey Cakes*. Oxford, UK: Lion Hudson, 2004.
Wink, Walter. *Engaging the Powers*. Minneapolis: Augsburg-Fortress, 1992.
———. *Jesus and Nonviolence: A Third Way*. Minneapolis: Fortress Press, 2003.
———. *Peace Is The Way: Writings on Nonviolence from the Fellowship of Reconciliation*. New York: Orbis, 2000.
———. *The Powers That Be: Theology for a New Millennium*. New York: Doubleday, 1998.
Wright, N. T. *Paul: Fresh Perspectives*. London: SPCK, 2005.
———. *Simply Christian*. London: SPCK, 2006.
Wood, Michael. "Climate Change: A Theological Reflection." *New Critic* 10 (Aug. 2009). https://ias.uwa.edu.au/new-critic/ten/wood.
Wooden, Cindy. "'No More War': Pope Continues His Teaching on Gospel Nonviolence." *National Catholic Reporter*, June 29, 2021. https://www.ncronline.org/news/justice/francis-chronicles/no-more-war-pope-continues-his-teaching-gospel-nonviolence.
Zaffron, Steve, and Dave Logan. *The Three Laws of Performance: Rewriting the Future of Your Organization and Your Life*. San Francisco: Jossey-Bass, 2009.
Zehr, Howard. *The Little Book of Restorative Justice*. New York: Good, 2015.

www.ingramcontent.com/pod-product-compliance
Lightning Source LLC
Chambersburg PA
CBHW050844230426
43667CB00012B/2134